# The Lyric Touch

JOHN WILKINSON is Research Professor at the University of Notre Dame where he teaches literature and creative writing, having worked in UK mental health services for three decades. He has been a Fulbright Scholar at the Nathan Kline Institute for Psychiatric Research, and Carl and Lily Pforzheimer Fellow at the National Humanities Center. *The Guardian* described his last book of poetry, *Lake Shore Drive* (Salt 2006), as "multiplex, visionary, ragged, and exceedingly strange because exceedingly true to reality".

# The Lyric Touch

*Essays on the Poetry of Excess*

JOHN WILKINSON

SALT

CAMBRIDGE

PUBLISHED BY SALT PUBLISHING
PO Box 937, Great Wilbraham. Cambridge PDO CB21 5JX United Kingdom

First published 2007

Printed and bound in the United Kingdom by Lightning Source

Typeset in Swift 10/12

ISBN 978 1 84471 395 0 paperback


Salt Publishing Ltd gratefully acknowledges
the financial assistance of Arts Council England

1  3  5  7  9  8  6  4  2

# Contents

# Acknowledgments

Drew Milne and Chris Emery encouraged me to assemble this collection, or something like it.

For practical help, I would like to thank Drew Milne and Andrew Duncan who provided copies of essays, and Cheryl Reed of The University of Notre Dame for retyping essays produced originally on a typewriter or Atari ST computer.

My debt to the original publishers of these essays is considerable.

The essays collected here were published previously as follows, in order of first appearance:

'Cadence'
*Reality Studios* vol.9, London 1988 [dated 1987], pp.81–5.

'Illyrian Places'
*Parataxis* 6, Brighton, Spring/Summer 1994, pp.58–69.

'A Single Striking Soviet: The Poetry of Barry MacSweeney'
as 'The Tempers of Hazard part 2: the Poems of Barry MacSweeney', *Angel Exhaust* 11, Cambridge, Winter 1994 [actually 1995], pp.55–74.

'The Line to Take: An appreciation of the seventies poetry of John James'
as 'Mexican Stand-Off in Practical Bondage Gear: An appreciation of the seventies poetry of John James', *Angel Exhaust* 13, Cambridge, Spring 1996, pp.80–91.

'The Metastases of Poetry'
*Parataxis* 8/9, Brighton 1996, pp.49–55.

'Counterfactual Prynne: An Approach to *Not-You*'
*Parataxis* 8/9, Brighton 1996, pp.190–202.

'Too-Close Reading: Poetry and Schizophrenia'
*The Gig* 1, November 1998, Ontario, Canada, pp.41–53 [Reprinted in ed. Romana Huk, *Assembling Alternatives*, Wesleyan UP 2003, pp.364–374].

'Mouthing Off'
*QUID* 7c, April 2001, Cambridge, pp.2–9.

'Frostwork and The Mud Vision'
*The Cambridge Quarterly* vol 31 no 1, Cambridge, March 2002, pp.93–105.

'Tripping the Light Fantastic: Tom Raworth's *Ace*'
in ed. Dorward, *Removed for Further Study: The Poetry of Tom Raworth*, *The Gig* 13/14, Toronto 2003, pp.145–160.

'The Value of *Penniless Politics*'
*Poetry Review* vol 93 no 2, London, Summer 2003, pp.62–70.

'Chamber Attitudes'
The present text conflates the two articles: 'Chamber Attitudes', *Jacket* 21, http://www.jacketmagazine.com/21/wilk-wien.html, posted March 2005 and 'A Tour of the State Capitol: Introducing the poems of John Wieners', *Edinburgh Review* 114, Edinburgh 2005 (dated 2004), pp.96–125.

'Faktura: The Work of Marjorie Welish'
*Chicago Review* vol.51 no.3, Autumn 2005, pp.115–127.

'Into the Day'
*QUID* 17, *For J.H. Prynne. In Celebration.* Brighton, 24th June 2006, pp.29–31.

'The Water-Rail of Tides'
Published as 'The Brain's Tent' in *Boston Review* vol.31, no.5, Sept/Oct 2006, pp.49–50.

Off the Grid: Lyric and Politics in Andrea Brady's *Embrace*
*Chicago Review* vol.53 no.1, Spring 2007, pp.95–115.

'Following the Poem' is a previously unpublished lecture, delivered at The University of Notre Dame in 2004.

*In Press*

'Unexpected Excellent Sausage', ed. Simon Perril, *The Salt Companion to John James;*
'A Poem for Liars', ed. David Hillman and Adam Phillips, *The Book of Interruptions;*
'Stumbling, Balking, Tacking: Robert Creeley's *For Love* and Mina Loy's *Love Songs to Joannes*', ed. Rachel Potter, *The Salt Companion to Mina Loy*

# Introduction

The present book is not a complete collection of my prose writing of the past thirty years; I have excluded articles concerned largely with mental health and public health matters, and literary-critical articles which now seem to me ungenerous or pointless. For reasons of space I have been obliged also to remove a number of shorter reviews, including those of books by Rod Mengham, D.S. Marriott, Drew Milne, Simon Jarvis, Andrew Duncan and Keston Sutherland. I regret this, but the exigency may stimulate me to more extended consideration of these notable writers on other occasions. Among British poets I would have liked to write about W.S. Graham, Allen Fisher, Veronica Forrest-Thomson and Mark Hyatt; again, this must wait. And the writing of some of the greatest American poets of the last half-century, Frank O'Hara and Barbara Guest, remains a summons to attention and emotional alacrity, and reproaches my lackadaisical ways.

The earliest articles have been lightly edited, mainly to remove asides I now find embarrassing, and to reduce traces of an oracular prose style. The articles were written for widely different publications, from mimeo worksheets to cultural magazines to peer-reviewed academic journals, and this shows. However, spelling and punctuation have been standardised to British usage of an informal academic kind.

Reviewing these pieces, the title offered itself readily enough. The collection finds a continuing preoccupation with the seductions of lyric, in a pulse of succumbing and resistance discerned within the poems it reads as well as in these responses. The poems include those of John Wieners, characterised by emotional and linguistic extremity, of Denise Riley, by lyric auto deconstruction and reconstruction, and of J.H. Prynne, characterised by intellectual ambition, astonishing rhetorical resources, and at the last, by the compensatory joys of the lyric counter-factuals they embody. I have been surprised to discover Laura (Riding) Jackson shadowing this book as suggestive of the costs which an excessive investment in lyric poetry might incur; and by an emerging understanding of Frank O'Hara as having instigated a dialogic lyric practice which suggests a way out of the romantic-modernist and individualist matrix inhabited (and quarrelled with) by the poets of excess.

This collection includes essays and talks concerned with my own poetry. Until recently I worked outside the academy; and even now I regret and resent the tendency to separate literary studies from 'creative writing'. While the writing addressed in the book is hopelessly 'unrepresentative', reflecting a sensibility trained in particular places at a particular time, such partiality goes along with an intense need to argue, for myself as well as for others, the value of poets scarcely heard of when I was writing. This is the kind of thing poets should do, and which the academy should better appreciate and promote.

I was taught to read poetry by two remarkable schoolmasters, Derek Rosser at Sherborne School and Brian Worthington at Clifton College. At Sherborne I enjoyed the several advantages of being introduced to contemporary poetry by Charles Verey, Thomas A. Clark and Lawrence Pedersen; of a school library with a fine collection of poetry of all periods; and of two bookshops (in this small town in a conservative part of England), each of them with a better literature selection than any bookshop in present-day Cambridge, and both selling a good range of small-press poetry books. At Cambridge I was taught by Stephen Heath and Colin MacCabe, and above all by J.H. Prynne. Charles Lambert introduced me to the poetry of John Wieners, and Geoffrey Ward and Rod Mengham to much else. Wendy Mulford opened my eyes to contemporary writing by women. The more recent essays have benefited from Maud Ellmann's fine scrutiny. With such advantages I should have done better and should have done more, but at least I can record my gratitude.

Mishawaka, IN
February 2007

# 1: British Poetry

# Counterfactual Prynne: An Approach to Not-You

The first poem in *Not-You* brings into focus a range of questions about poetic reading.[1] Given this poem opens a book-length sequence, can we anticipate its completion through what is to follow, so it will make sense in the light of cumulative information? Or knowing, if we do, something of the writing of J.H. Prynne, can we bring knowledge of established concerns and poetic procedures to make sense of these lines, as it were episodic in a continuing poem, or paralleled by previous poems? Is the reader to bring some specialised extrinsic knowledge to bear, and to what extent would that make the poem amenable? For instance:

> The twins blink, hands set to thread out
> a dipper cargo with lithium grease enhanced
> to break under heat stress

might conjure up a discourse around the affective operations of memory, owing to use of lithium salts in psycho-pharmacology as a mood-stabiliser, the twins then becoming cyclothymic polarities; and such an association then colours at once a provisional understanding of the poem. Yet this must remain provisional, given the oddity of 'lithium grease', which however tenable is 'lithium' within the provisional reading, suggests a different discourse reconciling 'lithium' with 'grease'. So the reader might advert to lithium in watch-batteries, associating both "same-day retread" and "mark | two transfiguration" with opposed accounts of time—either the repetitiveness of a contained and mechanical entity, or 'human time'. Still, lithium occurs chiefly as a salt, and it is difficult to envisage the chemical transformation of salt into grease, which metaphorically and chemically occupies another category. And the whole of this opening poem is fraught with contradiction, indecision, opposition and duplicity. It this the clew to follow?[2]

Several commentators have discussed the seeming non-referentiality and paradoxical authority of Prynne's definite articles, and of the specialised vocabularies he deploys. Who are the twins? To what discourse does a "mark | two transfiguration" attach, and do we need to know?

There may be two broad ways to follow, each branching into tributaries. The first is to seek firm footing in the opening poem, on the assumption it will provide a key to what follows. One tactic here would be exegetical, and lead into reference books and dictionaries. Perhaps any serious reader of Prynne is familiar with dictionary neurosis, whereby trust in one's grasp of familiar vocabulary, let alone of specialised vocabulary, becomes shaken; so I found myself consulting the dictionary for 'consult', lest I had missed some archaic or specialised shade of meaning, much as I looked for the origins of 'lithium' in the Greek for 'stone' and contemplated its kinship with 'lithography' and the processes of circulating a poem, before discounting that particular shade. There are pleasures and rewards to be discovered, as well as disappointments and frustrations, in such trawlage. But is the poem offered for the pleasure of the scholar alone? For this is a different matter from exegetical attention to a poem by Milton or Keats. Before Prynne's poem, exegesis seems pushed to take effect, effect might seem available only through exegetical activity—beyond the effect of frustration, which can be mulled over, but presumably is not the only or the main effect to be derived, or why would this poet proceed again and again, and why the authority which marks these lines, the impression that they say something which ought to be said?

Their authority is a puzzling attribute, by contrast with the work of poets with whom Prynne has been compared—the eschewal of authority has been a cardinal principle of postmodernist practice. This will be addressed below in a discussion of counterfactuals; sufficient here to remark that authority is connected with a consistent and recognisable syntactical or gestural repertoire—with the explicit quality of linkages. Poetic authority also requires that the poem does not make appeal to the reader by enjoining pity or sympathy, or explaining itself; or by asserting fellow feeling with a particular and envisaged readership.

A second strategy would be to assume that the first poem, rather than providing a semantic alignment for what follows, offers a circulation in little, and that to comprehend this poem's activity will provide guidance for the activity of the sequence as a whole. 'Circulate' refers to the experience of reading a poem so lacking in handholds, a potentially interminable re-reading which acknowledges the even spread of authority, where no title, no stressed statement, provides the reader with a seeming encapsulation, point of departure or heart. The twins open and close this poem, and the reader shuttles between their emblematic appearances little the wiser, but for a growing discrepancy between the poem's self-sufficiency and the unassignable matter it contains. Here is a poem of great formal integrity, bound by skilful vowel and consonantal patterning, organised into three-line stanzas, announcing itself as complete. Surely within this text the information is to be found which will justify its authority, whether at the internal semantic level through recognisable transformative development, through external reference although the poem seems cut off almost autistically from any recognisable world, or at the level of non-semantic poetic elements which will produce in the reader an affective response?

Another procedure assumes the poem requires the light of anticipation or retrospection to yield its sense. One might limit anticipation to what is provided in this book, in its physical presentation, in its title, in its dedication, and in the epigraphs which precede the poetic text. The dedication offers the book "For Che Qian-zi and Zhou Ya-ping and for the ORIGINALS", an enigma now unlocked by publication of *Original: Chinese Language-Poetry Group*, with an afterword by Prynne.[3] For the rest, inference is supplied with much material. This handsome slim pamphlet, a demonstration of what can be achieved with a xerox machine, is bound in a pale blue bearing a reticulated device reminiscent of microelectronics, and the second epigraph, "Love of semiconductors is not enough", is to such an extent in keeping as to produce an expectation that the poem-sequence will be 'about' computing. The first epigraph is more mystifying, but the discovery that it refers to counterfactuals, David Lewis being a mathematical logician interested in the logics of possible worlds, links to the book's title, overlaying or superseding a literary expectation of a relationship to Beckett's *Not I* with relocation into a logical discourse. 'You' at once conjures a speech-act, a direct address; 'Not-You' becomes monitory, implying that this poem eschews the world of speech-acts and might occur in a possible world where communication does not so depend. And this is the case with computing, in that the transaction of artificial intelligence takes place in a possible world without speech-acts. Indeed the world of artificial intelligence could be characterised as a world of 'truthfulness-by-silence', but as a world within which 'trust', which can occur only in transactions between sentient, moral individuals, is unavailable—hence, perhaps, "love of semiconductors is not enough". To summarise, the reader could embark on this book with the expectation that its operations occur within a possible, counterfactual world, and that this might give rise to ethical questions about human transactions and the prime requirement for successful speech-acts in trust. Will these poems occupy such a possible world *on account of* the absence of the necessary precondition of trust, will they occupy such a world *because it is the fate* of poetry to occupy such a world and trust is therefore an illegitimate expectation of poetry (and then, what is the ethical merit of poetic art?), or will they occupy such a world *by choice*, as a perverse recourse within the history of perverse recourses in twentieth-century art, raising then the question of the sustainability and ethical merit of such a choice?

These orientations bring to bear a literary and political weight of tradition. A reaction to the absence of conditions of trust within the experienced world would recall the dystopias of Beckett or Burroughs, but also those contemporary poets for whom the world of speech-acts is so far corrupted by commoditisation and the prior ownership and exploitation of all media for human communication, from words and acts of love to scientific papers, that the poet must crush, smash and conflate the verbal material to squeeze out or shake off the marks of prior ownership, releasing a lost potency of meaning.

That of the unavoidable fate of poetry recalls Laura (Riding) Jackson, and her disgust with the amorality of poetic truth, its heartless joy in the slipperiness of human communication. If it is the fate of lyric poetry to feign the intimacy of the trustworthy speech-act and invariably to break trust, at every turn exploiting the potential of language for at-least-duplicity, does not poetry actively bring about the erosion of the intimacy on which it presumes? The relative autonomy of the poetic domain then becomes deeply problematic, open to those charges levelled against the proponents of artificial intelligence as a model for human communication—both poetry and artificial intelligence would be reproached for an inadequacy linked to their totalising ambitions, slighting soul or consciousness which can develop or refine only in relationship to the trust ordained or negotiated with god or fellow human being.

That of choice would relate to the artistic strain of experimentalism, attached to popular metaphors of scientific discovery—a let's-see-what-happens procedure associated with writers such as Gertrude Stein and the Oulipo group and remaining attractive to some British poets. But the epigraphs enjoin a moral evaluation of procedure alien to this literary tendency. The question is begged: what would it mean to lift the dependency of poetry upon speech-acts? Why on earth (or in another contingent world) should one seek to do so?

A containing theory would be tempting—but given that the matrix of theory might act as a constricting device against which such an adventure is keyed (and this is a stricture important to counterfactual theory), it would be well to try a little rough historical description of the arena, before proceeding beyond the first poem to match and test the expectations prompted by epigraphs and title.

The urge to work poetically counter to the realism and empiricism which in so much British twentieth-century verse have seemed ineluctably drawn towards positivism or sentimentality, has marked dissident British poetry since the mid twentieth century. Whereas for Surrealists and for New Apocalyptics the strategy, in broad terms, was to deploy an unhinging ecstatics (whether or not referred to some presumed collective unconscious experience) as a disruptive force within the field of agency, characteristically this was drawn back to voice as a last redoubt of authenticity, the (fictionally) unmediated presence of the suffering or jubilant body crashing into the lists. This was so even for so fastidious a writer as W.S. Graham, and the reading voices of Dylan Thomas or George Barker have a physical resonance which might embarrass a contemporary writer. Authenticity in this sense tends towards a relative weakness in syntactical linkage and a reliance on vocalised rhythmic accumulation—to be metrically paratactical rather than syntactically so; this bardic quality therefore should be distinguished from poetic authority.

The voiced and voicing body is a more socialised recourse of J.H. Prynne's early mentor, Charles Olson, whose poetic theories give a primacy to breath which was elaborated by Robert Creeley into the voice of sexual intimacy or by John Wieners towards a gay and transvestite assertiveness. There is a mile of difference between advocacies of primary *voice* and speech-acts as purposive utterance, but in both the British and American—relatively discrete—poetical developments, primary voice tended to become attached to the celebration of will, by way of the proposition that to assert primary voice in a positivist culture was in itself possible only through an exercise of tremendous will, or alternatively a privilege of madness or reckless 'substance-abuse'. Both schools of writing, no matter how sophisticated or historically (or pre-historically) scrupulous in attention to the construction of the self, tended towards sentimental concession to simple *need* within a shrunken sphere of ownership: the more extravagant the gestures of inclusion, the more fatally determined and the thinner the writing.

The successive poetry was little more than a last twitch of the digestion, a madness painfully contrived, with only the novels of William Burroughs displaying the intelligence to conduct their own autopsy in the 'algebra of need'. But the example of Burroughs has no whit impeded the progressive fetishisation of the body in 'progressive' writing. Indeed, it may become possible to read much late twentieth-century Western culture in terms of body wars, where the physical site is contested by the forces of commoditisation, and by counter-forces for which the body remains the site of resistance to commoditisation, celebrating sexual hedonism (which occurs *at* rather than *between*), tattooing and SM, the excretions of primary process and so forth.

A catastrophic collapse in the conditions of trust is a given in contemporary cultural commentary, and as a relatively minor side-effect faces the reader of a poem with the question: to whom is this poem addressed? The poem can never be addressed to *you*, for you never will be of that certain gender, age, 'racial' origin, education, religion, politics, sexuality, experience of this or that... which is why the poems Faber continues to publish and the *TLS* et al to print, look so unloved and solicit love so pathetically, and why poetry reviewing has reached a nadir in expressions of personal liking argued stringently as liking for a particular chocolate centre. One solution might lie in a formalism where intimate speech-acts occur in a grid of transactional analysis, such that the poetry aspires to a tricky geometry of sentiment. This requires a sustained foregrounding of the formal constraints, as in Andrew Crozier's *Duets*, to work effectively, and runs the ever-present risk of bathos.[4] The approach Prynne adopts in *Not-You* is to go beyond formalism's reining-in, and to prevent any attribution which would permit a reading of the poem as composed of speech-acts or as modelled after a metaphor of speech-act.

This would explain the difficulty with which the first poem in *Not-You* faces the reader, whose model for reading any poem must be based in speech-acts, their ingratiation asking trust in order to deliver meaning. Not-You, then, but what alternative model is available? If neither trust nor reality-testing against a social and historical world assumed to be commonly accessible can be relied upon to negotiate these poems, then what binds them together, what principle permits them to be read as anything other than an arbitrary heap of intriguing phraseology?

The computing analogy can assist here, through supplying the principle of integrity. Integrity implies a logical consistency, but in database usage is subdivided into distinct types. Historically, Prynne's writing can be seen progressively to eschew semantic integrity in favour of referential integrity. The way in which database theorists use these terms is almost Saussurean; semantic integrity involves a check on external conditions (e.g. if a car with that number plate has not entered the garage, the entry is incorrect), whereas referential integrity implies validation within the information system (so a numberplate field within a database for transfer of ownership must be consistent with a numberplate field in a database for initial use of car numbers). Thus orientated, it might prove rewarding to enter this possible world in expectation of discovering a set of relationships and of transformations which do at least hold true by analogy with relationships and transformations with which we are familiar without making direct appeal to these. Hence some of the gratifications available from reading poetry of a more familiar kind are unlikely to be available, such as the experience of being touched directly by identification with the inferred persona of the poet, or the revelatory experience of recognising a thought or sentiment held as a pre-conscious *genera* (a term usefully coined by Christopher Bolas as the positive pole from trauma). The book may offer pleasures of another sort, those of involvement in possibilities beyond or outside those affordable by corrupted and ordinary commerce, and which engage the reader strictly, rather than either demanding a prodigious labour of processing an excess of information or inviting the reader to wallow in an unearned prodigality—a hypertextual paradise in which every turn is possible and in which every possible turn is right and true. These latter textual strategies would be too recklessly ungenerous or generous, and quite beyond any possibility of trust, being analogically untrue to any recognisably human world. Rewards, therefore, may be as constrained but also given as unpredictably (although as recognisably) as in the world we inhabit.

In considering relationships and transactions recognisable in a parallel world and endeavouring to follow these, thinking is given priority over thoughts. The poem's activity could be conceived, in W.R. Bion's terms, as marked by alpha-function, that is as processing sensory impression into a dream-work which according to Bion is active during the waking day. This is prior to 'experience'. Such a conception may be clarified if we call to mind a more conventional poetic procedure in which thoughts encapsulated as visual images (characteristically) are disposed across verse, and linked more or less explicitly as stepping-stones in a progress of thinking. Frequently in contemporary verse, linkages are implicit and left to the reader's adeptness as a verse reader to confirm within a framework supplied by a title and a declamatory concluding line. Some commentators on Prynne have read his poetry as an extreme development of such practice, whereas the linkages between elements marked rhythmically, syntactically and semantically, seem to me to be singularly explicit in Prynne: the processes of linkage attain a primacy over encapsulated thought. Imagery in its Martian parcels is notably absent in *Not-You*, and the reader tends to be carried by syntax—or to reach for a more phenomenologically-contextualised term, by gesture. This sequence of poems is apprehensible as an entity much as an individual human being is apprehensible through his or her gestural repertoire, remaining familiar even through drastic alterations in appearance; its linkages possess the inevitability and unarguable authority of dream. Such transactions might as much (or as little) lend themselves to algebraic formulation as Bion desired for psychoanalysis through the Grid he proposed for psychoanalytical notation.

Hence the knowing and not-knowing of the reader, who may find these poems both easy of acquaintance and quite incomprehensible. Hence also another effect: after putting this book aside for a month, on taking it up again the reader will be confronted with an unremembered poem—a new poem. For alpha-function is inimical to conscious memory, which relies on encapsulating storage; to return is like having learnt to ride a bicycle but then to discover a new landscape. But this is to under-state, for one's own mythologising baggage as participant reconfigures to some extent the text—you may have learnt to ride a bicycle, but this one feels radically different in its gearing and proportions.

For the commentator, who cannot be content simply to pedal his own bicycle into a science-fiction parallel world, the difficulty remains acute, as evident in the tendency of commentators on Prynne either to mine local exegesis or to raise some edifice in the air above a characterisation of Prynnian procedure. These poems stretch out too far and are at the same time too densely implicated to allow of a full account of the processes and transactions which occur across and between the poems, comparable to data-sets across which referential operations are conducted, or as the results of multi-table queries enacted on the data-sets which constitute the conditions of their universe. Paradoxically, these poems before whose publication the word 'rebarbative' had remained short of its potential, force the would-be exegete back into the position of the reader and enjoyer of poetry (the recourse of Iain Sinclair when reviewing *Her weasels wild returning* for the *LRB*).[5] Whilst to approach these poems naively is to invite repeated slaps in the face, that goes to demonstrate how well-taught is naïveté; what is required is the contrivance of a suspension of knowledge about poetry in order to re-learn poetry through engagement with this particular sequence of poems. It remains difficult to resist seeking within the poems some justification for propositions to which an approach through title and epigraphs has given rise.

*Not-You* consists of twenty-eight or twenty-nine poems (depending on whether pages 18 and 19 are read as a single poem), of which the first and final suites of eight take the form of trios of triplets, and the central twelve or thirteen are formally various. The cover device might propose thirteen poems in the middle section, showing two intersecting eights amounting to thirteen. The sum of the lines of the middle suite and the sum of the lines of the two suites of eight poems with epigraphs, are equal to 149. The first eight and last eight poems reflect the totalising, parallel-world ambitions described above, with the first eight featuring a language of equivalences, matches, balances, mimicry, stabilisation and maintenance, while the final eight are rich in database language, integrated in a high lyric manner. The transition from the first eight to the middle suite is heralded by a poem containing an empty room, whose final line asks 'remember me'; and the flurry of less formally stable poems which follows is marked by hesitations, lapses, phrasal drift and break, and one poem which appears to offer a narrative overview. These finish with a beautiful poem of two quatrains which enjoins trust through intimacy of cadence. The final group of eight announces a new set of checks and an 'anti-trust recital'. The equiva-lence in line count between the two modes supports a hypothesis of equivalent worlds, with one world composed out of personal and faulty but affectively powerful memory, and the other constituting a system aspiring to a formal integrity in which no data is misplaced.

Such a panoptic view invites impatience; who but an obsessional student of Prynne would count the lines? The student of Prynne is likely to do so on account of earlier numerological devices, e.g. *A Night Square* with its eleven poems of eleven lines. But the book does obtrude on the reader an unusual structural determinacy; the triplet poems feel often crammed into their form, concluding with a curt sign-off phrase, and this is not so with the central suite. Given the expectations teased out of the epigrammatic material and what the reader might infer from the concerns of the outer poems with matching and overlay, a *sense* of an implicit equivalence is liable to arise without discovery of such a contrivance. The attentive reader will recognise *Not-You* as a formally-structured *book* rather than a collection, and reflect on the propriety of that, given the book's thematics. Not a collection, and also not a sequence understood as an adventure through linear time; a reading which proceeds from establishing a foundation in the first poem and picks from stepping-stone to stepping-stone may well be frustrated. Rather than advance into the light, the reader must negotiate transactions within a system.

In discussing the first poem of this book, I found myself reaching for the term, circulation, and asking whether that poem might be regarded as a guide to the book it opens, a 'circulation in little'. The suggestion that it might encapsulate the semantic material of the book as a whole was found unreliable. But the reader's sense of circulating on the macro and micro level prompts a reconsideration; the error was to suppose that the circulation in little might be seized as introductory, as chronologically privileged.

Certainly transactions at different levels and the relationships between such sets of transactions are a preoccupation traceable throughout the first suite of poems, and for reasons of economy and reader's patience, I confine my analysis to these. From the already-explored ambiguities of the first poem, "shade over upon shade", the reader is introduced to atmospheric activity (including bird-flight), ground-level activity which is subject to attempts at marking, tagging and fixity to the lengths of "bolted to the floor"; and the cycles of diurnal activity and of physiological activity. Some of this may be traced through the succeeding seven poems; but this could be said to be no more than a dispersed imagery, and in order to demonstrate the transactional nature of the poems, they must be examined in a more particular and abstracted way—in terms of Transaction, Intention, Direction, Duration and Quantity. To appreciate their tight algebra, it is necessary to bear in mind that these are nine-line poems—every repetition, every parallelism is powerfully binding.

> **Poem 1:** *Transaction:* in-|decision *Intention:* to thread out, to whack, to break *Direction:* ahead, over *Duration:* at femur length *Quantity:* double, twins, alternative, two

**Poem 2:** *Transaction:* promise *Intention:* to praise, to please *Direction:* inside, together *Duration:* time rate *Quantity:* fifty more, poly

**Poem 3:** *Transaction:* choose *Intention:* to observe *Direction:* end-up, in front *Duration:* to length *Quantity:* everything, more or less, nothing

**Poem 4:** *Transaction:* in decision, intent *Intention:* to reach back *Direction:* on the low side, lifting, altitude, next *Duration:* be ready *Quantity:* the amount

**Poem 5:** *Transaction:* the best we took it *Intention:* to step, beat *Direction:* front, back, beneath *Duration:* by the hour, quite slowly *Quantity:* one, one

**Poem 6:** *Transaction:* pay-out *Intention:* to play, to equal, to break *Direction:* back, rises *Duration:* next month *Quantity:* one, a bundle

**Poem 7:** *Transaction:* market *Intention:* to pitch, to pack *Direction:* turning, falling *Duration:* so soon, no more *Quantity:* too high, lesser

**Poem 8:** *Transaction:* won, bidder *Intention:* to beat, to shun *Direction:* ahead, over (c/f poem 1) *Duration:* cut-back, dying year *Quantity:* twice (c/f poem 1)

Linkages are made forceful throughout, not only by the continual employment of the form 'to [verb]' meaning 'in order to' (which gains the force of violence), but by strong, injunctive verbs and by curt statement. Abrupt and violent verbs may appear repeatedly; across the eight poems we find "cut one hand off", "cuts to length", "cutlack portable" and "faction cut-back". The characteristic and much-noticed deployment of uncontextualised nouns (what twins? what cargo? what door? etc.) proposes connections made in a space we do not inhabit, a report from an exile in another universe—to my left is the door, ahead of me a cover over black swilled albumen—, except that no concession is made to the recipient, thrown back on reconstruction according to repetitions and parallelisms, and the nouns tend to be voided of any anticipation of yield through syllabic swapping, sharing and half-rhyme. The turns, the doublings-back, the sense of being propelled outward only to be flung back onto a familiar track, constitute the nearest poetic experience can approach to a big dipper ride—so Poem 8 returns recognisably to the transactions of Poem 1.

Authority or 'coherence' is reinforced by the poems' sound-world, which revolves around transformations of the pair blink/back. Half rhymes and assonance are employed insistently throughout—the mark of like and non-like. Such a process of sound transposition between what might be read as significant properties, the poet's selection from a remarkable lexicon, tends to diminish the impact of any particular term, no matter how recherché; and to invest with particular force the commonplace markers of linkage—'got', 'what', 'whose', 'there', 'this', in the poem in question.

But the impatient reader may expostulate: what after all do these poems mean? Do these transactions amount to something sufficiently analogous to the 'real world', for all their sealed-off composure, which may be transformed through the act of reading into the texture of personal experience? For whilst alpha-function may not perform such an apprehension—whilst it does not pre-digest—, it is the precondition for such apprehension; it makes it possible. And they do; and furthermore, they do so within tight limits. That is to say, they will not permit the reader the creative latitude of an author with an author's responsibility for what goes to press, an unearned prodigality; their meanings are constrained by legitimacy within the transactional sets.

The opening lines of poems 2 and 3 appear to erect a formidable barrier to interpretation, and for that reason invite close reading as a test of apprehensibility. Identification of their central transactions suggests that they will revolve around promise and choice. Poem 2 I reproduce in full, but the reader will need to obtain the book in order to follow my argument in Poem 3.

> Avian protection like a court plank as
> much as I do, the top-out fortunate
> conversion kit to praise what follows
>
> that rainforest, a rapid flick together
> on the glass excused. Phosphor alert badges
> reinforce the eye of last-touch gladness
>
> with the time rate to please fifty more,
> non-negative liquid poly he does well
> at the promise line, perched snug inside.

The mightily obscure first line comes on with a declamatory assertiveness, undercut by the amusingly crummy franglais pun in "court plank". But in reading Prynne it is important not to become bogged down by obstacles and over-committed to a linear unfolding. We have hypothesised that the poem will be organised around the transaction of promise, and that promise is linked to an intention to praise. How does this help? As soon as we focus on these words, "fortunate" is brought into the field, and "avian protection" starts to lose some of its obscurity—it would be legitimate within this semantic zone to think of augury, both in the reading of birds' flight, and to think of the augury associated with the geese of the Capitol, who provided protection through their noise and were associated with a prediction regarding Rome's fate. "Top-out", a term used for the completing of a building, may assist us in bringing "court plank" within the pale; a court plank may be equipment for the builder of castles in the air.

Moving towards the end of the poem, "non-negative liquid poly" is afforded by "the promise line" allowing a smug recognition and inhabitation of any possible outcome—auguries can never be gainsaid by the turn of events. It is "non-negative" in that it cannot be disproved or falsified, but can never be positive to the extent that the prediction can be trustingly acted upon. After all, the "conversion kit" of prediction makes it possible always "to praise what follows".

The central stanza refers to the self-confirming quality of predictions of ecological disaster; the "glass" which bears "phosphor alert badges" may be television, and the allusion would appear to be to ecological documentaries. "Last-touch gladness" is always available at "the promise line" in the calm contemplation of promised calamity enjoyed by the viewer. The "time rate" set on such disaster will confirm and please any number of TV-supper prophets. Ecological prediction is interpreted as a scientific analogue for reading birds' flight or entrails.

The poem avoids mere jeremiad through recognition that any moral statement—such as this is—arrives complete with its own promise; it courts (another shade) its own fulfilment. The "I" of "much as I do" is also reinforced by "the eye of last-touch gladness". "The rainforest", introducing the second stanza, is an instructive instance of counterfactual transaction in that it bears (with an explicitness unusual in Prynne) upon the postmodern contention that the reality available to the contemporary viewer, listener and computer jock is 'virtual'. A rainforest is as much to hand and as amenable to direct gesture in the suburban sitting-room (*that* rainforest) as for any rainforest denizen. More so indeed, since the signifier 'rainforest' with its halo of meaning for Western ecology would be more or less meaningless to the rainforest's inhabitants. But there is an important distinction to be made, in that Prynne has always been a stringently moral writer—precisely that aspect of his poetry which broadly post-modern accounts have remained blind to, symptomatically enough; the availability of "that rainforest", the virtuality of 'our' world, poses a real problem in its easy sense of responsibility for others' lives and needs (or a relativistic irresponsibility, which comes to much the same thing). The hedonistic surfing of signifiers typical of self-consciously postmodern poetry, is absolutely to be distinguished from Prynne's concerns and poetic procedures; when Iain Sinclair in *Radon Daughters* described his Prynne-figure Simon Undark as 'the conscience of England' he is closer to the mark than any previous published interpreter of Prynne.[6] "What follows" televisually and is confused through a "rapid flick together" in anticipation of the "announcer" in Poem 3, relegates "that rainforest" to its place in the programme, but does not absolve the viewer (and certainly not the producer) from responsibility for his or her response even if it to some extent determines it. The insane pluralism of choice is accompanied by the Cultural Studies lecturer's assertion that they had no choice at all—and although experientially true, this cannot be allowed to become normative.

Poem 3 shifts from the transaction of promise to the transaction of Choose, offering an account of a recognisable modern dilemma frequently addressed in Prynne's earlier writing: how to articulate an ethics of choice amidst endless promise, where the menu is offered for consumption ahead of the meal? The obscure "foaming metal" which opens the poem may now be connected with "phosphor alert"; the "hatch" from which we are fed and in front of which "this" (whatever is on now) may be observed, is television. "Our confidence is end-up like a roller towel" is a characteristically Prynnian witticism which tends to make exposition sound laboured—but in a roller towel the end goes up to be recirculated, and fresh confidence, fresh promise are guaranteed.

The choices offered by the channels do "titillate to the contrary" and any choice is haunted by the co-presence of brands as urgently attractive (perhaps a tilt at the complicity of rampant deconstructionism in the provision of ever more choice—'presence' hardly requires to be subverted); but there is a marked and continuing reflexivity in these lines. "Moralising" is to be distinguished conceptually from moral choice, but how is the morality of choice to be exercised when any purchase entails the consumer in a chain of unreckonable antecedents and consequences—and morality disconnected from the act of choice becomes merely 'moralising' as in any documentary's indignation? It is hard to miss the point in the line "blandly the announcer cuts to length"; after all, the indicative nature of statement in these poems which are manifestly 'cut to length' makes their author, as we have argued, a link-man extraordinary. It is this sardony which connects *Not-You* with the earlier poem-sequence *Down where changed* even if *Not-You* eschews that book's savage self-arraignment and baffled stutters. The 'we' of "we'll roam the proving ground and choose" is therefore apt; as ever, Prynne uses the first person plural with fullest acknowledgment.

When promiscuous promise attends choice, choice must be vindi-cated, and if that is so, "nothing counts more or less furtively"—"furtively" because no moralised huffing and puffing can discount, although it may disguise, both the inconsequentiality of choice and its consequences; it counts more as it counts less, for even choice at the armaments fair and a visit to the proving ground will light upon one shining missile, spoilt for choice. Whatever the effects of "lithium grease", precisely reckoned time which slides, blurs, and overlaps and erases accountability for actions, it is incumbent on us, urgently so, to weigh "the dipper cargo" in the interests of "just bearing", *Not-You*'s concluding phrase. Not-You indeed, for you will be offered absolution and every choice will have been right at the time.

But the fallibility and hesitancy of memory render it equally untrust-worthy (nationalism as opposed to the digital global village), and its "coming and going" tend to be governed by calculated or unconscious self-interest. In the central section of *Not-You*, the poems tellingly feel their way by contrast with the clipped stanzas before and after, and the recurrence of 'delay', 'shade' and 'recall', would seem to afford a "provi-sion beyond the fixed mark of | break-out liable detachment." As read-ers we are brought to recall the monitory consultation of the heraldic twins of the first poem, for whom "shade over upon shade" was but a retread, the nostalgia and myth-making of "alternative danny boy in-|decision" giving way to the pleasures of the proving ground. To come down on one side would be the most arbitrary moralising. *Not-You* is marked by a restless dialectic between the algebraic logic of counterfac-tuals and the broken articulation of 'human value', whose tentative and beautiful synthesis in the book's final poem it must be left to the reader of this article to encounter.

The question asked in beginning this approach to *Not-You*—a book which had appeared in both large and short measure as 'impossible' as a book of poetry might be—, may sound less like the rhetorical flourishes now conventional in introducing a discussion of Prynne, and more open to answer through such an account of reading the first suite of poems, and Poems 2 and 3 in particular. Familiarity with the specialised languages often deployed is not a prerequisite for understanding; recog-nition of the chief transactions governing the poem tends to define a semantic range which governs some of the more opaque vocabulary, and the verse's foregrounding of linkages consonant with the governing transaction, bound strongly by tight sound-patterning, is more constitutive of the meaning-universe of the book than any privileged encapsulation in imagery or appeal to common experience. Indeed, the poems show more wit—which is a transactional effect—than sentiment. Close reading has shown that the reader's work is rewarded by the emergence of a powerful moral account of transaction; the necessity for such work—which can be regarded in Bion's terms as a process of conception made possible for the reader by the alpha-function of the poems—, and its implication of the reader and the author, means that the reader is spared both moralising documentary and the easy recognitions and presumptuous kinship delivered through false intimacy. It has been demonstrated that to lift the dependency of poetry upon speech-acts and to strive for a poetry of internal consistency, avoiding direct appeal to a common landscape or a sociological constituency, does not result in autism or a more histrionic detachment. And Prynne's writing has been distinguished sharply from a range of contemporary poetic practices with which previously it has been compared.

Down where changed had appeared to this reader to herald a recourse to 'Truthfulness-by-silence' as the epigraph to Not-You has it, and as Laura (Riding) Jackson found necessary. But neither "expectation of truthfulness-by-silence" with its inference of an inaccessible counterfactual poetic world wherein poetic negotiation continues to be transacted (for such silence is a poetical decision, as Laura (Riding) Jackson's account in The Telling makes explicit—it is a continuation of the poetic work), nor "love of semiconductors" which allows negotiations to be conducted independently of speech-acts, can lead to trust. Prynne's courage in writing beyond the seeming impasse of Down where changed, was to refuse to become exemplary through silence, and to decline the formalistic temptation to devise a poetic programme and let it run (either by mechanical or evolutionary analogy). In a universe where trust is endless solicited by objects, persons and every stray phrase, Prynne has been drawn towards a counterfactual practice with its attendant formalism, but his scrupulousness, and his powerful moral conscience are not still, and enjoin a trust in his writing which is earned as by no other contemporary poetry.

# Tenter Ground[7]

When Devin Johnston reviewed the second issuance (to adopt its author's terminology) of J.H. Prynne's *Poems* in Summer 2000, he consciously was introducing the work of a writer "whose readership in the United States has been miniscule" but which "included a devoted following among experimental poets".[8] The situation had been little different in Prynne's native England, although the degree of obscurity needed to render a poet invisible is a nice judgement. Small press editions of Prynne's writing sold below the radar in quantities which would not have disgraced a major publishing house for any but school curriculum adopted texts. But the substantial Bloodaxe *Poems* (collecting all besides Prynne's relatively conservative first book)[9] obtruded the name Prynne on pages hitherto closed or innocent, even a *TLS* reviewer asserting that "Prynne presents a body of work of staggering audacity and authority such that the map of contemporary poetry already begins to look a little different".[10]

This judgment was echoed by reviewers in several prominent journals; but it was Prynne's apparent canonization in the volume of *The Oxford English Literary History* devoted to the period 1960–2000 that sparked a media kafuffle in England, whereby harmless professors were invited by the press to offer views on whether his poetry was 'better' than the alternately sainted and demonized Philip Larkin's.[11] The only way for the practice of lyric poetry to be made comprehensible in media terms is to identify its sociological constituency; if this poetry wasn't identifiable as women's poetry, black poetry, Northern poetry or simply deranged (and professors would not be trapped into anything resembling a value judgment), then it had to be intellectual snobs' poetry. When other taxonomies falter, in England class caricature never fails.

In the forefront of such splenetic response were tenured professors of creative writing, furious at the effrontery of a writing seeming to disdain self-expression: surely this restraint evinced a superior attitude, both to ordinary humanity and to the expressive gift whose cultivation embodies resistance to all Bad Things—liberal economics, environmental devastation, child sexual abuse and unhealthy eating.[12] The politics of such a response are not inherently ignominious, despite the ironies of institutionally profitable courses and prize-winning ambitions; and the new edition of *Poems* might serve to bring a set of political and poetical questions into sharper relief than Professor Don Paterson's animus could achieve. This is because the seven sequences added to *Poems* 2005 (six of them published previously as chapbooks, and the first four collected as *Furtherance*, published in the United States by The Figures in 2004) include writing at once unfeasibly imbricated and politically vehement.[13] While Prynne's poetics differ fundamentally from those sometimes ascribed to American 'Language Poets', both face a dilemma of political instrumentality encapsulated by the American poet Chris Stroffolino in calling impishly for a political and artistic practice bridging John Prine (a blue-collar singer/songwriter) and J.H. Prynne. The age of theory had for some while seemed so decisively and convincingly to have displaced political engagement into textual and conference 'interventions', that artists in any media engaged in political (or 'cultural') struggle, notably feminist, felt driven into theoretical practice, a phrase revealed only slowly as an oxymoron.

The present climate amongst radical artists feels explosive with disgust, as before and during the First World War—even if the tactics of the Cabaret Voltaire must be discounted as the box of tricks of indulged pranksters like Damien Hirst. A reaction against the hedonistic prescriptions of the postmodern has seen a powerful revival of documentary film and led to audible talk of class and poverty even in the United States; but for those working in the modernist and post-theory context, a return to realism is not a credible option. The extent to which Prynne's recent poetry might propose a late modernist poetics of resistance to neo-colonialism outside its immediate curtilage is hard to predict, although the move of politically activist young Prynnians in the UK into performance, promoted by the brilliant young theatre director and poet Chris Goode, marks a notable break with late modernist queasiness (especially in Cambridge) around personal display and publicity, and a determination to take highly challenging writing into the anti-war, anti-racist and anti-capitalist movements. In the same vein

CDs have featured collaborations with avant-garde musicians working at the intersection of electronic dance music and improvised jazz.[14]

Such considerations are abetted by the appearance since the 1999 edition of *Poems* of high octane critical writing on Prynne, whose apogee has to be Kevin Nolan's 27,000 word internet essay 'Capital Calves'. Subtitled 'Undertaking an Overview', this is where all critical writing on Prynne must now start, and indeed it is tempting to suggest that any serious writing on contemporary poetics must deal with this astonishingly erudite (and infuriatingly unfootnoted and sloppily proof-read) conspectus not just of Prynne's formidable oeuvre, but of philosophical poetics through Longinus, Kant, Hegel, Heidegger, Adorno and Levinas (to name a few).[15] Alongside Nolan's essay, a recent book by Anthony Mellors, *Late Modernist Poetics from Pound to Prynne*, offers a provocative thesis on the persistence of a suppressed modernist lineage adhering to the arcane and sacred beyond those quarters where it is acknowledged (for instance in Robert Duncan), a provocation both supported and blunted by close reading and detailed scholarship.[16] Taken together with *Poems* 2005, these two critical texts assist in considering how Prynne's poetry (and that of younger British late modernist poets, notably Keston Sutherland) differs from Language Poetry, and the implications of such difference both for theoretical poetics and for the practice of writing poetry in the Haliburton age.

The questions raised by Mellors are closely akin to debates which have surfaced recently among reflective poets in the United States, for instance in a fascinating discussion of John Ashbery's work on *Silliman's Blog*.[17] How far have seemingly revolutionary modernist and postmodernist adventures in poetry really disavowed the romantic elevation of lyric poetry to a divine discourse? A couple of centuries of repeated proclamations of a break with ontology (Mellors cites imagism as the model instance) seem scarcely to have dispelled the numinous vapours attending any conception of poetry as a securely-fenced linguistic activity. Unless circuit-breakers and dampers are introduced with conscious ingenuity, poetry's obscurity and separateness resonate with those tantalizingly just-beyond-hearing echoes which Westerners find definitive of spirituality; anti-modernists like Don Paterson are right to detect an anti-humanistic and hieratical tendency in this tradition of transcendent un-transcendence.

Such questions acquire greater historical irony in the United States than in England, since every American child learns that once the cultural and religious elitist T.S. Eliot found his proper destination in

foggy London and clouds of incense, the modernist home field was occupied by the rudely democratic descendents of William Carlos Williams.
Even John Ashbery has come to be praised routinely for his 'democratic'
love of Americana and of the ambient discourses which he so brilliantly
(and a little too easily) turns into silk purses. In the United States, the
contemporary reply to the anti-idealist challenge is that American
'progressive' poetry has become democratically 'open', whether an open
field or a jostling downtown.

Gerald L. Bruns' recent book *The Material of Poetry* exemplifies this
faith, taking a cue from Lyn Hejinian's celebration of poetry's freeing
from professors and elitists, and its potential for undermining all unde-
mocratic and unnatural hierarchies—both Bruns and Hejinian seeming
serious about this potential.[18] Expatiating on Hejinian's 'The Rejection
of Closure', Bruns writes: "For Hejinian … "open" means more than
open ended, playful, aleatory, or nonlinear; it also means open to what
is outside the poem. (Imagine a porous poem.) She writes: "The 'open
text,' by definition, is open to the world and particularly to the reader. It
invites participation, rejects the authority of the writer over the reader
and thus, by analogy, the authority implicit in other (social, economic,
cultural) hierarchies. It speaks for writing that is generative rather than
directive. The writer relinquishes control and challenges authority as a
principle and control as a motive. …""[19]

The proposition that the open text "speaks for writing" exposes the
naïveté of this program; it is not so easy to avoid exercising authority,
and the anti-hierarchical but unpublished writer may well question by
what process of privileged selection *this* writer's demonstrations of relinquished control are packaged and distributed, to be further consoli-
dated as authoritative texts through the attention of distinguished critics. She might also question whether *one* reader has ever been incited by
such texts to engage in political action; this before examining the texts
and considering their claims to 'openness'—sustainable only through
quasi-Trotskyite imputations of false consciousness to the non-profes-
sional and baffled reader. On the other hand, the idea that a writer's
'relinquishing control' will remove the bad spell sustaining authority
must count as magical thinking at its most inflated.

By a fortunate coincidence, Kevin Nolan in 'Capital Calves' seizes on
the same essay by Hejinian: "Writers like Lynn [sic] Hejinian can twitter
on about the 'rejection of closure' all they need to, sweetly unaware that
'closure' is merely relocated intact from a textual component into a
mirror image of the voluntarism that pre-selects it ('rejection')."[20] The

contemptuousness of Nolan's phrasing should not obscure the serious point: if 'closure' or 'authority' are to mean anything besides minor stylistic choices for poets, if they are to bear any relation to the authority of Haliburton or KPMG or the Catholic Church or 'patriarchy' or the institution of Medicine or the State of Slovakia—then the notion that a poet can simply decide one day that she will abolish them, must be preposterous. In fact, *this* is a religious conviction, comparable to a conversion experience: suddenly everything looks different! And Bruns' lectures proceed to riff on the way in which certain uses of language can stimulate a reader or audience to question the ontological status of the linguistic work; this poetics of encounter is what he means by a 'philosophical poetics', and it is definitively postmodern.

But the forces at work in language cannot be reduced to this dismissible thing, 'closure', nor can the writer free herself with one bound from the economic, social and linguistic orders within which she has negotiated her position during her development—*she can never be free and neither can any reader*. The historical irony is that the open text looks very like the would-be autonomous text, and appeals to exactly the same constituency; it is nothing but the would-be autonomous text in denial. Such denial makes for hectic runarounds and attention-grabbers—zany parody, stand-up routines, anything which might lure on board the charmingly innocent reader then whip the floor away from under her: now you try the trick on your own, my dear! To enlist poetry in energetic revolt can be exciting; but revolt tends to precede a settling down— either the depressive reckoning with economic and social reality, or a persistence in childishness. The more strenuous the commitment to naïve conceptions of openness, the more conservative becomes the undertow, freighted with nostalgia for childhood and its romanticised freedoms.

By contrast, the interrogative resistance to the delusions of autonomy in selfhood and in poetic text conducted in Frank O'Hara's 'In Memory of My Feelings' and pursued in his later conversational poetry, resistant also to the consolations of childhood which are Ashbery's compulsive and career-long resort, remains an important precursor to Prynne's ferocious rebuttals of the desert temptations of freedom. Kevin Nolan's essay can be read as an admiring protest against the scorched-earth poetics which are O'Hara's surprising legacy in Prynne:

But far from deploying poetry as the armature of a counter-Weberian strategy designed to pit 'institutional rationality' against a variety of literary estrangements, the very notion of autonomy itself has in Prynne's work become, increasingly, the site of attrition. [...] Yet the idea of autonomy may be ineradicable, not least because the dream of its eradication is the first evidence for its continuing presence amidst the debris of self evidence. [...] Some minimal and undiminished conception of autonomy is necessary if human personhood, even when relegated to authorship, is to continue, and for this to be ethically possible, some notion of resistance has remained formally central to much contemporary poetics besides Prynne's own.

Here Nolan alludes to radical poetry's role in resisting the systemic goal-orientation, the positivism exemplified in the Thatcherite proclamation and Blairite acceptance that There Is No Alternative to the rational interests of global capital, which individual fantasies of home-coming whether to God or to identity, serve merely to perpetuate. The danger lies in too comprehensive an articulation of the individual as the creature of ideological forces, a thoroughgoing deconstruction leaving the category of the human agent empty, a twitching puppet.

Nolan's protest is evoked especially by the seven books added to *Poems* in the 2005 edition. The first new book is *Red D Gypsum*, a text of thirty eight-line stanzas already the recipient of a critical analysis centring on the thematic of trekking.[21] This work takes its place in a lineage of Prynnian anti-pastoral whose earliest full expression was *High Pink on Chrome* (1975), the titles announcing the affinity. Chemical treatments, plant breeding, genetic manipulation: these are the countryside pursuits of our day which *Red D Gypsum* hybridises with financial instruments, specifically the hedge funds of which Lillian Chew, source of the text's epigraph, is a theoretician—thus the appearance of 'ferox' in the final stanza nicely unites a cannibal trout (such trout grow to monstrous size) with the name of a hedge fund.

Hybridity, not subordination, is the mechanism at work here, and this also is the principle of the text's manufacture. To call *Red D Gypsum* a text is to respect its self-reflexive cluster of terms for textile—pasture becomes a rug, turf is reduced to fibre.[22] Even food can now be woven, the mycelial meat substitute Quorn being an example. The dense weave of these stanzas is determinedly non-hierarchical in their plying of social, political, financial and scientific languages, but also formally their composition resolves into bands, strips and slats, with a modularly extended syntax whose sub-clauses or routines are often not clearly demarcated from the main clauses. With the exceptions of *Pearls That Were* and of *Triodes*, these new texts share certain characteristics with memory boards: that is, they consist of flat modules in non-hierarchical arrays, each intricately etched, polycentric and with switchable polarity. Such fretwork or mesh is the common term between textiles and electronics. For each text the stanzaic module is set and uniform, so in *Red D Gypsum* for instance, nine-beat lines compose eight-line stanzas.

Furthermore, the cadences of these texts are flattened. Consider the beginning and end points of the material added in *Poems* 2005, the first stanza of *Red D Gypsum* (1998) and the last stanza of *Blue Slides at Rest* (2004):

> Now trek inter-plate reversion to earth buy out
> as waters buried or get carrier up ready put
> across gypsum branch effaced, as root planed
> for don't now look to demand new birds in talent
> from turf stripped to fibre. Rip brace out here
> on the fringe reckless bestowing taint by the mart
> chosen, tamper nickel token lunge to bite you may
> cover down over, a flawless glucose shimmered sky.

> *Poems* 2005, p. 435.

> Go down in earth like a feather, front brace. Left over
> unrightful semblant will punish devoted machine knit
> parapet. Nip and tuck miniature grounded so. Into this
> world of darkness, of a kin deducted justified reproved
> to end without, companion hooded unseen. Attempt thus
> cut down as had never. Go with me. Within segment floss
> honour bright missing, on foot. Ignorant paramount will
> cadge a ride cranky dope appeal months and years, tell
> in mish-mash certainty head to black on. Better broken
> keep house yielding softly gnomic cataract depressed
> inwardly sent away. In care from hers avoidance transit
> accept in strong wardship, order holding trace and lock.

> *Poems* 2005, p. 575.

Apart from the conventional abjuration "Go with me", addressed to a "companion" who is "unseen" or "missing" in the second piece, this is a writing almost without pronouns. Without pronouns the residual sense of autonomy viewed by Nolan as the last resort of human political agency, is all but extinguished. Pronouns also are the chief grammatical element around which poetic cadence is organised, as they are the figures of delivery and reception, of agency and of yielding. Fundamental emotional and psychic movements of give-and-take, projection-and-introjection, and sadism-and-depression, govern poetic cadence, and they are associated with the development of a sense of self (comprising both autonomy and managed dependence) through language. True, a pronoun is implicit as the object of the injunctive verbs which govern eight of the twelve sentences in the two pieces, and the reader can hardly avoid taking this personally. Although at first the injunctive impact feels like an unjust berating, within the poems' weave the injunctions contribute to the sense of a world internally articulating through devices of devilish intricacy, or perhaps through computer programs—"buy", "get" and "put" being instructions in computerised market trading programs where decision-making cannot wait on human reflexes.

The absence of pronominal agency contributes to an almost robotic verse movement, further reinforced by the dominance of single-syllable verbs and nouns. This is "turf stripped to fibre" in the earlier stanza, "machine knit" in the book's last. But single-syllable words are nodal in Prynne rather than essential; they are knots in the mesh's reticulation. Thus "talent" is linked to "nickel" and "token" in a financial node, as well as to desire or partiality—but these attributes of will can now be expressed only in terms which re-animate the King James biblical sense of "talent" as coin. The word "brace" as used in the first stanza not only refers to some kind of support, but evokes in connection with "waters buried", "gypsum branch" (gypsum leached from fertiliser use), "new birds", "cover" and "glucose shimmered sky", perhaps a rough shoot in a fen landscape, a living off the land now implicated with the language of commerce—"buy out", "carrier", "demand". "Lunge to bite" tightens these scenarios through a single phrase uniting the raptor with the corporate raider.

The reticulations of this verse knit the components of a flattened landscape and a short-pile universe. In *Red D Gypsum* a root is "planed" and the sky's glucose contributes to the same economy as the fen's major crop of sugar beet. All activity occurs "inter-plate" (surely a pun on 'interpolate'), the sardony of "flawless" exacerbated in a space with neither floor nor ceiling, neither roots nor sky. "Bestowing taint" becomes the prime human activity in this flattened world, once all disposition and structure ("brace") have been ripped out.

Readers of Prynne have come to expect the closing passages of his works to perform a gesture of recognition towards the still uncorrupted or the ethically habitable, to allow some horizon which if not transcendent (and even in *High Pink on Chrome* it can sound nearly so), offers a little breathing-space; and *Red D Gypsum* does end with "vocal folds glowing deep unwinding", a space reminiscent of late Beckett but whose intense lyricism reconfigures flattened nature into a habitable room: "Vivid strips | of tree bark circle the room".[23] Although the tone of *Blue Slides at Rest* is almost vernal after the spoliations of *Red D Gypsum*, the closing passage cited above insists on its "machine knit" in a flurry of puns—"left over | unrightful", "nip and tuck"—and the room in which it comes to rest seems like a resort to maternal care, the only companion into the "world of darkness" being the internalised *holding* structure which the poem has gathered from the "paramount" She who oversees the poem.

Here then is the notable exception to the pronominal dearth in late Prynne: female pronouns dominate *Blue Slides at Rest* and *Triodes* as they did *Her Weasels Wild Returning* (1994), and the worlds of these poems are structured (or 'braced') by paramount women, there being no explicitly responsive male principle unless the entire texture of corruption is to be gendered as male (or has been male-engendered). The She of *Triodes* is Pandora, a Pandora whose political hopes are blocked at every turn in a Game Theory nightmare where state terror and the freelance terrorism of the dispossessed (for the setting is Palestine) have etched all possible pathways; while Nolan argues persuasively for the She of *Her Weasels Wild Returning* as a Penelope awaiting "a bloody new antistrophe in the history of conquest, marital and martial." The maternal presiding over *Blue Slides at Rest* permits a lyric inflection which rides an almost prelapsarian landscape (although what crosses the placenta can be fearful): strikingly, "Downy finish is | hers to ask after, the swan's road into Palestine not | yet level."[24] When Prynne read this poem at the first Pearl River Poetry Conference in Guangzhou, China in July 2005, he instructed the audience to close their eyes and to regard each word as a pinprick of light in a black screen, switched on then extinguished.

It is hard to reconcile such an instruction with the poem's "machine knit" of pre-birth, birth and early infant activity, with its still-insistent hybridity:

> Care taken, took into by a glance. Her hair loosened,
> cheek more red, plasma lactic acid dropping utter spread
> like raid to her knee, so freely downwards. Entranced

restricted cub in this tunnel, lissom case notes asperge
crevice woeful did they either.

*Poems* 2005, p. 573.

The connections are tightly plied between bodily and linguistic processes ("lissom case notes asperge"), and the child to which the poem adverts is no untrammelled sprite but a nipple-chewing Kleinian awaiting the language to propel him into his inheritance of hormones, gasoline and shamefulness. Still, the suggestion is that death can be—indeed, can *only* be—endured as a prospect through the deep but occluded psychic structure precipitated from the mother/child dyad and its intramural exchanges. This psychic chamber may also resound in response to particular poetic cadences, and even the most compressed of late Prynne poetic texts are rife with bitten-off and damped-down memories of earlier writing whose cadences felt deeply compelled. These residual, highly individual resources, which may be immune or at least resistant to contamination but are more likely to have become inaccessible to many who have been flattened in the most forceful vernacular sense, re-pose the political question: how are such resources to be made available politically, collectively?

The celebration of the 'open' too often welcomes back the transcendent via the cult of 'the body' as the home of authenticity, performing a manoeuvre now familiar on the post-modernist terrain, by re-installing pre-linguistic voice (expressed for Bruns in sound poetry) to summon the world back into substantial being. As often, Artaud provides the avant-gardist with a licence for such recidivism, but the logic is impeccable once the phenomenology of the encounter becomes the organising principle in the media welter, and Bruns' position is consistent. The abstraction of financial flows, signed off in automated trading, accompanied the rise of minimalist art: at a certain point of complexity, management becomes more important than the manifest of goods. The more 'theoretical' its 'concerns', the more art relies on the encounter—no longer is the viewer the connoisseur or the would-be home decorator, but she asks: what are the designs of this object on me, what is it doing here, and how am I supposed to respond? Just so the open text becomes an *environment* within which the reader performs her free response, in a zero-gravity space of indifference, a Buddhist world where designing languages have been neutralized. All is at play. Only the suffering body's screams, grunts, ecstatic yells and groans rip open the veil of appearances.

Given every toy money can buy, the Western child throws tantrums and expects praise for them.

Prynne's attack on body sentimentality has been remorseless, starting with *Wound Response* (1974). Like William S. Burroughs, he conceives of the body as soft machinery and biochemistry interspersing silicon and soil and gabble. Hence, as Nolan contends, there can be no 'home' to which Penelope can return. Indeed Nolan argues that a writing which from the start has refused such home consolations, basing its claims on an ethics of responsiveness, rather than the usual politics of representation attended by elegiacs for the loss of presence, necessarily was driven to seek an autonomy whose relation to experience then became principally one of shame. How could it be otherwise? Whatever autonomy poetry secures or claims, shames the author complicit with the historical and material conditions required for such relative independence; and whatever distance from corrupt discourse is asserted by the lyric text, its embedded cadences, its connective tissues, have been cultured in the factories of the human genome project—and patented for use. For Nolan, Prynne's late writing has fallen into an impasse of autoimmune struggle whereby the stuff from which it spins its network of resistance, is the very stuff which threatens its putative integrity; every agent has been 'turned' in advance.

This is the autoimmune dynamic. The system always threatens to eat itself; but how preferable is this risk to the nostalgia which has poets of oppressed ethnicities casting their laments for the homes to which they were never admitted, into the trophies of 'diversity' that *The New Yorker* admits to interleave the elegiac poetics of advertisements for sports cars doomed to queue at freeway toll booths? Here is a galloping consumption indeed.

Does *Blue Slides at Rest* offer a way out of Prynne's impasse? Only at the personal and poetic level, only by side-stepping the pileup which has preceded it. What are the alternatives presented by contemporary poetry in English, that is poetry which takes its poetic vocation seriously, more than the creation of pretty baubles? The alternative impasse of open poetry has been spelled out: it is based on an ahistorical and childish fantasy, destined to revert to the body or to metaphysics. Happily it practiced what it preached only for one historical moment and then fitfully, so now a pleasure of reading Lyn Hejinian's poetry is its "chatty asides, exclamations, digressions, gossip, confidences (all bedside mannerisms)", as that of reading Charles Bernstein's is its elatingly improvisational wit.[25] Such poise and charisma permit a continuing independence from the blights of spirituality and empathy; but the poetry attracts for the kind of qualities admired in *people*, and it surely must be troubling that what still is known academically as Language Poetry has found an audience through the attractiveness of its authors' personalities. But then, the politics of this poetry always had licensed the poet to do exactly what he or she liked.

By strict contrast, the politics of Prynne's poetry have afforded him little room for manoeuvre. A reader who can bear an unremittingly clear-sighted exposition of the full ethical and political implications of Western citizenship at the turn of the millennium has nowhere else to look: for at every other turn, issue politics offers its implicit and pitiful assurance that *once* equal opportunities are real, *once* animals are no longer slaughtered, *once* the carbon economy is replaced by a sustainable way of life, humankind will be back on track—even if most activists recognise they are engaged in a struggle without end. But after all, these are not separable ambitions. There is no imaginable version of contemporary British or American society which would not depend on organised exploitation. The very texture of Prynne's recent poetry is manufactured from these double and triple-binds, and outrageously the fabrications can be beautiful. But what then? *Blue Slides at Rest* feels like a revision of *Into the Day* (1972), an earlier birth song where "the compounded blood | and light makes lustre swerve in the dream", but now seeking any interstice for "the natural child" in the fabric of comprehensive corruption, even if only the grave. What if when you open your eyes, the lights have gone out?

# Into the Day

*Into the Day* was the book by J.H. Prynne which first compelled me; through the frustration of attempting to close-read these poems, I understood poetry I could barely describe might provide rewards greater than what readily submitted. This plate just couldn't be polished off. *Brass* might have taught that lesson, but I did not encounter it—too expensive for an undergraduate—until I knew *Into the Day*. What does this book mean at some distance in time?

English poetry then offered nothing comparable. The poem cycle begins:

> Blood fails the ear, trips the bird's
> fear of bright blue. Touching that
> halcyon cycle we were rested in ease
> and respite from dismay: strip to
> the noted bark, stop the child.

What goes on here? For that is the question I learnt to substitute for: What does it say? These lines sound like scene-setting, couched in historical narrative, proclaiming theme. Their syntax is correct, their movement lays down the law. Given though that "we" and "the child" are unattributable and fail to return in the first poem, and "bright blue" might be the sky or the kingfisher's (halcyon's) own wings, and given too the poem's refusal to explain its moves, here, evidently, was 'advanced' poetry. Advanced poetry meant textual derangement, extremity of personal testimony, chance procedures or parataxis, each inviting swift recognition before engaging its dedicated reading mode. None of these seemed apt.

The language of *Into the Day* differed startlingly from *The White Stones*, whose urgency was discursive and founded in an ethics of inhabitation. Although this cycle alludes to Charles Olson's poem 'The Kingfishers', it presents an emphatic shift in Prynne's poetic: henceforward he will cease primarily to "hunt among stones" but cue to measure, to time. Disputational syntax now gives way to a conductor's authority. Who is being enjoined, insistently and in a discourse whose adjectival sparingness brooks no argument? This writing's articles and deictics assert that we know the score. Outrageously, because the model of the poem as a medium for a man's speaking to men is so inculcated that a poem exhibited or staged, to be approached, read around, considered at different times and in different lights; or the poem as a score or plough-line to be followed; or the poem as orchestration (intellectual and musical) to be attended to or entered; none of these possibilities can offer itself until the speech model has been closed off as resolutely as these first lines achieve in face of the obstinate reader. Although the cadences of speech in high rhetorical mode charge Prynne's prosody here, they eschew the assumed intimacy of contemporary lyric.

This departure from intimate speech is by a notably different strategy from the parataxis so important to Anglo-American modernism, handing over the poem to exegesis for formal resolution. Of course, exegesis might be otherwise solicited; the assurance of Prynne's first stanza could prepare for allegory and a process of disclosure whereby the reader's struggle for meaning becomes itself a moral or religious training.

But the poetry does not need such strenuousness or devotion, even if it would attract it. The first stanza could be taken as a thematic announcement in a musical sense. Its elements will develop and both ear and mind follow their development with pleasure, within this cycle and in subsequent work of Prynne's (which requires an active memory). For instance, and reflexively, the ear closed in the first line is to be recognised in later passages both through its physical structure and through its attention to music. Crystal and quartz belong to the same thematic complex owing to their use in timing, in measure. A cluster opposing and closing the ear is announced in the word "bark", associated with other coverings such as paving-slabs, and with fear, blockage and aversion. There may be a link between covering and print, via lithographic stones and trays—in the second poem "circa 1430" may refer to the invention of moveable type.

Elements such as ear and bark will recur altered by their context, because they are incorporated in a poem cycle tracking a diurnal cycle, one of several by Prynne (the distinction between diurnal cycles and books of poems seems lost with *High Pink on Chrome* three years later). The 1972 first edition of *Into the Day* presents this diurnality visually with its black disks at front and back and its yellow disks dividing the two parts of the cycle. The corpus of Prynne's poetry, from *Brass* onwards, shares a character whereby what is presented seemingly as allegorical, is by degrees recognised as laid out openly: this is a poetry of open secrets. Some have identified the pilgrimage or trek as an organising motif, but its apparent teleology, as in depth, breakthrough or birth, is linked to recurrence rather than arrival or return and is more a heartfelt contrivance making it tolerable to go on. *Into the Day* inevitably returns to darkness, "from frenzy | to darker fields we go", but "in the set course" there will be day again and in these temporal and measured terms it becomes possible to say "we go". What do we do with what we cue to, with our stewardship, will then become the main theme. Therefore later poems will darken. Even in *Into the Day* for all its gorgeousness, oil spills from the lamp and becomes "an arab | tide," and what becomes of the first stanza's bird, is "its claw broken" or is it reduced to "the Egyptian plover's label"? Literal truths abound and must be seen for what they are.

What we hear and know of the world is constituted according to preset scripts, whether comforting, terrible or diverting, and our responses tend likewise, in assent, disinterest or impotent outrage. It is not invention we need from poets but the transmuting of information into current events. *Into the Day* inaugurated a project of the present day. Jeremy Prynne's current events configure the day like nothing else.

# The Line to Take: An appreciation of the seventies poetry of John James

In the late 1970s I was there when John James read at Kettle's Yard in Cambridge; could anyone in the audience have forgotten the exquisite antagonism between the poet and the place or failed to reflect on the frustrated sympathy between the two, out of which their antagonism was born? For the art of Kettle's Yard chimed with the elegant verse of John James' past and future, and John James wanted its domesticated artworks to be re-animated in him and in his verse, released from their confinement at his yelp; yet also Kettle's Yard wanted his belligerence which harked back to its founding myth and that of its modernism. And at this time, in poems casually reproduced or unprinted, James could rail against the painting and sculpture he loved as "the preoccupation of dull and stupid women" or wrench them into an improbable dialect (Richard Long and Howard Hodgkin in cod patois)—artworks descending politely from those which lived out their days at Kettle's Yard in the keeping of a dull cult of the madman domesticated and advertised. Yet wasn't the myth of the possessed artist, tracing his deliberate line at the onset of delirium tremens and selling drawings for absinthe into their museum servitude, paraded before us in this poet raging for Cambridge's connoisseurs of transgression? Here was the dialectic of modernism in all the contradictions of its relationship with the collection/home/museum, embodied in the offensive, licensed poet, in the audience which was the poet's support and appreciative clique relishing the shock delivered by this spectacle of modernism alive and snorting vigorously in the very mortuary of modernism. Here was the poet who loved art but was disgusted by its commoditisation, who dreamed to

Scriabin and Debussy but woke to Iggy Pop and The Sex Pistols, detourn-
ing the fan magazines and the most strenuous high art

> on the Bean Time line
> on the Bean-Sidhe line
> on the line out line
> on the rising line
> JHP and Siouxsie-Sioux make the feathered jump to Hyper Space
> Pure Chainsaw feeling in the Vat of TLP
> The Enemy of TV/The Enemy of Slow Decay
> the hard line on the fall-out line
> > (*A Former Boiling*)

into lines that railed against cold-warism, colonialism and the H-blocks
and the stagnation of British culture; here was the poet who appropriated the rhetoric of resistance from Irish republicanism and
Rastafarianism for a stuttering and fragmented sound-collage which
concluded

> wear it short but loose & full off your head
> but strip your neck to the nape
> not for my sake
> but as a gift
> > (*War*)

so making the hood of sensory-deprivation torture at once a fashion
statement, a wet dream and an ethical, political and aesthetic symbol.
Such an assault upon taste and its categories as *War/A Former Boiling*
(the latter being the high-rant Mayakovskian insert to the former 1978
text as punk itself became commoditised) could hardly have been
staged more pointedly than at Kettle's Yard where the machinery of
earlier revolts—and their factitious by-blows—had been beached for
contemplation. Contemplation was shattered by this performance
whose jarring notes rescued artefacts from their long slumber and
remobilised time (whose movement is felt only in clash, contradiction,
or more despairingly in accumulation) within the durance of the long-
stay ward.

Kettle's Yard had become the hushed, bleached and polished preserve
of a dainty modernism exemplified in the painting of the Nicholsons—
of taupe, cream and carefully wavering incisions, of 'natural' hues
should nature have been restricted to earth and chalk; that art where

work co-operates with 'natural processes' as it were meditatively, as if a peasant ploughed for the aesthetic pleasure of it or yet more philosophically were himself ploughed by the land. It is a place of 'surfaces' rather than shelves or floors, where pebbles and driftwood are arranged in heaps or swirls to gladden the eye beside a neutered Gaudier-Brzeska, where natural is also native and folkish and Alfred Wallis' paintings are as much an outgrowth of place as a Brancusi materialised as a product of stone through some 'respect for the material'. 'Place' in this aesthetic means a relationship between artist and an unspoiled and timeless visual setting, mediated by the work of art—the setting may be Mediterranean or Welsh or Cornish, but never suburban or light-industrial. Material means a substance which the artist has been the first man or woman to transfigure, or can feign to be so—hence the restricted palette, as though paint were applied from the naked earth rather than a mahogany Windsor and Newton case—or again, as though earth had urged its trace through the artist. *Respect* requires careful arrangement rather than anything suggesting manufacture, the considered, craftsman's mark or the cut along the grain rather than a routing, stamping, slashing or spattering which does the material violence. Honesty demands an even light, the eschewal of showiness; the artefacts must not be cluttered so compromising their individual authenticity, yet neither should they be isolated so as to dominate or compel. Some Buddhist trappings instruct the viewer in the correct frame of mind, contemplative, letting go of all desire, and resolutely avoiding vulgar considerations of value or of celebrity. The exhibits therefore were unlabelled, and surely a shell is as much an outcome of nature's artistry as that constructivist mobile.

Students could recline in low chairs to browse art catalogues, when admitted after tugging a bell-pull of weathered cork, the flotsam float of a fishing net. This is a so-English variant of modernism which creates a space even further sunk into vacuity than the English natural round of peasant and paternalistic proprietor. The coincident release of Ken Russell's film on Gaudier, its posters proclaiming 'All Art Is Sex', was a ludicrous but apt violation of this modernism so drained of desire, void of passion; where the only movement could be the turn of a delicate mobile but for the awkward padding of visitors scared to knock some winsome arrangement of seed-cases or of slipping on a thick white rug across the buffed floor, to crash into the grand piano and send a priceless figurine crashing. The *ne plus ultra* of such vacuity is of course the Tate Gallery in St Ives, whose touristic 'natural' setting has prompted the construction of a vast plein-air backdrop for an art which pales, sputters and sinks in the face of the sky's grand designs.

John James lurched into the withdrawing-room sanctum in a black bondage suit of synthetic material, some petroleum by-product, improbably strapped to make every movement unpredictable, stocky, hair brushed up black and spiky with Corimist no doubt, and he delivered lines like a flame-thrower: *War/A Former Boiling.* This was a thrilling poetry reading; Kettle's Yard was filled with tensely breathing flesh, and I felt fortunate to be sewn up into this literary cusp, when the famously mandarin art of 'Cambridge poetry' met a radical popular art and was set to break modernism out of the enclosure into which it had been designed for rainy-day idlers or to provide raw material for the research mills about. I should have remembered, looking about me, how any modernist movement needs its roustabouts, how the myth of the Dionysiac artist guarantees the human depth of the most hieratical art, as Gaudier-Brzeska's life-myth serves at Kettle's Yard to charge severe abstraction or merest whimsy with the sign of emotional and sexual revelation.

But this is to suggest that what was flung from the mouth might for a less partial listener have found its place easily amidst the furniture and ornaments as one more appurtenance, and this would not have been so. Much of the conceit of Kettle's Yard was the pretence that this was a home into which the visitor was received by the resident conservator, a home whose contents were artlessly arranged according to love and intuition and convenience. John James' poems of the time were as rough and informal, as 'street' as poetry could be while still bearing the traces of such a European-literary sensibility as his earlier writing had conveyed if not contrived to the lengths of pastiche. The poems would be neither commoditised nor domesticated; they contained and traduced commodities; they bellowed and stammered out of a body made more telling and threatening by its constriction, located as male, Welsh and working-class, and from which they would have to be detached to exhibit as literary art. This was a physical performance art let loose on the mummified art objects about and shocking in reproach, demonstrating what James had learnt in his collaboration with the artist Bruce MacLean; anything but home entertainment.

The puzzle is that nothing discernible followed, for this was a performance which could and should have travelled. The puzzlement is not mine alone; in a Radio 3 broadcast of highlights of a previous Cambridge Poetry Festival, the commentator had heard in the thunderous applause which greeted John James, the advent of the poetry of a new generation, and at this reading James had hit the Zeitgeist, that relationship with a wider than literary cultural shift which is the precondition for poetry extending its reach beyond its few votaries. Yet his poems remained firmly shut out from both the institutions of literature and the Late Show counter-cultural circuit which served those assiduous for what was happening wherever. Perhaps the poems had neither the laughs nor the straightforward constituency politics necessary for the gigging poet, although (unlike most Cambridge writing) they certainly had the punch-lines. As for dissemination from the audience, this was a time at which Theory enraptured the young and before Cultural Studies made it hip to attend to shifts in popular culture; it was one of those caesuras in the line of Cambridge Poetry, when readings were attended by an unchanging group and tuned-in students were elsewhere, competing in seminars. This group was augmented by the gratifyingly anxious and bewildered Friends of Kettle's Yard. The thrill was held and restricted to the energy line running between Panton Street and Gonville & Caius.

In keeping with punk aesthetic, James' writing of the time appeared in duplicated and xeroxed editions of a casualness which makes a Writers Forum pamphlet look like a major production—*A Former Boiling* could hardly be termed a publication at all; my copy doesn't bear James' 'Avocado' trademark or any publication data, but is signed and dated 'London July '79'. Neither *War* nor *A Former Boiling* was collected in James' next retrospective, *Berlin Return* (1983), although much earlier poems are included; 'Craven Images' starts with a sampling of the punk manner, and 'One for Rolf' (originally published in 1975) and 'Narrative Graffiti' feature the choppiness and pop culture borrowings of the Kettle's Yard material, but engrossed into a longer perspective and book-ended by poems in which the extended, zip gun line is dominant. The rumoured de luxe edition of *Toasting*, the third major extended poem of the late seventies (dated 1st May 1979), never appeared; its only outing was in the duplicated catalogue to the exhibition of the same name at the University of Sussex from May to June of that year, John James being poet in residence. True, the hectic improvisations of *Toasting* would have worked better as a headphone commentary to the paintings; the poem's loose recycling and relocation would have locked on, en face with repro-duced artworks, binding both. But if none of these poems was to have been exhibited as text, where are the tapes, and what an opportunity missed for video!

Was there also something of the reluctant rock-star in John James, a congenital tendency to withdraw whenever success outside the familiar and supportive constituency beckoned; or did he come to feel these poems too much of their time? The signs change; by the time of *Berlin Return* David Bowie had postured as a Nazi, and The Human League (to whom *A Former Boiling* is dedicated, the title borrowed from an early single) shifted foot from anger to irony and found a mass market as the precursors of The Pet Shop Boys. More generally, the impact of these poems would have been buffered by the Cambridge trademark and the long stand-off between a Cambridge disdain for publicity in the literary and cultural fashion pages where publicity might have broken. This is a great pity, since James is a considerable poet whose work could be popular—a rare thing in Britain—and is unusually conscious of image. Neither is image supererogatory to his writing, as I hope to indicate. It is hard to think of another British poet of any affiliation who might have been a fashion leader; but later on James was in tweeds and slicked hair well before Mulberry and today's City floor-traders.

Punk was the perfect have-it-both-ways aesthetic for a poet who had always shown ambiguity towards his talents and anything which might be categorised as art, "supine art & supremely useless poetry". Nostalgia for art tempered by aggression against art is the very manner of James, and his poems yearn to be anything but poems—they are "letters", a "theory", "toasting" and engaged in a permanent struggle against lyric grace as though it were the siren call of sensual abandon. Having discovered John James' poems as an undergraduate I was bewildered that a writer possessing mastery of the swagger line any young male poet would mug for, perversely should campaign against such a gift, strapping his lines into stumble, lurch and indignity. I now think of such perversity as emerging out of a discomfort similar to that felt by the poets of the Movement, also proclaiming working-class origin, at the institutions of art and literature in the wake of the Second World War. James is of a younger generation, one which still knew rationing but whose anger was directed not only at such institutions but also the meritocratic reaction against them which the Movement exemplified. *A Former Boiling* can be read as a tirade against the boredom of the fifties with its nagging assertion that you've never had it so good, and as a hymn to fifties discontent and rebellion into style—all coming round again.

In James the appeal of the more louche and romantic continental strain of modernism is coded as a turning from Anglo-American cod-classical and politically-reactionary modernism, and as a fifties dream of Mediterranean sensuality which occasionally makes him sound like the Elizabeth David of British poetry. The disgust at class barriers to advancement evident in the poems and novels of the Movement is paralleled in this poet of the next generation by rage at class betrayal allied to the appeal of abroad—where working-class solidarity, good food and painting drenched in light and heat would not be a compound oxymoron. Just as the dadaists and surrealists strove to arrogate Stalinism to their aesthetic as a kind of social mobilisation of the Id whilst at the same time seeking discipline from the Party for their hedonistic tendencies, so James' membership of the Communist Party of Great Britain might be seen as both romantic and a curb on individualist excess; a way of staying true to the political and social verities of South Wales whilst rejecting its cultural parochialism.

But for a poet to make such a political commitment in the Britain of the sixties and seventies bore a meaning very different from Eluard and Breton joining the French Communist Party. In Cambridge the CP was divided between a club of Left intellectuals and trade union activists in a way which could be caricatured as a split between *Marxism Today* designer communists and tankies—and James decidedly was on the tanky side. This had much of a town/gown divide, and teaching at an HE college in Cambridge must have done much to exacerbate and keep in good fettle a sense of exclusion:

> working away in a miniature Babylon in the muddy lowlands
> north of the city can be hard you know/ the indications:
> slow rural Tory pull in a mixed gig dimension of town
> & gown aggression/ heavy discipline over flank the people
> under Jesus and the Redevelopment Corporation/ the old
> Eastern Association long ago sunk deep into the land/
> 1,000 slum dwellers & reveries of a quick come profit
> hidden behind the running façade of the members room
> at County Hall/ no Red Stripe at the Midland either
> *(Toasting)*

James' poetry teaches, if it weren't obvious in the history of youth culture since the fifties, that the contradiction between attitudinising and a seriousness and consistency of critical engagement is a productive one; in this relationship attitude can drive cultural change, without it, it can only be a media. All the same there is something of the deep-dyed sinner's attachment to Catholicism about the politics of this poet who celebrates French food, wine, beer and sun and the pleasures of sex. Whilst selling the *Morning Star* might be anti-hedonistic, the materialism is filtered through the strain of romantic revolt; punk, after all, was regarded with grave suspicion by the hard Left as the politically naive expression of lumpen elements. As the translation of Tristan Tzara in *Letters From Sarah* produces a kind of sepia fin-de-siècle nostalgia and the punk phrasing of the poems at Kettle's Yard harked back to Club Dada, so communism becomes intensely evocative in James' poems of an outsider role sustained with style and preserving the rituals of lost community—both of working-class solidarity and its style revolts:

> reading the Star in the space left after the round
> then I harden my heart & polish my DMs
> gather my shirt from the line & press it
> sizzling black to the board
> with pointed strokes
> brush the old hair with Corimist a bit
> before we hit the local ready to kill
> an hour or two with gawping at the wealthy
> strangers in the pier-glass an empty space
> that fills up gradually with denim
> or elusive unintelligible crackle
> ('Variations on "Today Backwards"', *Berlin Return*)

James' verse is instinct with an active and resented nostalgia, personal, political, literary and filmic, the trademark firm and rising line turned both to arraign and to celebrate the persistence of the past in the present. This is stridently so in the most furiously charged of his seventies poems, *A Former Boiling*, whose head-on impact shunts periodically into lyric sidings dangerously close to Liverpool:

> but the stars burn above & below her head on habershon street
> As Pat Kisses the Blistering Cheek Of The Acolyte
> under the enamel pelican that tears its own breast
> black pudding again for tea
> tears & dripping & milky balm
> the hard-on against your soft brown pleated skirt
> in the alley your shaking fingers over the purple head line
> on the spurting arc line
> the little cries of ah line
> on the middle finger line
> the scar of dried semen on your brown stocking line
> they caned us on the hand line

What saves this from Liverpool winningness is that the nostalgia for a Catholic childhood embodied in Pat links to the most politically virulent expression of nostalgic hangover and cultural persistence in recent British history, the Irish republicanism which the poem both affects and believes in; what saves it from laddishness is Cousin Pat's sheer power as 'bleeding Celt flesh' surviving physical pain and cultural persecution as witnessed by the voices James hears calling from the H-blocks. Reading *A Former Boiling* it is not hard to understand why James may have winced away from its publication; it is a poem in which attitude becomes hard, and where the logic of aggressive nostalgia leads to that of the Armalite. Was this the point where the disjuncture between the Cambridge professional loving the good things in life and the life of the poem became insupportable, much as Auden came to find 'Spain'? I think *A Former Boiling* stands with 'Sister Midnight' as one of James' greatest poems, and it is the most indefensible because attitude seizes occasion by the scruff and gives no quarter—because it believes that to have a line is an equivalent virtue in poetry and politics.

Generally the line does not so govern context. The characteristic and effective device of an embodying persistence which both holds and tests what is loved is the undying echo, whereby phrases recur throughout James' mature work and confer a personal consistency. Indeed, given the number of translations, versions and direct quotations both literary and out of popular culture including song and graffiti, James' poetry might seem dependent on echoes. In one sense this is so, since any of us is dependent on these returns, wherever first acquired, which are arbitrary, circumstantial, and the heart of our being. But echo as a literary device might suggest a diminution of power and substance, a diffusion, whereas much of the warmth in the writing derives from this personal and loved quality of what might return involuntarily or be returned to as talismanic, so often attached to sensations of pleasure. The effect of this is paradoxical in the way that nostalgia is, inducing both rootedness and a sensual surrender. It both draws attention to the materiality of language and implies the persistence of experience (as its analogues, its markers) which language is unable quite to capture, either as involuntary memory states—moods reinduced by widely different settings—or as furniture, artefacts which recall the time and place of their discovery. To this extent when in the delivery of *War* loved phrases return ("creatures of an easy recognition" or "our casual blasé mean & cocky| how-would-you-like-a-punch-in-the-nose | attitude") the smash and grab of the poem is arrested and something of the aesthetic of the pebble collector and arranger becomes apparent. But the difference from Jim

Ede's curacy is in the disposition; the domesticity of Kettle's Yard is a sham because even where precious objects are disposed with seeming casualness or abandon, this has designs on admiration—it anticipates the viewer moving through and happening on the object during a passage which institutionally is made alert to surprise. In James' writing well-loved phrases are the repository of character, enabling the negotiation of the streets or of domestic and social life with some degree of poise and to others'—and his own—recognition. This is quite different from a self-consciousness which monitors the processes of response. It is striking that this writing's phrasal creature is so complete, that such a repertoire constructs rather than deconstructs a presence, powerfully suggesting that a materialist practice of poetry lies in exactly the reverse direction to that most commonly now avowed.

Phrasal repetition and variation shuttle across the poems from *Letters From Sarah* onward as large-scale rhyme, tightening a discursive universe which draws on otherwise heterogeneous ingredients and substantiating the sense of a person moving through specific time and place while retaining identity. This poet has style which verges on glamour. It is interesting to compare his personism with that of Frank O'Hara, the poet on whom James most evidently draws as a model—an unlikely model for a communist Welsh heterosexual poet. James' poetry is simply more phallic than O'Hara's, being line-driven rather than fluently stanzaic, and while O'Hara is of his milieu (which is infinitely extensive) James is located in it or against it, and the milieu is less elastic than a series of settings. James' theoretical bisexuality, which is a subject of 'Sister Midnight', is that "hanging over | of the woman in the man" introjected from his relationships with women and which makes his phallicism an object of contemplation, reflected back at him and admired.

This nostalgia for the phallus is refracted and multiple and even ironic, and the poems eddy about its stakes and are boundaried by its pale—within which the swoon is a delightful threat. The multiplication and dislocation of the phallus allows James within its delimited zone a sassy gorgeousness and look-at-me appearance of ease, unaffected by phallic anxiety, which is the heterosexual analogue of O'Hara's yield to his multiple selves' discursivity repealed (or at least mitigated) in the eyes and verbal responsiveness of friends. James did not need that particular guarantee, having his successful (his well-received) lines, as present and reassuring as Bill or Ashes at gallery opening or nightclub. But for both poets these jostling and responsive half-creatures, the others who make one's efficient self, are a provisional and perilous stay.

The disintegration evident in O'Hara's late verses, their clutching at straws 'for your information' (for the poem's, for his own), is answered by James' increasing reliance on a fixed lyrical persona, a phallocentrism, in *Dreaming Flesh* (1991). What indeed is dreaming flesh but a release from bondage? James' bondage was less a leather sheathing of the body as phallus than a bodily disarticulation, leg-straps effecting the disjunction of purposeful movement and its scatter.

The long poems of the seventies were a turning point for James, as 'Biotherm' was for O'Hara: both pushed to the limit a capacity for survival, tested through ungainliness, ugliness, chaos and rage in poems which seemed to leave them exhausted, such achievements as follow being dependent on the reader's acquaintance with the drama from which they have been rescued—and movingly so. The sense of exhaustion is manifest in *Toasting*, the last of James' poems in the series and written after I saw and heard him at Kettle's Yard: *A Former Boiling* had spat out every line in his locker while *Toasting* cast about for a decade's hook-lines, tasting and letting go. *Toasting* ends with

> a ritual of quiet entry
> into the prior & continuing existence of place some time
> no vegetation no path no road no boat no crop no goat
> no sheep/rock in the little pigeon river
>
> drifting slowly out of Africa
> walking is a time consuming process
> in which the distance is continually marked
> a ritual of conviction & care involving skill
> a thin scarf protects the children from the sun

This is beautiful, but with its sense of the increasing tenuousness of place and restatement of the aesthetic of care it hangs the photographic records of Richard Long's land art where they indeed belong, in Kettle's Yard, and it heralds the reconciliation of John James with the English modernist tradition, modest, craftsmanlike and respectfully appropriative. As we depart, the arrangements are unaffected and await the attentions of the next group of visitors, between 2.00 and 4.00 p.m. But years later this long-departed audience member hears the echoes of *War/A Former Boiling*, a poem which re-read in a new century still asks urgently, divorced from the imperative of one time and place:

> What's Your Game
> What's Your Number
> What's Your Line

# Unexpected Excellent Sausage: on simplicity in O'Hara, Lowell, Berrigan and James

In poetry there are kinds of simplicity as disconcerting as any flaunted complication—indeed more so, since their flirt of availability and their denial of obscurity ridicule a stiff-necked resort to the language of interpretation: a poem might wear a mask of its own candour, and for the reader to respond through saying, by way of more or less elaborate protocols, 'I know where you're coming from', seems as obnoxious as to refuse the assertively frank gaze, the proffered handshake. Like common sense, such straightforwardness claims the ground for any response. The interpreter risks being shown up as a po-faced curate of letters, wherever face-value is attached to self-evidence (on the face of it); shown up in his or her inaccessibility to joy, fellow-feeling or sympathy, or indeed to shame. How assured the poem, how wrong-footed the reader! So might a reader find a late poem by Edward Dorn, conniving in the poem's announcement that it has no side; it cuts to the quick or the chase and doesn't so much tell the truth as embody the truth. Because university trained readers have become accustomed to poems courting interpretation, another kind of designing, it is disconcerting to be rebuffed into examining the motives for such interpretative compulsions, exculpating our own shiftiness through our attributing of shiftiness to texts. But then in a triple take it may be found that a poetic display of honesty is one further shift or mask, donned in a knowing courtship and luring us towards an equivalence of face-value with honest substance.

Disconcertingly simple sensual pleasure might be thought the characteristic offer of the poems of John James, although sometimes it can

[47]

be difficult to distinguish swiftly enough between a gift and a pie in the face, or to see that a show of aggression clears the way for giving unexpected pleasure. Interpretation stalls: are you trying to get funny? what's this "casual blasé mean & cocky | how-would-you-like-a-punch-in-the-nose | attitude"?[26] The frank gaze hardens into a stare. You didn't take me seriously, surely? Well, I did and I didn't, I do and I don't, and if I hadn't I'd have looked like a different kind of fool. And there's a cue for much writing about language and presence while voices off-stage irksomely insist 'but it's only sausage'. Sausage, let it be said at once, is a serious matter in the poems of John James, and might legitimately prompt much speculation. The present short reading of apparently simple poems by four poets seeks to cover some of the bases by distinguishing various kinds of sausage before arriving at John James's.

James's poetry has strong stylistic affinities with the New York School, especially with Frank O'Hara and Ted Berrigan, but its affinity with French-language Dadaist and Surrealist poetry (rather than mediated through O'Hara or John Ashbery) is apparent in numerous versions, translations and direct references. Its Marxist politics are worn on its sleeve, and a distortion of what had been whimsical in the contrived simplicity of e.e. cummings and Lawrence Ferlinghetti is achieved through conflation of both the tough acts of Rolf Dieter Brinkmann and the flipness of Ron Padgett, giving his short poems a confrontational edge where the edges of his longer poems tend to subserve an authorial pose.[27] Flipness sours charm through an edge of dandy arrogance; and a stripped object presentation derived from early Brinkmann eschews ethical or aesthetic finesse—as though tipping the mud out of Williams' red wheelbarrow over the page. Both strategies push to the fore the conundrum affecting presentation of an embodied truth: whether the truth-claim is sustained in the poem or through the poem. More than once this question turns on sausage, much as it did for Ezra Pound.

The traps and enticements set by Frank O'Hara's 'Poem' beginning "Lana Turner has collapsed!", cause critics to flinch apologetically, like an anthropologist resorting nervously to respectful gestures when the meanings of a material artefact are more obvious and more unaccountable than its categorising proposes. Bashfulness is exacerbated here by historical context, for a famous anecdote has it that O'Hara threw off this poem during a ride on the Staten Island ferry (a very short ride) to a reading at Wagner College with Robert Lowell, Lowell said to have been discomforted by the circumstances of the poem's improvisation and so unmasked as a hopeless square. The point of the anecdote extends well beyond the gratifying one-upmanship of the hip over the self-conscious inheritor of a tradition, of the Irish adopted New Yorker over the Boston Brahmin: through its parade of superficial self-centredness as a mask for feeling then discovered to be true, O'Hara's poem exposes Lowell's painful negotiations with God in his early verse as a mask for monstrous egotism. Lowell's show of grappling looks as choreographed as tag-wrestling, a contact sport in which harm is mimed indefatigably; it is so serious that it can't be serious, and when O'Hara starts out "I was trotting along and suddenly", it is Lord Weary (an early Lowell persona) who thereby becomes laughable. How is it possible to resist this self-consciously unselfconscious jauntiness?[28] The poem, dated on the manuscript to February 9th 1962, is well known and included in most selections of O'Hara's work. It moves from news of Lana Turner's collapse which further stimulates a poet already bustling through New York streets with a companion, to end in the injunction "oh Lana Turner we love you get up".[29]

The neat overturning which O'Hara's 'Poem' performs is to admit to the fabrication of almost everything, itself included, so as to re-summon authentic feeling—or to invent the authentically inauthentic—in the contrived, the commercial and the scandalous. Lana Turner is reconstructed from a film star into a kind of edifice, which indeed she was as a Hollywood creation; even her collapse builds her up as a headline attraction blazoned across the page and placard, while behind the headlines she is found collapsed into lower case—a typical Hollywood trajectory. The headline which the poet reads (and which the reader reads), simultaneously exalts Lana Turner and knocks her down, but it is her being knocked down which makes her approachable comically and then tenderly. The first line of the poem reprises the headline in lower case (but rising to an exclamation mark) as an internal giggle, and it is with the word "hard" at the start of line 6 that the poem's dialectic converges and splits away and re-converges, and asserts a seriousness compatible with camp. "Hard" shifts the poem's gear from play with internal monologue (where raining and snowing and hailing might be analogues for psychological states) into assertion of what the *real* weather is up to, preparing for transcription of the real headline, out there, now capitalised. But O'Hara deftly undercuts any facile opposition between psychological state and the real weather—muddying the waters with the assertion that "the traffic | was acting exactly like the sky", blurring both the boundary between the natural and the fabricated worlds, and the distinction between natural and self-conscious processes ("acting").

At the same time "acting" undercuts the temptation to find an objective correlative in the meteorology; what is important is that this is all going on at once, and since the milieu is New York urban ('California' and 'Hollywood' are journalistic inventions), it's all about difference rather than separation.

Such disregard of any separation between the natural and the self-conscious and the humanly-made is central to O'Hara's urban aesthetic, and exemplified in 'Poem' itself. The poem purports to be conversational as though conversation were an art of improvisation, requiring no practice—whereas notable conversationalists often prepare their forays as carefully as O'Hara prepared poems. There are two main ways of doing this—to prepare in solitude or to test the anecdote or epigram in the live setting; the latter was O'Hara's poetic method, requiring numerous stabs along similar lines until a particular organising syntactic gesture reached its calligraphic perfection—or to socialise poetic writing through collaboration with visual artists and other poets, and through composing in public spaces. In protestant countries such poetic behaviour is almost indecent. Of course, the distinction between studio and live work can be drawn too tightly, and the greatest be-bop improvisers depended on 'wood-shedding', periods of retreat so as to refine or reconstruct a gestural vocabulary then further modified in live dialogue.

The present reputedly and perhaps actually improvised poem on Lana Turner's collapse attains such perfection, and its conversational manner is a flaunted fabrication, a brazen public secret as outrageous as the celebrity revelation. We (and the poem's conversational intimacy creates 'us') may suspect a revelation to be pure spin but consume it no less eagerly, and the slightest attention to ordinary gossip demonstrates how stirred and touched people can be by what they understand to be contrived. The film star is 'just like us', but if she were just like us our interest would be as casual as in scanning reports in the local freesheet of B or C's accident. Because she is *not* like us, because we know that the edifice of her headlined name is all falsehood, because there is no apprehensible person there but rather a set of projections into this cipher, entangling her movie parts and the parts she plays in gossip, with parts of us, the 'us' evoked by a calculated intimacy, we are moved by the 'real person' whom we feel to be suffering and whom we pray or will to be restored.

For Lana Turner is less transient than the sky or traffic; she bears the pathos of immortality much as this poem does, even as and because it rejoices in its ephemerality. Lana Turner will be held up by this poem forever, while the reality of the headline has long receded. The poem's conversational, throw-away manner is removed from speech-acts through a perfection of mendacity enticing the reader towards a truth outlasting the proclamation of the truth: that is, that real emotion captures us through tawdriness and flagrant artifice or mere accident, more often than through morally admirable promptings. Passing from the stressed enjambment of "head | hard" to "LANA TURNER HAS COLLAPSED!" the innocent reader is carried into a world which writing makes real, getting there only by way of unwitting connivance. But what is the status of this reality, when it's at home? It may be true of the weather that "there is no snow in Hollywood" although there is abundant snow on the filmsets and in the movies Hollywood produces—there is everything you could want or imagine in Hollywood—; but no way is it true of the weather that "there is no rain in California", even if there is no rain in the songs of California and no rain in the commercial art seducing people to relocate to California. Of course the weather page of the paper might justify the inference that there is no rain in California, but it would hardly announce it any more than the op-ed page would announce the Pope is Catholic. Even headline news may amount to no more than a decision to apply a particular rhetoric: a triviality or a truism would do as well—better—than an announcement that (to take a 1962 example) the US had begun defoliation of the Vietnam jungle with Agent Orange.

The assonance of "acted" and "actually" as the poem draws to a close, binds perfectly the dialectic of natural and self-conscious processes. A public secret of the poem is simply that it is written, and writing stops the conversational traffic and makes the accidental rain hard. Another public secret is that masks can be more trustworthy than authenticity. To adopt a mask is to concede to ritual or social prescription, and to announce yourself in a way which courts a specific recognition. At the same time it implies the possibility that behind the mask you are permitted to remain 'true to yourself' without your social status or provisional identity having impregnated your true self; a mask allows you to remain uncompromised, and engenders a particular trust when the mask is dropped. A profound difference between the poems of O'Hara and Robert Lowell lies in the figuration of truth in camp and in authenticity, and casts doubt on the project of presenting authentic feeling, on the possibility of authentic expression. An unusually simple poem of Robert Lowell's roughly contemporary with O'Hara's Lana Turner poem is 'Middle Age', with the poet enduring "the midwinter grind" of a New York which "drills through my nerves", and repeatedly encountering the image in memory of his father at the same age, forty-five.[30]

Has Robert Lowell collapsed? Surely not. Rather, with an access of self-importance unbecoming in a 45-year-old man, he is addressing his Father (bestowed with that capital in the line 'I meet my Father' lest we miss the point) in terms implying that his own suffering is Christ-like and therefore at least exemplary. Or perhaps his father is Abraham: the guilt lies with the victim who tempts the aggressor towards pity and away from patriarchal law. But Lowell suffers more profoundly than Christ, Abraham or Isaac, since instead of Mount Sion with all its symbolic grandeur, the doubly-unfortunate poet is condemned to the *via dolorosa* of New York's streets. New York's legendary bustle fails to infiltrate this poem, the city being transmuted into a kind of unpeopled Gethsemane; it means little more than the assault on the solitary poet of the ugliness human society creates—an assault he scarcely needs rebuff since unlike Christ, he seems impervious to temptation. Unaccountable though this attitude might be to a lover of New York, more disturbing is that Lowell's father attains no presence beyond Presence itself, descending in an annunciation of authenticity and bolstered in the third stanza by the language of liturgy, destined to be mobilised as a guarantor of Lowell's greatness. The substitution of "dinosaur" for 'giant' in the last stanza has it both ways: Lowell is walking in the footsteps of giants (and it is tempting to think he summons 'the' poetic tradition here too) while ruefully acknowledging that in the world of dereliction and decadence which is New York, his mission will be regarded as anachronistic. The briefly-interesting inversion in the third stanza does somewhat update the mission statement, with the discourse of psychoanalysis warping the discourse of liturgy, and thus laying claim to a reinforced authority: two great Judeo-Christian truth-telling traditions knit together in one posture.

This poem has no mask, but instead grabs the appurtenances of authority. "At every corner" and turn in its even metrical tread, as measured as a procession to the altar, it proclaims its own importance. What can be done with such simplicity, such directness? Efforts to unmask it are confounded by its impenetrable self-regard: on first encountering it a reader might be amazed to find that she is expected to infer that she is one for whose benefit Lowell has suffered—amazed, if she had not read the previous 324 pages of the *Collected Poems*. This poem startles in its brazenness, it does not need surprising into yielding its indecency; it proclaims it as its gift. The poem's highest achievement would be to allow access to Robert Lowell, whereas 'Frank O'Hara' highest achievement through his guise and guile, is to contrive access to the poem's inhabited universe; and this difference is epitomised nicely in the distance between "I was trotting along" and "where I must walk." Does Lowell's frankness disconcert the reader as Frank's triple-take does not? No, because the arrogance of Lowell's poem leads nowhere but to a too-recognisable and boring posture, either embarrassing in its insincerity or tragic in its sincerity—and such recognition kills a poem stone dead.

Second generation New York poets were often blind to O'Hara's guile. Ted Berrigan (1934–1983) seems to have been ambitious to be recognised as O'Hara's greatest fan, his determination to emulate O'Hara so unbridled that his poetic works evince spasms of panic at their author's incorrigible heterosexuality. Plenty of room remained for hero-worship to spill in other directions however, and it was Berrigan's youthful impressionability and omnivorousness that delivered, in his mid-twenties, the magnificent *Sonnets* (1963), raising pastiche to the highest art. These poems constructed a bridge between New York style demotic modernism and postmodernism, not to be crossed again until decades later by Charles Bernstein. Berrigan's own voice as it began to be heard after this unsurpassable opening to a career, sounds too often like a poet emulating O'Hara's most relaxed mode but missing the point—or rather, missing two salient points: a person's conversation becomes tedious if he's always talking about himself, and if he must talk about himself, the Warhol strategy of making the tedious fascinating, of flattening personal and affectively charged material into a mask which makes the obvious enigmatic, requires an impeccable control. Judging by his poems' overt content and increasing carelessness, Berrigan made the error of much of Warhol's entourage—unlike the platinum master, he did too many drugs. The resulting failures of discipline mar Berrigan's attempts at inconsequentiality. An example is 'In the Wheel':

> The pregnant waitress
> asks
>         "Would you like
> some more coffee?"
> Surprised out of the question
> I wait     seconds       "Yes,
> I think I would!" I hand her
>        my empty cup, &
> "thank you!" she says. My pleasure.

This poem appears in *So Going Around Cities* amidst numerous casual-aside poems, but none of them is quite casual enough.[31] "Surprised out of the question" is an annoying line in its combination of almost pompous self-regard and its over-literary play with the phrase 'out of the question'. Minus this line, the slight pun on the word "seconds" (meaning a second helping) might well have slid by easily enough, were it not for the archness of syllabic placement; the poem sounds like Robert Creeley trying to sound like Louis Zukofsky. In general Berrigan's trading in inconsequentiality is flawed in just this way, by an anxiety to be meaningfully poetic—leaving Berrigan to be out-insouzianced by Tom Raworth, who less than a decade later made inconsequentiality into the prosodic principle for a fleet, shimmering poetry.

The interest of 'In the Wheel' is that it marks a shift in New York poetry towards appropriation or ready-mades, here of classic Americana, and away from the intense zone of exchange and difference found in O'Hara's writing and in a completely other way (syllabically, syntactically) in the earlier poems of John Ashbery. Pop art is even more explicitly evoked in Berrigan's poem 'Babe Rainbow', named after a much-reproduced image by the British pop artist Peter Blake and created in 1968, the poem being dated 1968–69.[32] Perhaps Berrigan saw it in a shop in the King's Road, London at around the same time as the singer Melanie, who reminisced about her song 'Babe Rainbow' (released 1971):

> It was at a time when I was living in London, Chelsea to be exact. Well, nearly every day I used to pass this window in the Kings Road which had this painting of a lady wrestler. At first I thought that perhaps it was just an ad for some group or other. After a while I found that I was becoming fascinated by it, so one day I walked in the shop and enquired as to what it was, it turned out that it had been painted by Peter Blake, the guy who created the cover of the Beatles 'Sgt. Pepper' album. Then I began to identify with this lady wrestler. . . to the extent that sometimes I would catch myself in the mirror wearing her 'So What' expression. I suppose I was really hung-up with it.[33]

Regrettably Melanie failed to capture the 'so what' expression in her sentimental ditty, but Berrigan exploits a 'so what' aesthetic perfectly, even if his first line anticipates Melanie's "keep your glow on" refrain:

> Light up
>
> smoke

burn a few holes in the blanket

Burn a few holes in the Yellow blanket

burning

smoking

reading

Actually, despite the pop title this poem is more of a phenomenological reduction than 'In the Wheel' and evokes an artist more considerable than Peter Blake: 'Babe Rainbow' is exactly contemporary with the decisive phase of Philip Guston's shift in his painting towards what is usually called referentiality, but in Guston could more exactly be termed hallucinatory caricature. It seems unlikely that Berrigan had access to Guston's studio and to the work he was then producing, so it is more apt to consider Berrigan's poem an analogue in its relation to the poems of Frank O'Hara, to Guston's breakthrough into caricature in its relation to his own earlier mapping of colour intensities or to the painting of Helen Frankenthaler. The holes in the 'Yellow blanket' then might be considered gross marks of irresponsible appetite in the colour field, so personal as to be public and secret at once, as is the nature of basic appetites. After all, the capital letter for 'Yellow' suggests a colour on display, suggests paint—much as Guston's figures often muscle across colour workings reminiscent of his earlier painting, blatant and mysterious at once, part-objects in a world where objects and appetites have not been divorced: "By 1970, in a letter to Bill Berkson, [Guston] could announce with elation, "I have *never* been so close to what I've painted, not pictures—but a substitute world which comes *from* the world.""[34]

A breakthrough comparable to Guston's in this regard or indeed to Arshile Gorky's somewhat earlier parallel and populated world, was to prove beyond Berrigan (whose late poems were to be fine in quite another, intimate style), and indeed it would be necessary to look to Paul Celan's work or to J.H. Prynne's to find in lyric poetry such a 'substitute world' as Guston's. Berrigan at this time in his writing life seems to have been too dilettante to recognise what this poem might have heralded and to force forward with the single-mindedness exhibited by Guston. But even as an interruption 'Babe Rainbow' retains its enigmatic charge, always re-posing the question, what are we reading? A *notation* of appetite? A little more than notation perhaps. Or perhaps notation itself comprises the problematic. Launched with the injunctions, "Light up | smoke | burn…" the poem unexpectedly reports that it's the yellow blanket which is "burning | smoking", continuing to smoulder in the present participle with small need for encouragement. But then, can a blanket *read*? Such burns in the yellow blanket are readable in three ways—as charred punctures, as smoke-scribbles and as the signs, the language, which transits across "the Yellow blanket" of light laying out the world indifferently before these few holes are made. The original sin of our appetites causes the damage that makes the world readable in its differentiated intensities; "a few holes in the Yellow blanket" are the prerequisite for reading. True enough that marking introduces differentiations and intensities into the even coverage, but language itself becomes another blanket of total coverage. What makes this poem so much more considerable than Berrigan's other contemporary work is that the state of reading here encompasses all, while elsewhere the encompasser is Berrigan's own druggy sprawl—despite the back cover of *So Going Around Cities* bearing a photograph of Berrigan smoking and reading, sprawled on what appears suspiciously like a yellow blanket. That being so, these lines are language's burns or punctures within language, achieved through inconsequentiality: this is a text striving not to be a text so as to isolate, to differentiate its marks and allow them to be readable amidst so much text—in other words, it is a textual interruption.

The kinship with Guston may then be superficial in the shared references to basic appetites, and Berrigan's poem better aligned to Warhol's knowing blankness, where the mysterious ascription of cash and celebrity value encompasses all—physical pain and death included—and only the act of selection by the celebrity artist can interrupt the blanket coverage, if briefly, for the selection then to be assimilated into another financial circuit. Hence the ambiguity of Warhol's mass production of artworks distinguished by accidental variations, confounding two circuits of valuation. Nonetheless, much as Guston's paintings proclaim clearly that he stopped eating and smoking so as to paint, but that painting is an appetite as incontestable as eating and smoking, so Berrigan's poem shows he stopped to write (perhaps having put out a small fire) and that writing is a process as encompassing as reading—indeed, it encompasses reading having first been born from reading's interruption. This reminds us that Berrigan's poems notate perhaps more than anyone else's, the traces of a literary life.[35] Writing is at war with talking and reading but parasitically dependent upon them;

parasitically dependent, but possible only through stopping their tracks, and stopping their tracks achieved chiefly through irruptions of appetite, dragging things into the mouth, food or smoke. Writing leaks into these pauses.

Hence without O'Hara's conversational dialectic, Berrigan achieves an oscillation between the accidental and the necessary worlds in his pyrography, even if the seeming casualness of the writing threatens portentousness, a risk endemic to short simple poems. Berrigan's poem may drive back into the figuration of appetite as a differentiating language, a preference for this rather than that, making a hole here rather than there, being moved to open the mouth to put something in it or to utter something out. Perhaps, pursuing this logic, it was contradictory to encapsulate such motility in a finished product—finished, that is, in suppressing direct reference to the means of production—; but provisionality must represent a conundrum for the published poem, unlike the approximately-registered multi-colour silkscreen print, subject to accident on every pull. For only the finished text can be delivered through a book, and convincing workarounds were in short supply until Raworth's remarkable *Act* (1973), a sort of anthology of stratagems for having your cake and eating it.[36] What Raworth achieved was a reductiveness which is not egocentric: Berrigan's appetites were centred on his receptivity, and he failed to question how far down the social shaping of appetite might go. Where O'Hara bustled about socially and Raworth was to enact a linguistic dissolve, Berrigan characteristically was either sitting to eat or was horizontal and smoking. Ingestion so comprehensive must defeat the specificity of desire, figuring appetite as a void to be serviced but never knowing its objects, so leaving the world waste. In great contrast *The Pisan Cantos* of Ezra Pound fill a world laid waste, personally and by war, through a strengthening recognition that it is the small objects of desire rather than the satisfying of appetite in totality (with cocaine, say, or through social transformation) which enable survival and love: "le paradis n'est pas artificiel | but spezzato apparently | it exists only in fragments unexpected excellent sausage, | the smell of mint, for example, | Lasko the nightcat" (Canto LXXIV).

The meanings of food have already changed markedly in the nearer contemporary writing of the Welsh poet John James, one of the great sensualists of twentieth-century lyric poetry. To discuss John James's poetry in the context of the New York School is an obvious thing to do given his debt to the "Irish American poets" (Frank O'Hara and Ted Berrigan) and to "a 27-year-old poet from Tulsa | who recently "spent" a year in Paris" (presumably Ron Padgett who had a Fulbright scholarship in Paris in 1965–66, although Ted Berrigan went to University in Tulsa); but it is also misleading, given that James's *Collected Poems* presents workings of Tzara ('Letters from Sarah') poignant with that mixture of avant-gardism and nostalgia evoking neutral Switzerland in the first world war, alongside the highest-voltage Mayakovskian poem in English, the Irish Republican broadside 'A Former Boiling'.[37] Although resident in England since student days in Bristol, James is decidedly un-English in his love of French and German poetry, in his unembarrassed (and unembarrassing) celebration of the pleasures of the flesh, and in his Marxist and republican politics—which seem to legitimate a taste for the finer things on the grounds of international solidarity against a British suppression of the capacity for joy. In James's terms, revolutionary asceticism would be an incredible oxymoron. Witness the following short poem, at once simple and enigmatic:

**May Day Greetings 1971**[38]

eating a plate
from day to day
sharper than ever

blow your nose
in authentic
rigorousness

advance to bonheur

Comrades, let us advance to bonheur!—making sure to take your plates and glasses with you. A plate here is surely a plate of food—at first anyway, for then "sharper than ever" momentarily suggests a photographic plate, or even a fashion plate—looking sharp, that *sine qua non* of street action. But more seriously, food, and drawing strength from eating, eating *consciously* as we might say and for a purpose rather than routinely, this matters. Starting with the word "eating" ensures that "blow your nose" doesn't convey the drug reference it would in Raworth, but that it associates human achievement with simple bodily processes performed with conviction. To celebrate May Day demands everything you do being done purposefully, enjoining that terms such as "authentic" and "rigorousness" are as applicable to eating and nose-blowing as to revolutionary politics—thereby implying that political activity, which is about basic social being as well as serious stakes and complex analysis, should be as pleasurable and sensuous as eating. Authenticity for James seems here and elsewhere to invoke sensuous commitment (certainly 'A Theory of Poetry' is more about gratifying the senses than something called Theory) rather than an attested emotional investment or moral uprightness. Therefore "advance to bonheur" isn't a joke; what could be a greater thing to wish for humanity? Here is a collective prescription that anyone can follow unless actually starving, but one which needed some brass neck to proclaim early in the Heath Government, then sounding decisive about confrontation with Trades Unions, with Margaret Thatcher having recently been appointed Education minister and British troops being engaged in a civil war in Northern Ireland; a time when across the developed world the revolutionary hopes and achievements of the late sixties were rapidly shutting down, a kind of phoney war before the greater political assault shortly to be led by Thatcher and Reagan.

In the fifteen years from 1968 to 1983, a period of major social and political change, James published a body of work which equals any lyric poetry of the time in Britain, and whose variety as now fully revealed in the *Collected Poems* is remarkable. James and Barry MacSweeney were the only British poets to make good use of a punk aesthetic; while MacSweeney accommodated punk to his existing romantic anarchist outsider position, his language given consonantal edge and an odd authenticity through incorporation of not only Northern dialect but words imported from Chatterton's faked-up 'medieval' Rowley poems of 1777, James smashed his own glorious lyric line into fragments, performing acts of auto-vandalism in the collections 'Narrative Graffiti' and 'War' (1978). Never has the word 'collection' been better applied to publications than in the original duplicated, stapled productions, suggesting nothing less than a collection of body-parts after an explosion. The extremity of this move on James's part can be registered only through appreciation of what was being vandalised (and persisted also): a poetry of saturated evocativeness and beauty whose intensity at times can have an effect comparable only to Keats or Proust, the very taste and touch of sensuous worlds withdrawn and regretted immediately they are apprehended, most intense in a return complete with loss. When James recasts descriptive writing about the painting of Howard Hodgkin as the basis for 'A Theory of Poetry', it is because the same quality of dispossessed sensation overwhelming the senses with its involuntary return, saturates Hodgkin's canvases.

For any artist to be exactly where it's at for fifteen years is extremely unusual. Such a judgment is not only a judgment of quality, but describes an uncanny tuning to the Zeitgeist whose closest comparison (and one which James would relish) would be the recordings of David Bowie from *The Man Who Sold The World* to *Let's Dance* (1971–1983), tightly aligned to James's high period. Bowie provides an epigraph for 'Narrative Graffiti' in his comment "I am also my own medium" as well as contributing to the poem several lines derived from his 1973 album 'Aladdin Sane', one piece of evidence that 'Narrative Graffiti' predates 'War', as does 'One for Rolf' in the same *Berlin Return* collection, commemorating Rolf Dieter Brinkmann shortly after his 1975 death.[39] On first consideration the Bowie comparison seems out of order—as with James's choice of epigraph—since unlike Bowie, James does not embody style so much as allow himself to get caught up in it. Inventing John James is no part of his programme; indeed unlike Bowie (or Warhol who is Bowie's acknowledged master in this regard), James has no programme; the sensualist of the poems collected in *Striking the Pavilion of Zero* (1975) no more contrives an identification than the punk.

Neither Bowie nor James is interested in exploring his own identity as the site of authenticity, but James lacks interest even in identity play; he is in thrall to what seduces him rather than to his own propensity for being seduced, which is somewhat unusual for a lyric poet. He loves the objects of his appetite, which are not exhausted or consumed but return; such a relationship is reproduced through the circulation and savouring of phrases within his work, a technique doubtless learned from Ted Berrigan but turned to different effect. The final lines of 'Narrative Graffiti' are absolute: "You've just come back | I definitely love you".[40] Where Berrigan is the collagist of his own writing indifferently amidst other writing, James is drawn back repeatedly to sites of intensity even while seduced by new tastes.[41] Thus the vehement, agitprop James of 'A Former Boiling' does not repudiate the lusciousness of paint ('the bands of alternating colour') and the agitated James of 'War' can invoke both Robert Creeley alongside The Clash and Veronica Forrest-Thomson alongside Iggy Pop without strain or embarrassment, because high art and low-down rock'n'roll co-exist in the appetising world along with the woman of his desire—and with sausage:

> What's your name anyway
>
> Veronica/Veronica what/
> Veronica what's-the-difference
> inscription is its own form of condescension

but there are certain things in life
which have the power to restore you to your senses
such a chorizo sausage
& the works of James Osterberg
strike at the bone
at the back of the ear
like a bowl of exploding radish[42]

In reading these lines it helps to remember that the heyday of punk was also the high watermark of excitement with Theory prior to its institutionalisation in degree coursework, a moment when strenuous academic endeavour and a vigorous popular culture converged in a mission to subvert dominant discourses as embodied in 'classic rock' as well as canonical texts. This being so, there was considerable tension and competition between these subversive forces, between the Dionysian energies of punk and the less physical Nietzschian energies of some branches of Theory, each predicting the rapid recuperation of its competitor into its respective institution. James's lines capture the moment before Theory and punk settled on The Body as the agreed and fetishised site of resistance to almost everything. Here chorizo and Iggy Pop figure with particular force as explosive sites of desire exceeding the discourse of presence and difference, clearing a space for the brutal, in-your-face fragments that follow. The need to clear such space was pressing when lyric had come to be associated with a metaphysics of presence guaranteed by the markers of authenticity which James's writing had seemed to repudiate, but which lurked in the assurance of his lines—that is, until his assurance trailed off into the helplessly dangling conjunction at the end of 'A Theory of Poetry'.

Furthermore, 'War' appeared in the same year as Veronica Forrest-Thomson's landmark critical work *Poetic Artifice: a theory of twentieth-century poetry* (1978) and two years after the posthumous collection of poetry *On the Periphery* (1976) which made it painfully evident that a poet of the highest gifts had been lost. In James's home town of Cambridge, younger poets and academics were constantly repeating Forrest-Thomson's name; the more so as few people are evoked so vividly by their writing as she by hers, and few other writers' work moves between lyric and criticism as though indivisible. The poignancy of "Veronica what's-the-difference" lies in something as material and true as sausage: that the difference is that Veronica Forrest-Thomson was dead, and recently at the time this poem was written. To say so in as many words would indeed be "its own form of condescension" ("inscription" would be apt for a memorial) because she remains a presence who re-emerges as both a presence and an absence, while surely persisting as her writings under her name—what she had inscribed now exactly equalling her name's inscription (except for those like James who knew her). And for James poetry is a second order activity struggling to become as close as possible to a primary activity, but whose inadequacy to the purpose becomes the more apparent the more closely it approaches what is primary through a memorialising and under a name. No, James will not *inscribe* Veronica Forrest-Thomson; 'War' begins with the line "Is she really/", and she really is, she really isn't. Against naming is posed "the power to restore you to your senses" which could be read in a strong sense as the power to remove you from your inscription both as your name and more widely as your being in language, so as to consign what identity you have to the senses which respond to "certain things in life"—a deceptively casual phrase where every word tells precisely, summoning the ethical world of *The Pisan Cantos* with its minute attention to human and animal goings-on.

James's poetry is tensed between what at once seduces him into being and restores him to his senses (taking him out of himself so as to bring him back), and the poetry's own betraying trace; however much James might denigrate inscription for its approaches and fallings-away, its traces gather substance and become in themselves intoxicating. His mistrust in the throes of linguistic intoxication (reminiscent of Keats) is expressed in the determined return to his senses—James fears poetry will be the death of him. But maybe the bracketing of inscription, the bracketing of presence, might have been a deadly practice? This is too much to think or bear. And so:

After Francis Amunategui[43]

The appearance
of a hot sausage
with its salad
of potatoes in oil
can leave nobody
indifferent…

It is pure, it
precludes
all sentimentality,
it is
the Truth.

What could be more straightforward than this? Francis Amunatégui is not the missing poetic link between Giuseppe Ungaretti and Bertolt Brecht, as the poem might encourage us to speculate, but the author of *Masterpieces of French Cuisine*. While this information may undercut the poem's literary pretensions, at the same time it destabilizes the categorical proclamation of 'the Truth' by placing the simple dish within a distinguished culinary tradition, and furthermore by situating it within a particular discourse under the name of a gastronomic author—much as we are inclined to place the simple poem within the tradition of, say, the dialectical lyric or (if it were by Thomas A. Clark, say) the sophisticated naïveté of *A Child's Garden of Verses*. The more we contemplate this poem the more we understand that we have not fallen on a simple sausage, and that nothing exciting appetite like this—stopping short of consumption at the point of passionate contemplation and appreciation—could be termed *simple*; and furthermore, this applies to the poem as much as to the hot sausage presented. Or whose picture is presented. Or whose literary progenitors are half-present.

James's poem is phrased exquisitely, through its tripping prosody, in a way which draws attention to the very language which signals towards the object of desire. The it-ness, the quiddity of the sausage and of the poem are hung exactly on the dangling "it" and the line break of "It is pure, it | precludes". But is it the sausage which embodies the Truth, or its appearance in the gastronomic canon, or its illustration in the cookbook; or is it the elegant signal made by this poem in the direction of the sausage, or is it the poem itself? Or taking to heart the Brechtian admonition in 'War'—"don't knock fresh bread if you've always had plenty | on the shelf"—Truth might then lie in the poem's adverting to a material want extending to starvation, prevalent still and found even in Europe, and surely the poem asserts the irreducible centrality of food in our lives, and of its preparation to all cultures? To say this is to labour the point, to explicate the self-evident, where the poem's skill lies in its poise at the node of several possibilities not perceived as choices, as possibilities or as contrived ambiguities, and where just a smidgeon of self-consciousness (as with Berrigan's 'In the Wheel') would have marred it.

The simple short poem can present real difficulties for reading. This essay provides the evidence, in making a meal of a few short poems by writers of notable ambition and achievement, but who also published poems disarmingly simple in ways that put the reader at risk of looking foolish through over-ingenuity. The successful simple short poem has it both ways: the charm of Frank O'Hara's poem suggests a pre-lapsarian poetic, or rather pre-modern in a way which pushes the dawn of modernism back to some notional advent of self-consciousness—but of course it is thoroughly modern and knowing to a fault, as we all are. John James's *Collected Poems* could have supplied many such charming examples (almost anything from 'Letters from Sarah' would do), but Brechtian pith is rarer than charm, in English anyway, and moments where James eschews full orchestration demonstrate the poetic precision required to confound and therefore reinvigorate the devouring reader when writing in an open idiom, keeping appetite alive but its objects complete, even and because their elusiveness is conjoined with their vivid presence, their consumption with their sustaining power. This simplicity precludes attitudinising and literary showiness as well as sentimentality, and poetic resources must be deployed with extreme discretion. James is as expert in this unadorned manner as in the "delicate smears and caresses" of his longer-sustained poems.[44]

'After Francis Amunatégui' oscillates between referentiality and self-containment: the poem tells the truth or embodies the truth. These two readings can be accommodated, but cannot be reconciled into stability. Taking the poem at face value might ask us to eat the full-colour plate of a sausage; or do we have a taste for textual presence verging on sententiousness, but surely amused? Whether the sausage is pixilated or half-screened or a textual hallucination, we know when we read this poem that here—somewhere—is the wanted sausage, the ceaselessly found and removed hot sausage grail. It is an honest feint, an open secret, an unexpected excellent sausage.

# Illyrian Places[45]

The commendation by Douglas Oliver which adorns the back cover of Denise Riley's collection *Mop Mop Georgette* adopts a tone which crescendos from the reverential to the millennial, proclaiming that "poetry's future probably lies in the direction Denise Riley is taking" and concluding that "her poems have got to reach the widest possible public because poetry itself needs that to happen." Reviewing for *Parataxis* two of the pamphlets collected in this volume, Nigel Wheale acclaimed Riley's writing as demonstrating "what poetry is 'for'.... fierce ethical moments that bear on any one's behaviour."[46] Both Oliver's and Wheale's celebrations are decidedly unusual in tone; they share a calculated antipathy to the critical discourses which tend to surround 'serious' contemporary poetry, being insistently ethical, concerned quite directly to assert what is right in the teeth of what each would condemn implicitly as, on the one hand, rampant moral relativism associated with postmodernism, and on the other, the separation of poetry from life with the professionalisation of its reading. In an irritable response to an earlier version of Wheale's article delivered at the Cambridge Conference of Contemporary Poetry, James Keery has turned on Riley's writing, denouncing it as "offhand", vitiated by self-consciousness and by a "fatal reflexiveness", "arch", "pedantic" and as a tissue of cack-handed plagiarism.[47] From the pulpit of *PN Review*, Denise Riley stands accused of precisely that schedule of postmodern sinfulness from which Oliver and Wheale regard her writing as singularly exempt—as exemplary in surpassing. What then are the qualities of Denise Riley's poems which have generated this curiously de-centred debate?

At first blush, these poems would seem unlikely participants in this skirmish. Why not Charles Bernstein or Bruce Andrews, wearing postmodernism on their empty sleeves? But the emptiness of their sleeves is exactly the space where Denise Riley's poetry deals in Narcissism and its politics, no mere strategy but the tribulations of the postmodern heart. The insistent question is recognisable in the question Narcissism asks: "What strength has a self based on the internalization of others—indeed, to what should we ascribe the sense of selfhood which each of us seems to have? These are repetitive queries of contemporary experience: behind the mirror which the self needs to persuade us of its own existence, is there anything real? "Look, you can love me too—I am so like the object"; possibly, I am so like everything that I am nothing at all."[48] Could any formula better describe the claims Riley's poetry makes on its readers? What are the responses of Oliver and Wheale but an identification with the narcissistic pursuit of the ego-ideal which, as Janine Chasseguet-Smirgel has it, "implicitly promises the coming of a world without any father and a correlative union with the almighty mother, the one before the breaking up of primary fusion, even with the one before birth"[49]—or after death, as readers of Oliver's later poems might add.[50] But where these critics find themselves in resonance with the breathtaking, oceanic promise with which Riley's poems frequently come to rest—for instance, the stanza on which the sequence of 'A Shortened Set' finally converges and then rolls out: "In a rush | the glide of the heart | out on a flood of ease." (p. 24)—Keery can only recoil from the marks of narcissistic detachment, seeing a shallow manipulativeness. 'A Shortened Set', which arouses his especial ire and thus solicits a close reading here, consists of fifteen fragmentary lyrics which collectively Keery designates "so-whattish", borrowing a phrase from the poems. The matter of the set follows the travails of the narcissistic ego, patching together, displaced and alienated from derealised feelings, testing the potency and authenticity of feelings, assuming a male identity to discover the loved self as female, requiring another's presence but only to serve for container, seeking to become its own parents in order to give itself a full, new birth. As Keery and Wheale note, and as *Mop Mop Georgette* acknowledges, the poems are freighted with appropriations from popular song, and as Keery and Riley fail to acknowledge, borrow substantially from the poems of W.S. Graham—the anonymous are named and the named left anonymous. Here indeed is a repertoire of narcissistic devices, but in knowing use, deployed by a writer familiar with psychoanalytic literature, as her prose writings demonstrate. The risks are extraordinary in being consciously taken—the mirroring of a mirroring, the reflexiveness of reflexiveness—in the endeavour to stake the possibility of ethical being on this slippery, endlessly removed ground. Whether this is found maddening or moving—and I find it both—depends on the reader. Certainly it is courageous and not to be mistaken as 'confessional'—the data of a life, of the poet's experience, are not confessed for a frisson, but the conditions of that experience; the "fatal reflexiveness", the "self-consciousness" identified by Keery possesses the definite property of being our shared condition, even as it is a condition which for each cannot be shared and does not admit of sharing. This is the donnée from which Riley *begins*:

> All the connectives of right recall
> have grown askew. I know
> a child could have lived, that
> my body was cut. This cut
> my memory half-sealed but glued
> the edges together awry.
> The skin is distorted, the scar-tissue
> does damage, the accounts are wrong.
> And this is called 'the healing process'. (p.16)

Imagine the sentences here linked by the mathematical sign for 'almost equals'. Each sentence has similar weight, and points to an equivalent. Imagine each line as separated. Each line carries a pointing gesture, this thing, that thing, and the equivalences between sentences are reinforced by consonantal echo and by half-rhymes, as those between lines are reinforced through a shared rhythmical abruptness. As Stephen Frosh puts it, "external objects have to become the mechanisms for self-esteem regulation" and the body here is a collection of external objects *par excellence*, but it is one thing too, it is a repeated thing. This is strange enough, that difference should so reduce to sameness, but the final line quoted is the most interestingly characteristic, charged both with sardony and with real faith. Recognition of despair and self-doubt and of their all-pervasiveness, recognition of the mismatched materials from which the ego is sutured, is and must be the very prerequisite for their surpassing, is and must be the position from which the healing process might start, and as it will be undertaken, however hesitantly *and* grandiosely, in this sequence of poems. Keery quite fails to understand this, his reductive reading taking the poems as merely symptomatic of what they set out to heal and what they, when successful, actually *do* heal (provisionally, and so far as a poem can), for the reader released from reading. The extent to which each may do so for any reader, depends on how far s/he is willing to stand on the ground of their self-consciousness, what tolerances s/he might have for a narcissism which hammers as insistently as 'Let's Dance' in the seventh poem.

1.                               This
   representing yourself, desperate to get it right,
   as if you could                                    (# 2, p.17)

2. The slap of recognition that you know.
   Your feelings, I mean mine, are common to us all:  (# 3, p.17)

3. In this I'm not unique, I'm just
   the only one who thinks I'm not, maybe.            (# 3, p.18)

4. There has been damage, which must stop at me.
   I think that's finished.                           (# 5, p.18)

5. You're being called across your work
   or—No I don't want that thought.                   (# 6, p.19)

6. It was my party and I wept not wanting to.         (# 7, p.20)

7. It is called feeling but is its real name thought? (# 8, p.20)

8. The ex-poet's beside herself:                      (# 9, p.21)

The log of reflexiveness extends throughout the sequence. It strains credulity to imply that the author of *Am I That Name?* has poeticized in this vein blind to its symptomology, nor to its consonance with the much-discussed 'postmodernist condition'—of the impossibility of the presence to oneself, of feelings as ideologically interpreted physiological events which therefore have their truth only in an otherwhere-owned discourse, of the self as a party, a meeting-place of discourses both intoxicating and alienating. What, then, are the personal politics which derive from and can surpass this condition; how is the wholeness of others to be apprehended and asserted when one's own provisional sense of wholeness depends on the expropriation of parts of those others? If Riley had an answer to this, then Oliver's and Wheale's encomia would be fully justified, and if that answer were to be found in poetic process, Oliver's millenarian expectations of poetry would be fulfilled. This would be too much to expect, if not too much to hope. But where are the signs of Riley's contention with this narcissistic insistence, and what legitimises my predisposition, the parti-pris which knowledge of Riley's prose work encourages? First, there is the recognition of commonality to which the second and third quotations above bear witness. To acknowledge narcissism as a shared disfigurement ameliorates the exemplary status of the narcissist, and even if what is shared renders sharing impossible, the paradox of sharing enables an intellectual, if not a feeling, mutual understanding—hence the seventh quotation. Secondly, as a concise reformulation of this paradox, stand the otherwise odd and unaccountable phrases "A | perfectly democratic loneliness" (# 2, p.17) and "the social democracy of loneliness" (# 8, p.20). These phrases represent a wager of trust across narcissistic barriers and vectors of exploitation. Thirdly, stand the sequence's two final poems, which are separate by virtue of their poetic formality, and so disrupt the third level of equivalences—from poem to poem, whereby until this pair, no weight of authority, no priority could be assigned across each tactical re-start. The final poems, by contrast, are authoritative in their stanzaic stitching and in their 'connectives of right recall'.

In this first of these, Riley scours the earth for the origins of her own image, starting with those parents who abandoned her and moving on to lovers, but recognising her definitive inadequacy:

> at admitting unlikeness or grasping the
> dodgem collision whose shock isn't
> truth but like the spine says is no
>
> deception.                    (p.23)

To admit unlikeness would be to reach the psychoanalytic grail of integrated maturity, and this is no more open to Riley as a completion than to any of us. But to know so does make it possible to avoid the collusion of narcissistic love, and this poem ends by allowing the equivalent more-or-less integrity of others' feelings, if no axiomatic integrity of self; although it might be argued that the resultant "out post-sexual" has through this apparent act of grace withdrawn into a narcissistic redoubt, unable to entertain the claims on her which to admit others' unlikeness would bring through an intolerable breach. After all, there is no ready escape from this predicament, no gesture of generosity which would short-cut the healing process.

The last poem's oceanic slipway, cited above, represents an accommodation in ethical terms as prescriptively unsatisfactory as withdrawal; the two may be different sides of the same coin. Such a judgment begs a question regarding the poetical achievement of the sequence; that is, in terms of the ethical bearing of the specifically poetic process. I would judge that 'A Shortened Set' does carry ethical force in the emergence out of narcissistic fidgeting and squirming, of a poet knowing herself sustained through the love of others even in her isolation. Caught in the bleak Docklands landscape of the final poem, her rest nonetheless is "social", and here the adjective feels justified, after the lines: "A friend's shout | blown inaudibly." (p.24) Confident in the friendship whilst unanxious to appropriate the words, after the earlier poems' tissue of borrowings and anger and fear of retribution, the poem briefly becomes 'unanxious' and capable of trust. Has it been worth the journey? Yes, for to reach this release as an admitted creature of equivalence and so-whattishness has demanded unusual resourcefulness, investing these verses with a power they would not have carried had they fallen glistening from the air. But this seems entirely a poetical healing in which so-briefly the reader shares (for succeeding poems remain under the narcissistic spell, and the reader is not so readily released); more questionable is the suggestion of Oliver and Wheale that Riley's writing offers a guide to right living in the face of what Oliver calls "cynicism, sentimentality, or grandiose forms of lying." To consider that question—of the poetics of a possible life—requires turning to a poem of more overtly social and political concern.

'Laibach Lyrik: Slovenia, 1991' opens *Mop Mop Georgette*. It is a fine poem, in which the construction of ethnic and sexual identity is explored personally and in the contemporary Slovenian setting. It helps to know that Laibach is a Slovenian rock band which has intrigued and puzzled Western commentators since well before Yugoslavia's dissolution, a band whose po-faced ironies have been sustained with a consistency so ferocious as seemingly to accede to a fascistic commitment to blood and purity. Some typical strategies have been setting speeches of Marshall Tito to triumphalist marching rhythms, performing banal Eurovision-type songs in Wagnerian style, reading the camp excesses of Queen absolutely straight and to chilling effect, and hymning the glories of Slovenian culture in German. Laibach seem committed to celebrating Slovenian nationalism in terms which reveal that nationalism as a thoroughly mongrel invention—which in a double irony emerges worthy of celebration as such. Riley's names for this invented national identity are Istrian and Illyrian; the Illyrians were the people of an extinct and unrecorded language, so to speak Illyrian would be to speak something unknown, to stutter and halt *and* to bring to light, to speak in tongues "like "the unconscious""(p.9), out of a national identity no-one recognises and which is unfixable. This "lyrik" is not a lyric, but is stitched together from clearly different poetic modes, as identity is stitched together out of different modes of being—for instance, the Illyrian dilemma is identified in sexuality: "*A hesitant gap now stretches its | | raw mouth: I will become this sex | and Istrian.*" (p. 9)—Istrian being another double identity, a region which historically has been shuttled from state to state. 'Laibach Lyrik' is one of only two poems in *Mop Mop Georgette* which treat directly of the struggle in others to assert and maintain a working identity, the other being 'Pastoral' where men strive to dominate the landscape, fantasizing themselves as landed gents. Both poems are remarkable for their generosity, refusing the easy ridicule which the 'good jackets' of 'Pastoral' would elicit from any other writer sharp enough to trace the pastoral power relationship Riley discovers in the healthy pursuit of hill-walking.

'Laibach Lyrik' opens with six stanzas of primpingly beautiful travel writing and cultural 'response' which would look quite at home in a Faber Poetry Introduction volume but for their musical deftness, before a descent from italic into Roman and the injunction "Cut the slavonics now". Indeed this reader felt foolish to have taken on trust a passage which began "*The milky sheen of birch trees*" (the sort of thing only Tarkovsky is allowed by sophisticated Westerners). But then, a poem of shifting frames is unprecedented in Riley's writing, where always the voice has been trustworthy through its constant admission of untrustworthiness ("love me"). The continuous passage of thirty-five long lines which follows is reminiscent of James Fenton in its exact account, journalistic in the best sense, of a visit to Ljubljana followed by conversations with Yugoslav exiles in London, troubled by their definition as Bosnian and Croatian and troubled still more by the internal necessity to adopt such an identity:

> ... But that blood lost means I must take that name—
> though not that politics—must be, no not a nationalist, yet
>   ambiguously Croatian
> must be it through the dictates of those deaths alone. We should,
>   all should—
> look forward, must rebuild...' She stops, I'm seeing present
>   history
> glance round it for support. I'm hearing it at work to stammer its
>   imperfect story
> go on too long, be conscientious, grab at straws, then reach its
>   edge of tears.
>
>                    (pp.8–9)

The entire passage is immensely assured and affecting, and its amplitude, its tactful and generous containing, resonate throughout a reading of the book which follows; here alone Riley seems to forget herself.
But not, after all, for long. After a stanza break, she returns, conjuring
herself within this roomful of inconsolable and mutually-consoling
disputants: "as a dark stand of trees, still, sealed black, outwardly silent
but vibrantly | loud inside with others' gossip about itself, like "the
unconscious"" (p. 9). This is announced as a tactic of management
through irony, but it is not irony which mars the passage but rampant
and ravenous envy, "rage born of envy reined in only by a desperate
defensive withdrawal from real relationships with others": "the
grandiosity of the narcissist stems from the strategy adopted to overcome the painful splits produced by inner rage".[51] The withdrawal is
plain in the dehumanization of the disputants, "the room splits into
clumps and fights", and "the evening's tongues go scrapping...", and
grandiosity is marked strongly in the lines quoted above. But the poet
preserves this painfully revealing record to switch tracks, as in 'A
Shortened Set', into an impeccably balanced, conscious of self-consciousness, dialectic lyric—the negation of the negation of the negation. Quite
simply, the six quatrains which follow are peerless—they must be what
Oliver means by "poetry itself needs that to happen". They begin:

> The settling scar agrees to voice
> what seems to speak its earliest cut.  (p.9)

I would like to dwell on this pair of lines, for they are exemplary of this
art. The murmuration of these settling lines arrives like life speaking
its origin, yet that origin in birth is itself registered ambiguously; it is
caesarean and therefore an achievement of human artifice, and it is
proto-vaginal, as the poem comes to acknowledge. Unafraid of speaking
its origins, it nevertheless implies that genital identity itself is a human
wager. The shifting reassembly of voice through a tissue of 's's, hard 'c's
and long 'e's works counter to the lines' forward motion and rocks and
lullabies; this is a maternal holding, mother of its own song, and in its
holding it is all potential of combination and identity, with no directedness of determination. "Agrees" looks forward to 'A Shortened Set'; the
agreement is physical, as in the lips' agreement "to voice". The precedent
narcissistic rage turns back to empathy with the exiles; the question
'what is true?' becomes suspended in the acceptance of 'what seems to

*speak'*, which is where perforce we must start from, quieting rage, settling the scar. But

> *A rage to be some wholeness gropes*
>
> *past damage that it half recalls—*
> *where it was, I will found my name.* (p.9)

This rage is of another kind; it is the appetite of the old child to establish her separate name, but the ground on which that name is established is always contingent: surely we depend for our names on the 'damage' of our birth (although poignantly we may know that 'Denise Riley', an adopted child, did not), but whilst we may *find* our names there where we enter the language, we do not *found* our names there:

> As you do not live your life fully defined as a shop assistant, nor do you as a Greek Cypriot, for example, and you can always refuse such identifications in the name of another description which, because it is more individuated, may ring more truthfully to you.. Or, more commonly, you will skate across the several identities which will take your weight…[52]

But the verse lines travel beyond the implication that a simple choice is available, have been informed by the predicament of the Yugoslav exiles; the name is founded upon an inaccessible, damaging as well as life-giving, 'essential nature'—that is, we found our names by negotiation with what we find, which remains elusively present-and-absent. The pronoun 'it' has become unstable; its reference might be the scar, or the rage, or the wholeness, each of which is a force insubmissible to will; only that shift into the present tense, recessed from governing presence—"*where it was*"—allows the margin for individual agency: '*I will found my name.*'

> *A hesitant gap now stretches its*
> *raw mouth: I will become this sex*
> *and Istrian.* (p. 9)

Yet no doubt at all, that "*raw mouth*" is no choice: what is said, the voice which speaks from the "*hesitant gap*" works in the marginality of freedom. To be given birth, to give birth, the mouth, the caesarean cut, the vagina—this doubled-over-doubleness which speaks may recall

Irigaray's écriture feminine, but here is no residual biological determinism imbruing a politics of discourse. What is this that "*I will become*",
this sex which is an incision in the belly, or this sex which is the child's
sex? The modifier "*and Istrian*" names even whilst it will not assign; it
insists on a wholeness which is irreducible taxonomically, which
belongs to no state. Now the earliest cut, the wound recalls Bosnia and
its people's enforced reassignments, people whose identities are become
"*spent shells*"

> *A greenish patina*
> *may roughen these spent shells*
> *for future curious songs.*          (p.9)

Time and distance will enable more songs such as this one, which is
founded on the shifts of the irretrievable. The poem now moves with
choral grandeur to conclude out of the

> *opened and reopened mouths that form*
> *the hollow of a speaking wound, we*
> *come to say, yes, now we are Illyrian.*          (p. 10)

The first person plural here rests on a necessary fiction, neither the 'we'
of pairs or of a given sentient humanity, but a "we" of the deeply disaffected discovering an affective ground in a hollow which is as much a
speaking *womb* as a "*speaking wound*". The multiple doublenesses, the
'*resonant cities*' of meeting lips resonate where the child, the heart of the
city, the individual self have been torn away. It is in this lisping, stuttering, emptying and refilling space of the sound, the mouth, the womb,
that the pronouncement "*yes, we are Illyrian*" may form. While the art-
terrorist tactics of Laibach may have provided Riley with a point of
departure, the not-place reached in this concluding lyric passage is an
excessive emptiness beyond their reach, and for its simplicity of diction
and confidence of movement allied to a productivity which I hope I have
started to untease, deserves recognition as something unique in current
British poetry, and which frustrates the conventional sort-filters of
'complexity' and 'simplicity'.
     Several of the shorter poems in the first half of *Mop Mop Georgette*
share something of this quality, if none other partakes in its reach
beyond the travails of the narcissistic ego. With the poems collected
previously in *Poetical Histories* and those which follow, doubts start to

accumulate and to play back across the surface of the earlier poems.[53] Poems such as 'Cruelty Without Beauty' and 'So Is It?' capitulate to a rage which threatens to lay waste the world. So driven is this rage that quotation becomes a matter of arbitrary excerpt, every pause or transition being but a blank wall at which the helter-skelter car jerks ninety degrees with a sickening shock to swoop down further:

> this hot scowl on songs marks rage for
> closeness just not found in a true human love—
> burn, work, burn blue, since one clean word on
> someone's blank makes salt well under any tongue,
> am I to go unswollen, arm across my shoulders
> good, that's who off the end of a wrist? (p.50)

—a viciously retributive tissue of fear which touches base in a pair of lines whose seeming doubleness is no more poised than the ambiguity of the confessions of a justified killer:

> Yet no-one should say to me, Nothing's enough
> for you, ever. But I do want to kill and die. (p.51)

In psychoanalytic terms, these lines expose the close relationship between narcissism and borderline personality disturbance, and whatever the symptomatic accuracy of this writing, it becomes necessary to ask whether the knowingness, the reflexivity which is paraded throughout this poem, is any kind of saving grace. The answer would have to be No. Faced with this writing and its self-knowledge one is right to demand a revolt against narcissism as such, rather than this working with the narcissistic grain which cannot divert or obstruct its pathological logic. To reach such a conclusion concurs with a troubling experience in reading Riley's poetry. Almost any individual poem may be profoundly satisfying to feeling and intellect (as much as any poetry being written), and yet to read a collection is to feel resistance rise, to feel that something is being progressively *taken away* rather than given. This is the stranger given the incredible beauty of many shorter lyrics, instinct with moving breath as the best of Schuyler or Graham.

Yet the poems do circulate, but for a few exquisite (painful and beautiful) moments of perfect poise—like gaps in the clouds out of which generosity floods—, trapped within the narcissistic orbit; one yearns for release, for a writing which does not so repeatedly reassemble the writer's looking-glass, no matter how lovely the fleeting figure of self-invention there revealed, no matter how suggestive the finely-tuned points of surpassing, no matter how deft the founding of each name. What this reader chiefly remembers are those more modest, epiphanic chinks where a real exchange—with landscape, with another—briefly occurs; that, and those Illyrian formulations which so swiftly dissolve. The fragile yet tempered grace of the best of this writing does not hold except in a following silence, or turning the mind to quite other activity. Whilst these poems singly yield so much matter for meditation, to read a collection of this extent is to feel tormented, as by the spectacle of a behavioural experiment, the food snatched from the yearning mouth. To say that "poetry's future probably lies in the direction Denise Riley is taking" would rely upon Denise Riley discovering a prospect reached forward from where she has founded her Illyrian name; for the cumulative effect of this book is to obviate all hope for the future. The future which *Mop Mop Georgette* contains and devours is a cruel one; frail hope is snatched and disintegrated by a tireless and apparently omnipotent, insatiable hunger, sardony does prevail. Oliver is right to the extent that no other poet is half so unforgivingly and intelligently attentive to his or her struggles to come into full being in a narcissistic culture; the eventual disappointment of this reader can be put down to the strength of his own attachment to the ego-ideal which haunts Denise Riley's writing and for which nothing will ever be good enough.

# A Single Striking Soviet: The Poems of Barry MacSweeney[54]

From the start, Barry MacSweeney's writing has been uncannily open to influence, and it is a task to discern of what gestural elements his nonetheless distinctive lyric voice is composed. The work following *Just Twenty Two—And I Don't Mind Dying* (1973) has a crushed, hectic quality, an insatiable fetishistic slide of greedy substitutions, which is unmistakably MacSweeney's; what preceded it was for the most part a series of part-ventriloquisms which in retrospect can be read as an accumulation of the materials out of which the later gallimaufry heaves into nine-days-old activity. Where MacSweeney has striven to be culturally true (as in *Black Torch*) his writing has seemed less convincingly pressured; his truth lies in a concoction, one extraordinary instance of which is to be found in the markers of Northern-ness in his writing, derived as much from Thomas Chatterton's invented Rowley language as from authentic Northern dialect. By this unlikely route, his later writing arrives at a Northern-ness as convincing as that of Basil Bunting's *Briggflatts*, the reference poem for Northern English writers of MacSweeney's generation. But in order to understand MacSweeney's later achievement—which I think very remarkable indeed, and which has involved a courageous forfeiture of the rewards any one of a number of earlier guises might have brought in the process of mixing his basic *mirepoix*—there is value in returning to the earlier work: this may help in identifying elements and intentions consistent in his poetry throughout all its stylistic vicissitudes, amounting to an unusually sustained if perverse stance.

MacSweeney's first collection, *The Boy from the Green Cabaret Tells of his Mother* (Hutchinson, 1968), amounts to an anthology of the poetic fashions of its time (1965–1968), running through replica Liverpool poetry, ersatz Russian megaphone-poetry, fake Carlos Williams, Bunting, Olson, Dorn, Rimbaud, O'Hara and (surely a first!) exercises in Prynne's *White Stones* style. What is most odd about these contrivances is their flagrancy, and flagrancy has been the leitmotif of MacSweeney's writing, reaching its full flowering only in the sexual delirium of *Jury Vet*. But here is the flagrancy of the rip-off artist; it is one thing to be influenced by O'Hara, another to write a Northern working-class, heterosexualised rip-off of O'Hara's best-known poem:

> a girl in a hoped miniskirt leans against the white door
> of the CLOTH MARKET CAFÉ
> its 10:30 a.m. here are cabbages jewish
> artichokes granny pippins & button mushrooms

and so on . . . Such exercises in style, as here, can be a delight to the knowing, their frequently unwitting parodies being tokens of true esteem. The Prynne workout includes such lines as:

> we have the decision
> without bitterness, with
> a *resignation*
> to the facts which are *these*:

and is dedicated to Prynne lest the point be missed. The assertiveness of the first person plural wrenched from Prynne's geological historicism sounds plaintive, the italicized key-word pulled from the philological web sounds close to defeat; but these shadings throw into relief also the embattled moralism which underlies Prynne's historical strategies. The bathos of MacSweeney's piece lies in his arrogation of Prynne's discourse of value and coinage to a romantic conceit of the poet as new-minter. The least successful imitation is that of Edward Dorn; Dorn's political-ethical discursive sweep is quite beyond MacSweeney, and to title a poem 'A Letter, This Far Away, Tonight For Liberty', after one of Dorn's best-known poems of the period, 'A Letter, in the Meantime, Not to be Mailed Tonight', was reckless. MacSweeney is unable to reach beyond some rather banal tourism of partitioned Berlin—"the black acorns are thunderclouds over Europe". But this is the price of shame-lessness, and in shamelessness lies the strength of the more interesting poems in the collection. Too many poems in *The Boy from the Green Cabaret Tells of his Mother* were vitiated by shame; MacSweeney simply had to pull poems into line with the contemporary doxology of Love Is All You Need and of authenticity. A war between the desire to stand forth as authentic and an intoxication with the possibilities of the medium demands on the one hand repeated gestures of sensitivity and senti-mentality, and on the other, headlong plunges into the discourses which spellbind. Put another way, his love of poetic text cannot be sustained as far as lyric truth, with initially interesting poems too often resolving into a gesture of love or beguilingness borrowed from popular culture and hugely unconvincing. Predictably MacSweeney jumps out of the dense linguistic thicket in which the lyric persona has become implicated, with a *faux-naïf* restitution of the Edenic Real Me, standing forth in tones of an infuriatingly coy sentimentality—this declension remaining, of course, the single trick of Brian Patten.

If his introduction to the collection is to be believed, MacSweeney embarked at the age of 15 on a programme of reading, especially in post-Romantic French lyric poetry, of startling precocity, and his interest in Decadent verse is apparent in some fine translations of Paris into Newcastle. But at the same time he was being marketed as a poet for "unabashed boys and girls" (in Bunting's yucky phrase). Two examples will suffice; the book's first poem, 'To Lynn at Work whose Surname I don't know' (a winsome title), starts with some finely-worked lines derived from Baudelaire:

> The sun always goes down
> like this between the
> staithes of the High Level Bridge,
> dragging of golden plate across
> the sewage,
> and then breaking it
> among the rooftops of the
> wharf-side houses and stores,

breaks into some social realism about navvies going home, and collapses abjectly into a final stanza which starts

> now i think i will come to you
> and ask you and pour the Tyne
> and the sun's bangles....

and so forth in a manner too depressing to quote further. Both title and concluding stanza constitute a bashful framing device, apparently apologetic for the poem's opening manner. This is a very early poem, but even in a later piece which adumbrates some of MacSweeney's fully-developed preoccupations, sentiment is worked in against the grain. The poem is quoted in full:

> 2<sup>nd</sup> Telephone Song
> Emeralds, spa-rock chips
> quartz slivers if all these
> fell on this same stretch
> of black straight path &
> rickety hedge none cd
> compare with the
> cracked gaunt slip of finger
> nail pointing as
> some bright star thru
> years and years & joy
> along which we sailed
> in eyes of storms in
> sunshine & rain
> (yr bright fingernail
> brings yr voice past
> terraced wardrobes a
> grocery store the motor
> way to this humble bright
> & oh so willing nest
> of outward going concern
> for you for you for you

The density of fragments, of fractured objects, is posed against containers as bodily substitutes—the wardrobes, the grocery stores—and against human commerce, represented bleakly in the asphalt of the road. Wholeness here is vacancy or a mere assemblage for trade, whilst fragments glitter as precious stones or stars. The valued "you" is a "cracked gaunt slip of finger | nail" or a disembodied voice which lodges in no container but drifts, or becomes another *thing* held in the receiver; this celebration of dismemberment (might the emeralds be her eyes?) will be exploited in MacSweeney's later writing, infatuated and distressed by unstitched fashion details. *Our Mutual Scarlet Boulevard* (Fulcrum, 1971) collects poems from 1965–70. Those which are contemporary with *The Boy from the Green Cabaret Tells of his Mother* lean strongly towards the sentimental, but their greater integration suggests a process of re-working in the intervening period. In a 1974 interview with Eric Mottram in *Poetry Information* (18, Winter/Spring 1977–78) MacSweeney cites the example of William Carlos Williams, rather dismissively; but although strongly imagistic, the majority of MacSweeney's poems suffer from an itch to ensure the reader (in the first place the loved woman) receives the message, a message frequently duller than the image-complex would permit the less-governed reading. Only a few brief pastoral lyrics are permitted to exercise a charm unaffected by the determination to offer the selfless, unqualified gift, expressive of mutual appetite and exchange:

Io!

hail pounding
on the red roof.
made love till
7 a.m., six hours.
no breaks, just
to lie parallel
and talk. hail
on the roof
plovers at the spring,
kettle on the boil.
Insatiable.

Restraint of a kind associated with Williams is a rare virtue in MacSweeney, and this and the lyric 'Country again' associate the possibility of restraint with desire satisfied, in a way reminiscent of a handful of happy pastoral lyrics by Mark Hyatt—a poet commemorated in the dedication to *Fog Eye* (1973), whose title poem is MacSweeney's best and last exercise in the mode, and is one of the few I miss from the selection in *The Tempers of Hazard*. Within this group of poems from 1965–1968 appears quite unaccountably the great poem 'The Last Bud', bearing little evident relationship to writing before and after—for the second half of *Our Mutual Scarlet Boulevard* consists chiefly of exercises in the style of early O'Hara and his New York followers. Given the depth and range of MacSweeney's reading in post-Romantic French poetry, the skill in manufacture is to be expected; a *mélange* of Tzara, Reverdy and Surrealist entertainment together with jokey and affectionate reference to a set of friends, offers the same kind of pleasure as the work of Ted

Berrigan. But MacSweeney's poems do not rise out of a productive milieu, but more from an extended epistolary network which leaves the poet relatively isolated except in the act of offering the poem; the density of cultural referents smells of the lonely room in which friends' suggestions for further reading are pursued, rather than the rapid sharing which poems ride as of a collectivity. Neither does MacSweeney achieve either the hedonistically scattered persona of an O'Hara, or the muscular who-you-looking-at swagger of O'Hara's most adept British translator/transformer, John James. By comparison, MacSweeney has no style; he is too anxious, too self-conscious, too concerned to have something to say about Life or Pain or Love. The most moving moment in this writing is when anxiety becomes vertiginous:

> sleep safely fall in
> to no replica;
> our fondled noose
> & closed shop, sleep well
> watch that no
> body bites. No
> one at all.

This short lyric can be associated with 'The Last Bud' through ache; loss with the fear of loss, crossed by ambiguity and guilt, is the sole principle of personal integration throughout MacSweeney's work. The processes of integration and disintegration govern the writing collected in *The Tempers of Hazard* with the exception of 'Brother Wolf' and 'Fools Gold', both of these resorting to flagrant imitation. The stable self-in-discourse is attainable only in replica; guilt performs a contraction, but opens to the sweep of the past, and the guilty, mournful lover is the figure who releases tides of integrative memory, receding to leave the self contracted to a mere bleached marker, life's plenitude available only in reminiscence. The contrary movement whirls out in a savage celebration of destructiveness, constellations of contested fragments, a bee-swarm of fascination. But this is some years ahead, when the spell of the unifying myths of his time and of received poetic models had been broken. It is important, though, to recognize the quality of those models. Loosely associated in the public mind with the Liverpool poets—his ticket to the radio and television appearances credited in the acknowledgments to these first books—, MacSweeney possessed from a start a restless intelligence which alienated him from both the gelatinous culture of the prevalent mainstream verse, and from writers of a lazily sentimental counter-culture who offered direct and untroubled access to a repertoire of self-patenting feeling. MacSweeney's early writing offers the spectacle of a serious but unsolemn autodidact growing up in public; it is pretentious in the best sense, struggling against the tyranny of cultural circumstance, and marked by an appetite for learning and for technique subservient to an intention only dimly discernible (to the writer too, one presumes) before the sequence of *Odes* which inaugurate his fully achieved work—where his relations with the claims on his sensibility become characterized by a paranoid disintegration and reorganisation.

The journals in which he published during the 1960s and early 1970s included *The English Intelligencer, Grosseteste Review, Collection* and *Resuscitator*—the house journals of the early Cambridge formation—, as well as the organs of the Northern movement of literary independence. However, MacSweeney has remained a lone wolf, one of those writers like John Wieners or Stephen Rodefer in the US, who may be affiliated temporarily with a particular school, but can never be *of* a school. Temperamentally, MacSweeney is not one who belongs; neither through deliberate adherence, nor through others' appropriation of his work to their programme. In part this may indeed be because MacSweeney is not distinguished for technical innovation, and because a wolfish streak impels him to give offence to any possibly welcoming constituency. Any stability of integrated identity which might be offered through a belonging, seems to be subject to especially virulent attack—so in *Our Mutual Scarlet Boulevard* he puts the blacksuede boot into political protesters who "dribble conscientious phlegm, | oozing melodically | in tune with each world tragedy"; they are "chanting maggots in chorus". This seems unhinged, explicable only in terms of a pathological need to ensure his own pariah-hood, and something of the same mechanism is evident in later poems (wisely not collected in *The Tempers of Hazard* with those of the same period) in which misogyny runs uncontrollable. This has certainly been an effective strategy for ensuring a lasting neglect; where was MacSweeney in *A Various Art*? Who has written of MacSweeney except Maggie O'Sullivan, herself a writer spurning association?

MacSweeney would describe his resistance to attachment or patronage in terms of pride, and a significant insight into his poetic is furnished by his essay on Thomas Chatterton, *Elegy for January*, published as a short book by The Menard Press in 1970. The example of the Marvellous Boy, who died two hundred years before aged eighteen, has been inspirational to generations of adolescent poets, but the consonance between Chatterton and MacSweeney is far more than in the shared precocity of young working-class poets charged-up with a sense of their powers, and feeling victimized by a literary establishment. Chatterton was the author of the poems of 'Thomas Rowley', which he presented, as a series of manuscripts discovered in the muniment room of St Mary Redcliffe Church, Bristol, to the celebrated antiquarian and *pasticheur* Horace Walpole. Acknowledging to Walpole his humble origins, he was advised to apply himself diligently to his apprenticeship. His furiously resentful response to the snub was the overture to a self-destructive frenzy of resentment and pride, leading towards an early death through poverty and starvation—the haughty refusal of his land-lady's charitable offer of food in his final days, clinching for MacSweeney the iconic status of Chatterton as the poet who would live only on his own self-making. MacSweeney declines to mention the theory that Chatterton perished owing to amateur self-medication for syphilis, at that time treated with arsenic and mercury.

The key dyad is pride and pastiche, and the purple passages conclud-ing MacSweeney's touchingly awkward recital of Chatterton's history contain a remarkable resolution: "Can we allow ourselves to grow neatly into bigotry? Is that, too, a necessary portion of our making? Then it is better to be unnatural." The resolution can be taken as the key to MacSweeney's later writing, permitting him to discard sentimental gesture, and to embrace pastiche as holding out the promise of self-authorship and self-destruction. To write from the heart has proved, in MacSweeney's earlier work, a sure way into the inauthentic—either towards acceptance and capitulation to the fate his class would deter-mine for him, or to collusion with commercial or official middlebrow culture. Much as Chatterton created himself as another (and MacSweeney's other youthful hero was Rimbaud), so MacSweeney has successively recreated himself. But where information collapses the historical, where any stance is itself subject to too much information, and where information is the densely glittering miasma in which the contours of personal construction melt, an alternative persona has proved unstable. Chatterton did seek to sustain himself through exer-cises in the journalistic poetry of the time; poetry is no longer a calling in demand at Grub Street, but MacSweeney similarly pursued a career as journalist, immersing himself—at the cost and at the advantage of an abiding rage—in the very midden where false authenticity is generated.

Although he speaks approvingly in *Poetry Information* of the discipline of compression enjoined by journalism, the formulaic lie of the contemporary tabloid is as much anchored to a Great Heart as were the graceful sentiment and the scabrous satirical jibe in Chatterton's time. "I'm 16, 17, from a working-class background, that has no literary connections, that knows nothing about the outside world really. We lived in a close community of a housing estate. I didn't know what the hell was going on", MacSweeney reminisces in his *Poetry Information* interview, where six years later he continues to nurse his resentment at the history of his co-option by a literary establishment eager for a best-selling voice of youth, culminating at his candidature for the Chair of Poetry at Oxford University, an advertising stunt contrived by his publisher through strategic payments to a brace of Oxford MAs.

The humiliation of being paraded as a 'natural', a dole-queue voice from a generation in protest, has continued to haunt MacSweeney, and his determination to remain unnatural has been stalked by that eighteenth-century sense of unnatural as incapable of feeling gratitude for the patronage of his betters. Such unnaturalness, as devoid of the sympathies which are determiningly human, has been embodied for MacSweeney in the figure of the wolf, the scavenging animal dependent on the proximity of human settlement but marking the limits of the humanly tameable. In old age, MacSweeney fears, "we cannot hunt any longer, but lag behind for scraps" (*Elegy for January*) like the tamed dog. With his Chatterton essay MacSweeney shows himself obsessed by youth and as such, more a creature of contemporary commercial culture than he would admit; but both he and Chatterton have suffered badly in their reputations from their absorption into a youth-cult, and MacSweeney laments in his interview the failure of reviewers to attend to his poems, rather than to his sociological significance as a poet. The integration and compromised acceptances of middle-age are MacSweeney's horror, and it is remarkable that the poems collected in *The Tempers of Hazard* leap directly from an extended youth, a continuing preoccupation with youth culture (in his thirties MacSweeney was alert to the rise of punk), to old age in 'Finnbar's Lament'.

But 'The Last Bud' preceded *Elegy for January*. Before collection in *Our Mutual Scarlet Boulevard* it appeared in an eponymously-titled pamphlet (Blacksuede Boot Press, Newcastle, 1969) along with seven further poems, which the later collection publishes in the same sequence, and prior to this the poem had appeared in *The English Intelligencer*. 'The Last Bud' with its associated poems indeed opens out as the last flowering of the 'natural' in MacSweeney's work, and is by some way his finest achievement before the *Odes*. As with a handful of other poems of the same period, it appears to draw largely for its relaxed, flexible verse on the Romantic conversation poem, especially Shelley's 'Letter to Maria Gisborne', allowing a kind of controlled ramble in which the convention of address to another draws a world of disparate objects and concerns into a focused fiction of intersubjectivity:

> —Upon the table
> More knacks and quips there be than I am able
> To catalogize in this verse of mine:—
> A pretty bowl of wood—not full of wine,
> but quicksilver;
> > (Shelley)

> Grasping at thin things for support, but
>  finding nothing but books, devices, verbal
> chicanery, & cosmological range
> > (MacSweeney)

For MacSweeney, even the objects of his intellectual curiosity become a mockery, the evidence of frauds practiced upon him and a taunting reminder of his baseless and hopeless pretensions, whereas for Shelley they compose a world of preoccupation into which the absence of the loved one arrives as a disintegrative shock: "You are not here!". 'The Last Bud' also echoes O'Hara's 'In Memory of My Feelings' in its overall organisation and movement, both poems ending with superb and positive acts of resignation, although MacSweeney remains closer to the Romantic figure of self than to O'Hara's teeming inhabitants; in 'The Last Bud' MacSweeney is imperilled by the depredations of treacherous and fraudulent erstwhile friends and fellow poets, who stand in place of Shelley's local representatives of kindness—hence the abnegation of "I am finished with your kingdom of light". The other immediately evident echo—especially when the briefer poems are read alongside 'The Last Bud' (see 'In Sunlight the Bankrupt Gamblers')—is of John Wieners' *The Hotel Wentley Poems*. This is more difficult to show, being the lyric expression of sustained dignity in utter bereavement and nakedness, a measured walk through Hell, where the lines of the poem wrap about the bereft in an always-tentative but never failing motion:

> My middle name is Joseph and I
> walk beside an ass on the way to what

Bethlehem, where a new babe is born.
        (Wieners)

That one lends me virtue, and I live
 thereby; he knows the grammar of the
most important motion, the song in a flame.
        (MacSweeney)

Both Wieners and MacSweeney are poets for whom the gifts of poetry
and of human love are the only saving graces when all else betrays, and
of these human love is bound in its time to betray; there are parallels
also in their later development towards a poetry of transvestism in
Wieners' case and a poetry of fetishism in MacSweeney's, which will be
discussed below. All wholeness becomes disavowed in the course of the
poem. Generation and parenthood are dismissed. Once again the ego is
a mere empty container, but this is welcomed—all contents are to be
expelled, all affection voided:

I have only one half of my parenthood.
The other isn't dead, but he lingers on
this side of breath with the tenacity
of a rat. That breakdown in relations
doesn't even bother me now. I just want
to be left to be inhabited by my furniture if needs be. Or the music of an
empty room.

Once voided, the objects of affection turn to attack, and even the inani-
mate objects surrounding the poet partake in a paranoiac reanimation:

And the new reality, the real, is full,
kicks you over, tells tales, whistles at
you when you walk, leaves you for someone
else, but leaves no sentiment (spelled
sediment)…

The one ward, the one redemption, lies in another's unconditional
love and care, the one to whom the poem is addressed. But how will the
cruelly empty self, beset by enemies in those case out, answer such love?
The poem starts in the wake of betrayal of that love; treachery is the
shared lot, and she whose true gift was betrayed is destined as Israfel
(the angel who sounds the last trump, according to the Koran) to cast

the poet into limbo along with the entire Circle of traitors. What has been rejected—what must be rejected—is a fulfilment, a satisfaction which is grounded in others' exploitation. The treacherous rejection of proffered love is preferred to the satisfaction which relies upon another's self-immolation, and the third part of the poem is saturated with disgust at both service exacted through imperialism and at the freely-given self-denial of love, even, in the poem's most startlingly nihilistic lines, back to the earth's originating maternity:

> That dark
> continent of man has lived very well
> since this ball of dust aborted itself
> from the sun's legs.

For all of this account's investment of 'The Last Bud' with a literary history, the poem has nothing of pastiche about it; throughout its 200-odd lines there is never a false note, never a momentary lapse into off-the-shelf sentiment. The poem belongs with Andrew Crozier's *The Veil Poem* as the finest fruit of the English rediscovery of High Romanticism in the 1960s, but while Crozier's poem rises to the heights of a great cosmological hymn, MacSweeney's ends with a back firmly turned against the human world of love, of daily labour, and of fellowship in creative endeavour. The poem performs a scorched earth exercise on all MacSweeney's previous writing, and fuelled by the disgust and resentment documented in the *Poetry Information* interview, thrusts away friends, patrons and lovers in favour of a glorious darkness and emptiness, an absolute independence conceding and receiving nothing:

> Enjoy the warmth, soak in
> the lukewarm sea, wave your naked bodies
> about like freedom flags. Ahead of me
> is brilliant darkness, and the king
> of night. This is a signed resignation;
> I am finished with your kingdom of light.

This is no mere rhetoric; *Elegy for January* spells out the decision in plain prose, and henceforward the natural, vulnerable, speaking first-person identifiable with the poet, will appear in MacSweeney's writing only at great extremity as a residue when all else has been stolen and traduced,— in the poem 'Wild Knitting' which occupies a summary and reorientative position relative to the writing of the late Seventies and the Eighties, similar to 'The Last Bud''s relationship with foregoing work. MacSweeney's curricular stance is now established, but it is a stance supported only by part-identification with a number of rejected, humiliated and outlaw figures set for early destruction, inherently unstable itself and reaching towards unstable supports. To Rimbaud, Chatterton and Shelley will be added Jim Morrison, some of the more tragic figures of late Seventies punk and the Delta blues singer Robert Johnson (*Hellhound Memos*, The Many Press, 1993). Their instability is a condition for poetic success; where MacSweeney has relied upon the authors of an achieved *oeuvre*, his writing has become absorbed to their gestural repertoire to the extent of intimation; this was so with William Carlos Williams in some early lyrics, and becomes so with Jack Spicer and J. H. Prynne in the books *Brother Wolf* and *Fools Gold* (both 1972) respectively, reprinted in *The Tempers of Hazard*. Where in more recent writing he has cut loose from part-identification, the results have been vertiginously unstrapped. This writing, which together with 'The Last Bud' constitutes MacSweeney's justification for recognition as a major British writer of the late twentieth century, is what I shall now consider, bypassing *Brother Wolf* and *Fools Gold* except for their additions to the gestural repertoire.

## II

> BREVE ME BRYGHTE clean green pearl. Breve
> Brine supercharging urchin spunkette
> Dribble into. All you
> drab caffeine mums-to-be.
> Shaved pork elbows, cumridden bras
> & laddered leather. YOU
>
> floordragged, roughened
> by violence, bangled
> tits &tots.
>
> VIXENATED HORNON LIPCRAWL.
> BLONDE & REALLY GINGERED UP.

This short passage from 'Streeters Into Red', one of the *Jury Vet* sequence of poems printed in full in *The Tempers of Hazard*, turns the repeated question of the intelligibility of modernist verse towards one of acceptability. For the language of the sequence as a whole, sexist seems a barely adequate description and misogynistic would be inept; pornography and the pages of *Vogue* offer a delirious description of womanhood to which is counterposed only a figure of virgin innocence. Are we faced with a personal pathology, or with virulent social satire—or that especially charged combination of the two exemplified in the early novels of William Burroughs, before pederasty became matter for his celebratory nostalgia? I think the last, and that MacSweeney takes a step outside Burroughs' Private Dick persona to displace undercover observation to an industry outside the body, collapsing the fashion spies of glossy magazines, Special Branch and Security Service operatives, newspaper reporters and the machinery of jury selection for secret trials, into the perverse organizing principle of these poems, scopophiliac, coprophiliac, fetishistic, sniffing and prying, unwrapping, smearing and ejaculating. Every sexual perversion is mobilized against the persistence of unregulated love, with marriage and parenthood brought into the technical repertoire of surveillance. Only conscience is absent conspicuously; the work of repression becomes actually the work of paranoid disclosure, as the fantastically finical and prurient files of the Stasi have demonstrated. How is this reflected in the poems' procedures? As Tony Lopez has observed, the basic verse-form and ejaculatory rhetoric have been taken from Michael McClure, the poet of sentient meat, complete with a pitching between upper and lower-case, scatterings of wild punctuation, lines drawn across the page and at once transgressed, and a roughly central line-justification. In McClure these devices serve a biological determinism of a consistent, well-researched and celebratory tenor, although rampant egotism always favours the McClure genetic stuff—whose recipients are blessed indeed. McClure strives strenuously enough for the ease of the ego into the ultimate orgasm, an orgiastic merging into basic transhistorical creativity afforded by Woman—whose breasts, womb and anus are full partners in the quest. By contrast, the lines of *Jury Vet* are incessantly being thrown off-axis, clotting, sputtering into singularities, running across margins; but the most decided difference lies in their lexical miscegenation. McClure makes inventive use of scientific discourses, but these are incorporated into a seamless and untroubled lexis, where *Jury Vet* is a babble of privileged, up-to-the-minute information from a variety of well-placed sources which are not confined to description—they interfere, they pronounce rules which seem arbitrary to those who are neither slaves to fashion or victims of misidentification: but then, *Jury Vet* contends, nobody is proof against what Wieners calls the "terms of language, love and fashion".

The passage printed above starts with a Rowley-esque anachronism; 'breve' is 'set down in writing', and the injunction to "BREVE ME BRYGHTE" at once places the first person at the mercy of the language he handles or is handled by. What is an "urchin spunkette"? A pubescent receptacle for spunk I presume; and the passage moves from woman defined by her purity and this year's colour ("clean green pearl") to masturbatory fantasy, to woman as used and violated through perverse sexual practices, through childbirth and through domestic violence, with "bangled | tits & tots" hinging together sexual, maternal and domestic violation. These all are "dribblings into" MacSweeney's brevet, his "VIXENATED HORNON LIPCRAWL", which after a dividing line is transformed into "Fingered Up | crawl" and a passage of fellatio in language of lust, disgust, pornographic detachment, passive submission, near-rape, desolate loss and nostalgia for physical contact. This is achieved in five short lines through use of street slang ('pony' for penis), neologism ('gangness' for the condition of being ganged i.e. gang-raped, ganged-up-against, and drawing a sequence of lovers into one gang), local dialect ('bint' being derogatory Northern argot for 'girl') and arch Frenchisms ("creamery de la femme"). For MacSweeney, it should be noted, French is the language which destroyed British (especially Northern British) speech—as his 'Ode: Resolution', has it:

> French words dominated
> Chaucer's day.
>           They ate away
> the oak & rose.
> Strangeling
> Changeling
> (*Odes,* Trigram Press 1978, p.37)

The fantasy of an honest tongue, of men speaking straight to men, underlies this, but cut across with the irony of Chatterton's manufacture. Certainly in *Jury Vet* this cod-British comes closest to an open authorial voice, but it is a voice in despair, drowning in a welter of intrusive of these tongues being that of the fashion industry, an Anglo-French hybrid. Elsewhere in the *Jury Vet* poems, Jamaican dialect, punk lyrics, tradenames and terms distorted and misspelled in the manner of tradenames are mobilised in a sadistic cracking open of the female body and of the body of the text; for instance, Elvis Costello's lines "You want her broken with her mouth wide open | because she's this year's girl" introduce the poem 'Pink Enamelled Tosspot' which ends with the pivotal and centred line "Your single body's a striking SOVIET!"—'striking' as in air-strike. It should be noted that the body does not *contain* a Soviet; the only bodily content in these poems is strewn and spilt, with shit, menstrual blood, spit, piss and sperm defacing the outer garments of high couture which are inadequate even to assemble the limbs and organs into an articulated presence. This decidedly distinguishes such garments from their use in an earlier poetic treatment of women's clothing, John Wieners' *Behind the State Capitol, or Cincinnati Pike*, where once formally-organised 'male' lyrics billow after transvestite makeover, to be signed triumphantly with the name of a Hollywood starlet or Jackie Onassis. MacSweeney is not in love with transformed surfaces— the "single body" is a whirl of female parts, sheathed or flapping, a swarm of furies. They may be marshalled, as in the first passage quoted in this discussion, may be a fusillade of shots of a single model in differ- ent settings and outfits, as in 'Pink Enamelled Tosspot' where the model appears as an estranged wife on whom fantasies are projected, but never resolve into an individual female. The "striking soviet" gapes with sexual organs; she convenes a quim, a cunt, a clit, a manhole, twitch- root, slit, fanny, patent lips—the plurality of body-parts is illusory, it is a plurality of names.

There is no doubt that this is shocking to feminist-influenced sensi- bilities, and that it is meant to be. Absolutely no cover is afforded by clothes, shoes or makeup, which serve merely to tear off the lips or a calf, to colour-code limbs and organs and announce that breasts are crucial this year as the neck was last, moving the pruriently forensic eye down one space in its fetishistic focus, only for the eye to roll disen- gaged. *Jury Vet* represents the extreme of MacSweeney's disaffected vision of a culture given over to flagrancy, to a depudorating atomisation of the individual conducted through his and her inven- torising by unaccountable and disguised interests, reaching into all inti- macy and rendering sexuality a cruel and infantile set of exploitative, operative acts.

One way to understand the late writing of MacSweeney would be as an instance of aesthetic paranoia. Within contemporary society, the particularity of aesthetic sensibility is bracketed out and accorded no value beyond its own circumscribed domain. MacSweeney has repre- sented and challenged the autonomy of the aesthetic by trying to live out its lone wolf myth. MacSweeney's writing seeks to move out of modernistic aesthetics towards a political engagement, and at the same time suffers the inquisitive tentacles both of secular forms of truth which render subjective particularity a mere sociological or linguistic construction, and of laws which render political and aesthetic acts nugatory—particularly the invisible hand of the market. Striving to break out of an aesthetic citadel, he discovers the keep already has been invaded and reduced to rubble. *Jury Vet* struggles to reconstruct an aesthetic domain from the debris of selfhood. On the other hand, the State of the Nation Addresses which frame it in *The Tempers of Hazard*, 'Colonel B' and 'Wild Knitting', evince the contrary motion, striving to enter poetically the political and ethical. A backward glance at the *Odes* shows one stage in MacSweeney's journey towards this categorical breakdown. Lone wolf figures such as Chatterton and Jim Morrison have ceased to be exemplary as fully-constituted beings, historically proof in their achievements and representative significance against the forces which destroyed them physically; rather they come to be distributed as fragmentary discourses amongst the discourses which seized and traduced them, most notably the false-aesthetic embodied in the fashion industry. The wolf which adorns the cover of *Odes* is caged, rather than on the prowl. 'Colonel B', which recycles many phrases from the *Odes* as well as sharing its lexis, is left stranded between the contrary movements, neither registering the incursivity of (im)moral society which precipitated the fragments from which it is built, nor successfully transgressive in the ethical and political domain—the appearance of The Maggie Beast occasions no more dread than the comical devil figure in a Mummers' play.

Against this, 'Wild Knitting' is an extraordinary poem, clearly joining the poetical and the political in a unified gasp for survival and clutch for the shreds of dignity. Again MacSweeney confounds the nostalgia of left-liberalism; the desolate Albion on which the poem opens fails to usher in the conventional lament for broken communities and hand-wringing over the fate of the unemployed—MacSweeney, after all, is one of few poets who has worked always outside the public sector, and his libertarianism is calculated to offend social workers grossly. But this is no gratuitous offensiveness—the poem arraigns the death of politics, and will not collude in the authoritarianism of a bankrupt labourism or chapel morality. Holding to his outsider stance, MacSweeney directs withering scorn at victims, apathetic and abject in their masochistic desire to become the objects of authority, unable to negotiate the particulars of their lives:

Boss me
Up
or I go Bostik nostril
& totally Sickrude, need to be
ordered, regular fishcakes & spam
every day I write the book
the bad book. Join the army
of deserters, council estate dogs
shitting in the beck, rimless cars, porn
videos & snuff movies on the rental

Like poetry, the political is invaded by false pledges, of security in the "council estate dogs", of mobility and independence in "rimless cars" and in intimacy in "porn | videos & snuff movies". All forms both of pleasure and of control are alienated, but alienated, but alienated pleasure and control are *all there is*. For it is a mark of the development of the outsider stance, that the outsider himself is profoundly affected, is structured similarly to the objects of his scorn. 'Wild Knitting' is driven and squeezed and torn between deep emotional necessity for external structure in the shape of work and marriage, and disgusted humiliation in the workplace and home:

What sulky
bends & nascent gloom
the wife brings home
with lentil puree
on a stick
to beat yr frying head
& make you see SENSE, that biggest
of boys.

And yet, after "I wreck the cot & cuddle corner in my head, burn the children", the spirit of Albion returns in the form of the Wife in passages of celebratory love as moving as any in recent poetry:

Always bless & Do. Wrap me in fantastik kiss crusts.

You the wronged woman. You the complexity. You the seeker
of buses & trains. You the wandering wife far from
home.
You beneath the curlew-whooping sky, sinking
in my northern arms. Dimming forest of touches
blest with Real.

It is time to register just how skilful is MacSweeney's versification, and how acute his word-selection. This passage hinges semantically about the word 'bless', which derives from blood and is related to the French *blessure* or wound. In this word is compacted profundity of physical need, resentment at hurt and the bestowal of grace, as these are embodied for MacSweeney in Albion/Wife. The consonantal handling swings around the wounding noise of the 'k's, and open submission of the 'w's; sound organization around consonants rather than vowels has an affinity with Bunting's *Briggflatts*, with Rowley, with medieval Midlands poetry such as *Sir Gawain and the Green Knight* (regarded until quite recently as a 'Northern' slingshot against the effete Chaucer) and with the abrupt consonantism of Northern slang. Posed against this is the mellifluousness of French and its fashion language, as in the whispering confessions of infidelity in part 14 of 'Wild Knitting':

> Here. Here! all; my knowledge of buttersoft beige
> kidsmooth sandalettes of Enzo Albanese & all the
> Sparked Up peccadilloes in Paris & Bordeaux.
> Hotbank Seine summer with celandine salad.

'Wild Knitting' is a fantastically beautiful poem of hopelessness and ugliness, which ends in a first person plural which is fully earned and which dares to proposed a way of conduct, uniting the Wife in her "squaw madness" and "my scrapheap head" in the politics and the poetry of negotiating life on earth, neither in preparation for life after death, nor in subservience to overarching codes of behaviour or ideological eschatologies:

> now that the sky
>    is a blue desert,
> starved of love: we go for the
>    ruched field

This is not a 'political poem' of the sort which amusingly would intervene in the excuse for politics which makes for our governance; in the end it is far more ambitious. MacSweeney takes seriously the Thatcherite adage that there is no society, for society would require men and women fully political—and poetical—in negotiating the particularity of their mutual lives. By a strange twist, the lone wolf is turned teacher and an example of social living; for after all the wolf is a social animal. *The Tempers of Hazard* concludes its selection with 'Finnbar's

Lament', an elegy for love departed which moves with the dignity and assurance of 'The Seafarer' and whose virtues and beauty are so apparent as to require no exposition. Instead I would summarise by asking how to estimate the odd and ill-digestible writing of Barry MacSweeney, responding with the following high claims:

*First*, a poetical pursuit so reckless of reward and recognition, a courage remarkable even where an activity can carry few expectations of appreciation, must be admired. *Secondly*, a refusal to rest within the limits ascribed to poetical activity in post-enlightenment culture, thanks either to blind affection for process and for products in themselves, untroubled by their political and ethical matrix, or to a cheerful equation of readership's extent with instrumentality, or to deployment of confused metaphors of linguistic disturbance allowing the fiction of political force—this too is admirable and unusual, and to my knowledge has been shared only with J.H. Prynne amongst contemporaries. *Thirdly*, the repeated radical remaking of a poetic whose finest achievements arises at the point where a poetic programme is relinquished—*vide* 'The Last Bud' and 'Wild Knitting'—testifies to a principled restlessness and self-interrogation, to be distinguished from the hedonism of poets who surf the waters their own excrement pollutes. *Fourthly*, an abiding honesty which lays the work open to the opprobrium and dismissal of the casually judgmental, refusing to be representative of any social current, always true to a subjectivity which is scrupulously and painfully interrogated.

# The Value of Penniless Politics

A few evenings ago I returned to my temporary Greenwich Village apartment and handsetted into C-SPAN, a cable gesture-broadcaster of wall-to-wall democratic process calculated to send the parish pump's greatest enthusiastic scuttling to the trough for a cold and bracing douche of consumerism. My viewing served up a well-choreographed 'demonstration' of Hispanic lobbyists protesting against a democrat filibuster delaying the nomination of Miguel Estrada to the US Court of Appeals (often a step towards the Supreme Court). The paraded stars alternated between silver-haired Southern state legislators, impeccably Anglo, deploring the introduction of racial politics into the legal domain of pure uncontaminated reason, while shamelessly schmoozing their Hispanic voting base; and Tex-Mex recording stars, several claiming long friendship with the Bush family and talking of their gratitude that in these times a great man leads the nation. 'This great nation of ours' (whose?) figured repeatedly, the other insistent trope being the embodiment in Miguel Estrada of the American Dream. The American Dream in his progress via Columbia and Harvard Law School to the pinnacle of his profession, certainly trumps the reality of his actual, toxically conservative politics.

Witnessing this insulting farce, unlikely to be chosen by poor Hispanics in New York City in preference to a Spanish language soap, was to be reminded of Douglas Oliver's poem *Penniless Politics*, first published in 1991 in London by Iain Sinclair, revised and reissued in 1994 by Bloodaxe in Newcastle. This edition, please note, is still available. Betweentimes the poem made a print debut in New York (having been tested in public readings) as part of *The Scarlet Cabinet*, 'a compendium of books' by Oliver and Alice Notley with I imagine a small readership—450 pages of poetry and weird pastiche prose would require electric shocks to command many readers. I fear that *Penniless Politics* might be neglected despite unusual media attention for its 200-copy first edition sparked by Howard Brenton's enthusiasm in *The Guardian*, reprinted as foreword to the Bloodaxe edition (the Bloodaxe website giving Brenton and Oliver equivalent billing).

One reason the poem seems little discussed may be that Douglas Oliver as poet was one of a kind, a kind which shook off any constituency as soon as it assembled. Here I would like to suggest what that odd kind of poet was and could be in others, and how his poetics led Oliver, an Anglo-Scot who mocked his own plumminess, to write a narrative satire on US politics introducing (amidst various 'non-poetic' matter) a draft for a revised US constitution. This poem must not be forgotten; whatever its poetic merit, if that can be separated from any other sort, it should engender disputatiousness beyond the usual internecine poetic strife. It is impossible to read *Penniless Politics* without thinking about what its extra-literary as well as literary consequences should be.

Poetry may be a lying art, but lyric poets often mean what they write when they write it. Douglas Oliver made sure he also knew about it, but further was interested in the way in which he and others knew, and the implications of knowing for action in the private and public worlds. His poetic was concerned above all with pragmatic ethics. Avant-gardists may cite string theory and grant-holders check the obscurer stopoffs in their British Council itineraries, but whatever, in lyric poetry knowledge almost always stands secondary to style and to affect, and to exemplify how any of us might live personally and politically lies way off the lyric territory. Proclamations of personal liberal or revolutionary sensibility are not in question—Oliver had no interest in posturing.

So Oliver's poetry was primarily an ethical rather than an ontological project, perhaps uniquely in post-Romantic British poetry, and stylistically he employed whatever suited that purpose—or turned to that purpose the writing styles developed by those close to him at different times. With his first book, *Oppo Hectic* (Ferry Press 1969) he was recognisably a 'Cambridge poet' albeit a journalist passing through who found friendship and intellectual stimulus among Cambridge poets (by no means all university-connected); this book and his first novel, *The Harmless Building* (1973) left recognisable traces behind in the poetry of Peter Riley for instance. But whereas in Riley the terms of Trust, Love and Kindness were systematised within an ontological framework derived from Merleau-Ponty and Heidegger, for Oliver they were located in a pragmatics of goodness founded in his experience as the father of Tom, a Down's syndrome baby—where his own goodness was conceived as no more than what the goodness of the child had afforded. This experience made possible an innocence beyond all the waddings of irony, a possibility responsible for the most unprecedented passages of Oliver's poetry, including some in *Penniless Politics*.

I don't wish to imply that Oliver was theoretically naïve by comparison with Riley or other Cambridge poets; published in 1973, *The Harmless Building* famously (in Cambridge at any rate) could claim to be the first novel in English to include Lacanian jokes. Much of his working life was spent in Paris, as a journalist working for Reuters and Agence France-Presse, and in the final period of his life teaching at the British Institute. He was always restive intellectually and persistently if kindly challenging. Born on September 14th 1937 in Southampton and brought up in Bournemouth where Mary Shelley's body and Percy Bysshe Shelley's heart are buried, Douglas Oliver died in Paris on 21st April 2000.[55]

Perhaps it was the theoretically sophisticated who were naïve; *The Diagram Poems* (Ferry Press, 1979) looked as interestingly hermetic as a Cambridge reader could wish, its imposing format featuring en face with the poems, elaborate doodles comprising circuits, cartoon animals, and the tracks of Tupamaros guerrilla operations. The poems were headed with brief prose narratives of guerrilla attacks on banks. This macaronic presentation had already been deployed in *In the Cave of Suicession* (Street Editions, 1974), a profoundly odd book of narrative, oracular dialogue and lyric poetry touch-typed in semi-darkness in a Derbyshire cave (hence orthographic errors such as that in the title) and discoursing with Tom, his dead son. The test that any ethics should be equal to an encounter with the death of one much-loved, remained fundamental to Oliver's writing. This was hard to reconcile with the presumption that lyric poetry might embody a privileged and sufficient way of knowing, not unheard-of in Cambridge at that time; *In the Cave of Suicession* and *The Diagram Poems* employed poetry among several instruments for its fitness as a medium of production and delivery, just as the novel *The Harmless Building* spouted verse when necessary.

Oliver's introduction to *The Diagram Poems* plainly sets out the ethical ambition as extended from its earlier more personal domain:

> But whether the guerrillas were right or wrong, you were dreaming quite obliquely, as you tapped the stories out, of how an authentic politics

might combine the mildness of your dead baby with the stern wisdom of a judicious elder minister: some beneficial balance, instead of revolutionary flamboyance and a dictator's response of iron rule. Only a fool, while ill-informed, supports anyone else's violence…

That last comment is characteristic; Oliver may have been a liberal of an especially generous kind, but although regarding the abject as the suitable position for a white male he was tough-minded, and *Penniless Politics* is filled with challenges to authorial and others' too lightly-acquired assumptions, enthusiasms and purported experience.

At this point I wish to jump forward to *Penniless Politics*, vaulting across some of Oliver's most remarkable work including the narrative poem denouncing Thatcherism, *The Infant and The Pearl*.[56] I began with a vignette of US political process as shown by C-SPAN; but yesterday evening (10th March 2003) I turned to a local station to watch a city hall debate about the expected war with Iraq, overwhelmingly hostile. During an interlude, one of those venerable pundits in whom American TV delights, was asked why the country was on the brink of war: "Why? Why?" he choked— "Because out of the South West dust a fanatic, a *fanatic* with *Jesus* in his eyes came to send boys from the Bronx to die, and said to Kids in Baghdad, on *their* birthdays it won't be candles on their cakes that get burnt, those kids will be set on fire and burnt by *our* missiles." His rage was so extreme and his age so advanced that I expected paramedics to rush into the studio. *Penniless Politics* registers simultaneously both the outrageously obvious corruption of American democracy, and this rude, demotic energy and honesty—the residual but still-visible radical power encapsulated in official ideology.

Oliver took that power as seriously as any right-wing militiaman does, with the crucial difference that his sense of the 'Hooman' as he called it in *Penniless Politics* exists in an intimate if constantly frictional relationship with diversity. He lived in New York City's Lower East Side from 1987 to 1992, as recounted in Alice Notley's excellent essay 'Douglas Oliver's New York Poem'[57]. Notley does so impressive a job in summarising the complex plot of the poem that it makes any attempt of mine redundant, and she positions it exactly to its historical moment— closer to 1999 than to now, judging from her bemoaning of US politics' "lack of powerful symbols and of connection with scary forces. What if the President of the United States had to talk to the keeper of the Delphic Oracle from time to time [....] What if he had to face the gods before he decided policy?" Now we know.

But needs must describe the poem briefly, with Notley's help. Supposedly written in ottavo rima derived from Tasso, although played very fast and loose, by a Francophile Brit living on the Lower East Side, the poem contains multitudes—a real New York poem in the Whitman tradition. Notley explains: "The plot of the poem turns about the founding and progress of a new political party, called Spirit, without power or money. Invitations to the party's first meeting, instigated by Emen, a Haitian immigrant and Will, an Anglo-Scots immigrant, are by chain-letter. Crucial members of the party, the poem's characters, include Hispanic Dolores Esteves, a Cuban boxer named High John, African-American Ma Johnson, a young Korean woman (Republican) Yuhwa Lee, Juan her Hispanic boyfriend, the middle-aged Chinese man Peter Sung, the Jewish lawyer Lou Levinson." The storyline of the poem recounts a version of urban regeneration which—improbably—benefits the residents of the area regenerated, and which is driven by fun, spectacle and a considerable amount of sex (in forms tending to mock existing power relations).

It is a pity that Brenton's foreword to the Bloodaxe edition uses the poem as stalking-horse for a sour swipe at "the post-communist, postmodernist, 'ideas are dead' miasma that is poisoning us" (post-feminism being a more welcome turn no doubt). But Oliver never set up the politically-engaged narrative poem as a standard for poetic conduct for himself or for others; his nimbleness was such that he could place voodoo and Spirit at the heart of *Penniless Politics* and at the same time poke fun at Will's lyrical effusions and irresponsibilities—*and* that those effusions then drive and further elaborate the pragmatics of the poem. Indeed this 'satire' works as a credible counter-factual to the sorry crack-blighted housing projects, visible and miserably inhabited legacy of a policy of 'benign neglect' and 'planned shrinkage' brazenly articulated in 1970 by Nixon's advisor on urban policy, Daniel P. Moynihan, and implemented by successive City administrations; a policy of community destruction recently pursued by the sainted Rudy Giuliani.[58] Oliver's satire exposes such wicked folly not through denunciation primarily, but by way of an expressive counter-factual realised fully in its lusts, its zest, its quarrels, its errancy—it produces a world we might wish at our best to inhabit; and whilst because we are so rarely at our best it never will be realised, we are brought to desire urgently to mobilise the spirit of Spirit in ourselves and for each other, and even maybe to promote some of Spirit's wholly pragmatic and sensible programme.

Yet what could be more 'postmodern' than a voodoo spell kludged out of stanzas borrowed from the author of *Jerusalem Delivered*, and alive with the voices of half the world as mediated through their shared American experience? [59] Oliver's poem vindicates the politics and artistic practice of 'diversity'—he relishes the linguistic, cultural and political encounters of Korean small capitalist with cool gay downtown lawyer with disillusioned turncoat Marxist journalist (who's that then?) with Hispanic drugsmoney launderer with African-American sporting icon. Oliver likes the edges, the bumpy seams, not melange or gumbo. *Contra* Brenton the only real irritants registered are presumptuously totalizing and prescriptive accounts of humanity—specifically, sub-Marxist dogma and Islamicism as distinguished from Marxism and Islam. Even so Oliver doesn't carry a torch for enlightenment scepticism; his position is consistent with what some social theorists have termed 'thick multiculturalism', distinguished from a 'thin multiculturalism' accepting difference so long as qualified by an emphasis on individual self-determination founded in rational scepticism.[60] Oliver's position acknowledges community as well as individual rights inasmuch as they conform to the 'kind', the humane ('kind' being a crucial term for Oliver's writing). Here, evidently, the space opens for a critique of the dread 'essentialism'. The powers of spirit and of lyric poetry expounded in *Penniless Politics* are founded in that romantic protest which was the historical forerunner of 'thick multiculturalism' and convinced of the inexhaustibility of common human potential; the poem's new US Constitution derives from this romantic vision of diverse expressions of a shared spirit, rather than the enlightenment-descended test of shared rationality so exclusive in its influential modern restatement by John Rawls.

Oliver demonstrates beyond doubt that a postmodern poem *can* be stirringly political. Postmodern artworks have a weakness for the monumental in scale compensating for their shiftiness, too long, too widescreen, too loud; but the brilliance of *Penniless Politics* as a long and ambitious poem lies in its use of animating narrative. Here of course it departs from postmodern cliché, where narrative is always conflated with 'master narratives'. Oliver's narrative is essentially farcical (Brenton cites Ealing comedy), a convention which gives ample space to subservient narratives in versions of their vernacular and empowers them; each farcical mishap comes right, and guiding interventions and signposting are always guyed and teased by those uppity subservient narratives.

Strong narrative is necessary to this poem; unlike some other readers I find Oliver's handling of formal rhymed stanzas insufficiently adept and propulsive to manage thick multiculturalism without a storyline. Even within *Penniless Politics* the superiority of Oliver's free verse seems to me obvious in 'Will's Incantation', both the most preposterous and the most deeply moving section of the poem, and from which I quote a short portion. Its freedom though depends on the narrative and linguistic milieu already established:

> Oh Lord—Who is Lord?—Oh Lordess
> you are the bridegroom to Justess,
> which is female, a black mare of night,
> arise in your stable, Christess,
> in your groom's leather leggings arise:
> provide the stirrup that burns
> under the instep of the jockeys of night
> riding the black night mares
> shadows racing down the lost perspectives of street lamps
> past burning automobiles of darkness
> fires in the streets of lost civil rights
> the lanes of invisibles down lanes alternative to the fast lanes
> dearborn angel in black
> angel more than us arise from politics of contest
> not to end contest, but to add spurs and stirrups
> to the one, true race of our time.
> Come to this stable, Judaic Christess
> from your Italo-Irish Protestant cathedrals,
> take at last the white wafers of guilt from my mouth
> my tongue coated as if with thrush
> in my sorrow-song at those we have outlawed
> who die on the margins, in garishly-lit hospices
> or in African countries stricken with plague;

—that last line looking ahead to Oliver's last published book, *A Salvo for Africa* (Bloodaxe, 2000). This passage exemplifies how embarrassing Oliver can be in his innocence ("streets of lost civil rights"), and the importance of such embarrassment—a point Brenton gets right in talking about the alarmed leftist response to his championing of the poem. Oliver is unworried about looking foolish—this is part of his shtick, the white middle-aged male intellectual getting down on the dancefloor; the project for which the poem operates is too big for the poet's dignity to be material, and what the poem might animate is more important than its finished objecthood. Abjectly in the spirit of Spirit I admit having been one of the "middle-class well-educated whites" mentioned by Notley, who shrunk prissily (and in print alas) from Oliver's willingness to make a spectacle of himself, failing to appreciate how closed, how exclusive are the politics of standing on one's dignity. The refrain to the 'White Crossroads' section still makes me cringe, but such risks in ventriloquising the oppressed allow (for instance) the progress Lordess/Justess/Christess above, which (along with the invention of new pronouns) effects a bouleversement for which its 'politically correct' equivalents have striven ineffectually.[61] *Penniless Politics* feels like a stand-up act, taking pratfalls, sometimes even boring, but when it hits its stride the hits come thick and fast and thrilling.

Responsive then to the oral, semi-improvised poetics of contemporary New York, sure to gladden Shelley's heart in Bournemouth, reminiscent of Oliver's contemporary Barry MacSweeney (who died two weeks after him) and whose most moving writing was guided by the mute girl Pearl whom he taught to read, much as Oliver's was by Tom, this writing knows no shame in its pursuit of the good. Douglas Oliver was a good man, both unselfconsciously and deliberately, and this is the first thing those who knew him say. I cannot think of another writer becoming a good person as an outgrowth of his or her project of writing or whose goodness animated his writing. Whatever way this worked, it makes a lovely and more than ever required demand.

# Tripping the Light Fantastic: Tom Raworth's Ace

As published by The Figures in California in 1977 Tom Raworth's poem *Ace* is a long, skinny poem in a short book, and as read publicly by its author it is a long poem in a short time. *Ace* repudiates the monumental and cannot be dwelt upon by the silent or intoning reader; it runs out of breath and breath will die, light flickers. Here is no structure to set against time's passing; rather it seizes time, teases it out and recompresses it in an instant: this poem understands time as light, the striped steadiness and breakup of the cathode tube image, the perceptual blink of an eye, the flicker of memory. Where is the poem's centre, the aperture through which it scans the world and might meet the reader's visual passages? Ace in a hole we learn at the outset to be exactly *offset:*

> drill
> another hole
> near the edge
> of the label and
> play it
> from there
> with a light
> pickup
>             (p.11; *CP*, p.201)[62]

Labels on LPs were designed either with a studied indifference to the hole punched for the record player's spindle or alternatively with the hole as their central organizing feature. A hole at the edge of a label would fling off-bias the lightest pickup arm. No stability then; sound and light not so much as referred to a centre, and the label's guidance discounted. These lines were written prior to the invention of CD

[105]

players, where laser light does pick up sound information; here light falls on the surface and retrieves distortions of what has been encoded as for perfect reproduction. The poem's instruction for off-centre drilling might be taken by a reader as a warning (for instance against 'drilling down' to the individual line or word) or as encouraging a reading which does not strain for an impossible fidelity; and this article therefore is not so much an account of *Ace*, for nothing could be more absurdly out of key with the poem's evading of summation, as the scratching of a pickup destined to be less skittishly entertaining than the tracks Raworth has laid down. An instruction of comparable weight, however, would be to remain aware that 'centre' identified as the source of organizing power is no more than a metaphor, and that to allude to a displacement does not discount the possibility—even the likelihood—of an organizing point of reference above, behind or to one side of the centre of the label, or even permeating or distributed through the pickup's output in sound or in the silent sounding of the reader.

*Ace* is the first of the long skinny poems which were to become characteristic of Raworth's published work of the late seventies and the eighties, at once all over the place and immobile, shapeshifting, mercurial and sustained. Against a hop-skip-and-jump metric its rhythms weave, decay, accelerate, even relax. Reading is never obstructed by recondite vocabulary or complex syntax—although a vocabulary rooted in the vernacular may run the risk of turning recondite. The poem's thinking is endlessly distracted but its distractions return unintentionally (or seemingly so), spiralling in and out of each other, but never denying their reference to a subjectivity—not so much reliant on a subjective *agency* as played though the subjective sensorium shaped by the writer's close human relationships. Where lyric performs its work between the self and other, *Ace* cannot recognize such a distinction; to distinguish between the internal and the external would produce a record which is

>        STUCK
>        STUCK
>        to be
>        accepted
>        for the apple
>        in the picture
>        mister raworth

          (p.46; *CP*, p.214)

—a passage which brings to light a difficulty in quoting from this poem. Where ordinarily a quotation is adduced to support an argument, the contention may be refuted by pointing out ellipsis in quotation or a studied suppression of context. The difficulty with *Ace* is that any excerpt wriggles free of the grasp; what it appears to say (or supports) will be compromised by what precedes and follows regardless of where the incisions are made. But this has its compensations, since like a cut worm any section of the poem achieves independent life.

Such an accommodating quality has little in common with literary procedures designed to unsettle radically either the reader or hegemonic culture in the service of an ideological challenge. Although Tom Raworth's poems are unconventional procedurally, they do not advance on the reader promising or threatening his or her moral or political improvement, and they proffer nothing whatever to society for all that their fleetness might offer much. They invest with a new meaning the term *light verse*, which had come to be synonymous with harmless comedy, but in their principled unpretentiousness and lack of disdain for pleasure they also have a relationship with light verse as commonly understood, and can share light verse's hedonism and (contrary to some claims for Raworth) its sentimentality. I like *Ace* particularly because it resonates so strongly with a cultural moment which remains precious to me—it shares that moment's unashamed optimism—and because it continues to spring ahead "in think," "in mind," "in motion" and "in place" (these being the subtitles of its four sections) and does so distractedly, forgetfully, hedonistically.

Returning therefore to that cultural moment I think *immediately* of

> that riffle
> of the deck
>
> (p.16; *CP*, p.203)

and then I remember

> morning
> release
> plays softly
> spins
> fixed
> tracking
> sharp molecules
>
> (p.72; *CP*, p.223)

—since this was the time at which the record deck ceased be simply the site engineered for a flat response (the elusive goal of the hifi nut) but became an instrument for variation, like a deck of cards. In the mid-seventies, scratching and toasting by Jamaican DJs (precursors of hiphop) became influential in British music, leading to extensive musical exchange and collaboration, among the most successful being The Slits' *Cut* album with Dennis Bovell producing (1979) and the most discussed for sure being The Clash's *Complete Control* single produced by the great Jamaican studio auteur Lee Perry and released on 23rd September 1977.[63] *Complete Control* offers in one brief bridge passage a musical experience close to the reading experience of *Ace*.

When *Complete Control* was released, many were disappointed at the limited evidence of Lee Perry's involvement—expectations had run high that The Clash's music would transmute into an exemplary reggae/punk hybrid to serve the anti-racist politics of the time. Instead, *Complete Control* starts and continues for much of its course with the oddly bouncy, accelerated oompah-pah of much second-rate punk, its lyrics a vehement whinge against the record company—another punk convention. Then something extraordinary happens, in an episode of a few seconds incorporating silence, distorted noise, inarticulate cries and punctuating drum jolts jarring against the so-far crashingly obvious rhythm. This Lee Perry episode holds at once the vastness of curved space in which sounding planes shift and overlap, and the impact of extreme compression; it is both violent and profoundly calm. It also prepares for the return of the interrupted song so as to invest the cry "This is Joe Public speaking | I'm controlled in the body | Controlled in the mind" with an authority which renders all the earlier rockist posturing negligible. Resisting the invitation to produce a cultural hybrid, Perry's intervention (to use a shopworn but apt term) of but a few seconds effects a radical transformation of time—extension itself suspended and pinpointed—demonstrating what could be done with fairly crude recording technology:

> rock
> baby
> sleeps
> scarlet
> light
> snares
> pause
> to

slow
movie
halves
nice people
they turned
me in
SPACE
SPACE

(pp.32–33; *CP*, pp.210–11)

Hitherto the main service of modern studio technology had been to construct the immaculate or complex product in place of recording performance, a development similar to the elaboration of the lyric poem as it too became detached from performance.[64] What was new about both scratching a record and Lee Perry's studio practice was their improvisation with and against the current of time. The commercial pervasiveness of hiphop has dampened if not wholly buried the radical oddity of using a record deck to play bursts of music backwards and forwards rapidly, and Perry's studio techniques—the skeletal dub sound which stripped down the original 'plate' to a warped drum and bass with bursts of show-through, contributed by example to the development of sampling technologies.[65] The relationship between the two techniques is strongly evident now in the preservation of the scratchiness of original samples (easy to clean up digitally) and even in the addition of scratch noise to samples which were digitally produced in the first place.

Time warp affected publication and reception of the poem too so that it was both anachronistic and anticipatory from the start; specific to the moment of *Complete Control* in its publication by The Figures, this serendipity was produced through a series of misadventures, the poem having first been printed for the Goliard Press in 1974 but not released by the printer owing to problems on the part of the publisher in settling the bill. As an endnote to The Figures' edition describes, a flash flood destroyed the first edition in 1975. This 'flash flood' evidently was triggered by the unreleased poem whose

FLASH
FLASH

(p.37; *CP*, p.212)

was a taunt too many for any dark basement to contain. The poem also may be held responsible for the commercial introduction of the CD in 1982. The poem's internal conflations of time presumably created this disruptive temporal force-field.

The interrupted, untimely, sleepy or greedy reading of poems notwithstanding, it continues to be the case that most poems assume reception in real time, that is, that the time brought by a reader to a poem will be roughly equivalent to the time occupied by a public recital of the poem at a conventionally slow pace and with the careful identification of semantic signposts through sequential and predictable metrical stresses (which in professional readings on public radio, for example, are accorded a bludgeoning intensity). They assume beyond this that repeated reading will yield more subtle and local effects, and there will be a continuing relationship between work done and seman-tic/affective yield. This accumulation down a timeline differs greatly (it goes without saying) from the relationship between time invested by the poet and the poem's semantic/affective productivity, but differs also from the operations of memory. The involuntary return of poetic frag-ments into the memory alters the relationship with the poem so that rather than being one of *extraction* from the poem by the reader it becomes one of *reinvestment* of the reader by the poetic fragment, in curved time—or (simultaneous) times.

A frequent technique for achieving this is the sequence (an unfortu-nate term), although to avoid reception as a continuous progress through time, a sequence must establish a careful equivocation between the tendency of any section to assert a discrete and finished identity, and the tendency of the whole to override divisions. Raworth has avoided this most characteristic of twentieth-century forms, probably on account of its inexorably architectonic tendency.[66] The reader's constru-ing of the poet's world-creative intent through identification of echo points within grand sounded structures—chords drawn to the hole in the label—would freeze what must remain *in motion*, the play of light in its arbitrariness and irresolution. Just so the darting, wayward improvi-sations of Lee Perry in the studio, the foil to further improvisation by a DJ, engage the listener in a way very different from the sculpted sound-scapes of some drum'n'bass derivatives from dub through which s/he is paraded as a diminished figure.

For Raworth memory is "a light | pickup" (p.11; *CP*, p.201) flickering through the sensorium and whereby no impression can be registered and meaningful except in the light of memory—hence the strange formulation "part | of ace":

> early
> lyrical
> passage
> words
> any
> tape
> but this
> part
> of ace
> one
> form
> for moment

(pp.71–72; *CP*, p.223)

The playing of an ace is what settles a game or any exchange in an instant. A part of ace is a contradiction in terms—indeed, the philological derivation of 'ace' is "via French *as* from Latin, 'unit, unity.'" But this feels less contradictory in considering the incursions of memory, which when it seizes its fragmentary object is at once total (and totalizing) and an infinitesimal fragment, the fragment which reinvests, which restores the fullness of identity while bodying unmistakably the frail contingency of any continuing identity. In other words, it is only in the recovery of a memory—however trivial inherently and in itself (and there can be no such thing as a memory 'inherently and in itself') that we recover ourselves completely while knowing this completion, this selfhood, is as contingent as anything could be. Thus the shiver, the flicker of memory and of becoming-an-entity which *Ace* plays again and again.

How though can memory be instated socially, how can it be shared without traducing its nature through its instatement structurally? In its repetitive reproduction the remembered event is drained of meaning and affect—

> lingering
> on every trait
> out of focus
> certain
> territory
> for fire
> fattens

that's mohawk four
four one hundred
coming
through
splashed
wall
paper
good as
gun
SHOT
SHOT
under
SPOT
SPOT
light

(pp.51-52; *CP*, p.216)

—and becomes pornographic; memory is not an effect of stereotyped repetition. Both the 1977 and 2001 editions of *Ace* carry a red star logo on the cover which reappears on a grainy image on the half-title page whose most decipherable element is a sober-suited gent seemingly loading a machine gun. The logo above him and to the right, superimposed rather than present in the news photograph, encourages a reading of the image as a pre-operational guerrilla commemorative, reminiscent of a celebrated picture of Patty Hearst or more recently of Gaza Strip suicide bombers; that is, a staged memory, locked against the flow of time. But this reading surely would entail a tonal misrecognition. Newsprint, television, the speed of mass media and the instant conversion of political and other human commitments into an even stream of data (*Ace* on the page resembles the punched tape of early computer storage): in associating *Ace* with these mass media, Raworth implies nothing like the spurious claims for "intervention" linked to the propaganda of the deed or to situationism—interventions which would stop the flow of events for memory-by-design. Rather I think Raworth's poems point to the shaping power of *inattention*, the remembering that occurs out of a flickering stream, as though the inattentive mind were a decoder of gestalt and this function would be imperilled by premature apprehension of any fragment or by conferring on it an historical significance.

A supplementary or rather a comprehensive meaning of the ace card lies in its unity: a unified theory of everything derived from quantum mechanics. Thomas Young's original experiment of the 1880s demonstrating the wave characteristic of light can be modified to provide evidence for the wave behaviour of electrons using a medium known as a scintillator (poets might wish for such an instrument). This produces a flash of light when an electron passes though, whose voltage can be recorded. So far so classical, but the twist in quantum mechanics is that a further modified experiment demonstrates the electron to be a particle; as the *Encyclopaedia Britannica* has it:

> ...the answer to the question whether the electron is a wave or a particle is that it is neither. It is an object exhibiting either wave or particle properties, depending on the type of measurement that is made on it. In other words, once cannot talk about the intrinsic properties of an electron; instead, one must consider the properties of the electron and measuring apparatus together"
>
> ('Quantum mechanics: The interpretation of quantum mechanics', 2002 DVD edition for Mac).

The poetic form of *Ace* exhibits a similar characteristic in being particulate or wavelike depending on its reading. The poem can be received as a succession of "sharp molecules" (p.72; *CP*, p.223) or wave peaks and troughs that may travel, stabilize, obliterate, radiate and emit, just as experience and memory are managed through the poem. Much to the point for the following discussion, memory is both laid down and recalled socially, among friends and familially through the distracted, unattended-to wave activity between them as much as committed through a particular focus on the event.

Which ace will trump? That depends on the game. The image of an ace which precedes the poem's opening in The Figures' edition effects a compromise between an ace of spades and an ace of hearts. I think this points to an important social repository of memory, in family and in love—an inattentive accumulation which comes profoundly to shape all attentiveness. Many literary, critical and biographical acres testify to this shaping work on the part of the original family matrix, but acknowledgement of the psychologically shaping work of acquired family is relatively unusual, with lyric poetry in particular more commonly regarded as an extra-familial activity conducted at some peril to family life. *Ace* is dedicated first and foremost to Val Raworth, the author's wife, as is true of the author's successive versions of his selected poems, *Tottering State*— not to mention separate book after book.

In reading *Ace* and associated poems, it seems to me that the account of Raworth's writing which I have heard often—as radically de-centred and ahumanistic—must be fundamentally mistaken, even if the centre may not be where the label leads it to be expected. Perhaps we have come to expect of lyric poetry that the personal centre announce full-on its suffering or celebration, and where disappointed in this tend to assign the poem, if it appears sophisticated in vocabulary and resistant to easy thematic translation, at once to the category of writing under the aegis of Theory (that singular thing). The human centre to Raworth poems seems obvious enough if sought in the acknowledged condition for the poems' existence rather their subject; it is both their matrix and their horizon. What their acknowledged condition permits to deploy in the poems is a lyric persona entirely without angst, without a scintilla of an inclination to auto-analysis, nomadically—or flirtatiously—disengaged from proceedings while acknowledging with unusual straightforwardness what it relies upon to sustain them. The presence of friends ("friend" is a word whose recurrence in *Ace* is insistent), of Val and of children in and around these poems does not introduce the self-centred scrutiny of a relationship, what friends, partner and children mean to the poet as a man beset with such unpoetical responsibilities—such a posture would seem presumptuous here. These relationships form the home base, the condition of the poems' nomadism and the permission for the poet's nomadism; so both *Ace* and *Bolivia: Another End of Ace* end in expressions of love for Val and of a child, of love flickering across separation and unity as the ground of the poetic undertakings:

> heart
> and heart
> so far
> apart

(pp.83–84; *CP*, p.225)

and

> heart
> and heart
> so far
> a
> part

(p.100; *CP*, p.229)

*Bolivia* ("another end" which is not an end) is indeed neither more nor less than one trace of the effect of Val working through the language of *Ace*.

Would it not be strangely unresponsive to ignore this foundational truth which Raworth proclaims to lie outside the poems and even outside language, which constitutes his linguistic practice and decidedly is not constructed through it?

> the true direction is always a glancing off—there must be an out—all truth is not *contained* in the language: it *builds* the language. ("Tracking (Notes)"; *Act*, p.43)

This surely is unequivocal enough. There was a time when I found Raworth's characteristic domestic resort sentimental, as though it were a lapse from a bravely unsupported linguistic project (look! no structure!), but now I find such honesty moving and even a reproach to both the callowness of some 'linguistically innovative' poetry and the self-obsession of some other styles of 'radical' poetry. That is not to propose unexamined dependency on another person as a moral good, although it is at least an advance on unacknowledged dependency, but to suggest that self-supporting linguistic systems may be as indicative of fantasies of motherless origin as compulsive self-unpicking may be of fantasies of fatherlessness. The one is as reliant on a hidden matrix of intent as the other on the internal structurings of authority. Domestic stability and a circle of friends might also provide a latitude for flirtatiousness, a more morally ambiguous term than nomadism perhaps.

But the proof of the pudding lies in the poem, it being a necessity of lyric writing to trick and lie its products into the light by some means or other. What seems indisputable is that Raworth's poems are different from any others, and I am suggesting that this difference can be described in terms of a lightness made possible by the poems' being relieved of the necessity to construct an entirely adequate world, and without relying either on the reader's identification with an authorial or fictional persona, or with a subordinate relationship to another text or set of texts whether poetic or theoretical—indeed a remarkable feature of Tom Raworth's writing is the repeated sense that it is knowing and prognostic theoretically rather than driven extrinsically by theory as institutionalized.

It is then both a strength and a weakness in Raworth's poetry that nothing is examined but everything is registered; nothing is established but everything is possible; glances off the environment mark the photosensitive paper. Such an abdication may let the poet off the heroic modernist task of re-creating the whole world again in each poem, even if such projects tended to relax as a developed body of work took some of the strain—to the degree where *The Maximus Poems* peters out in cryptic addenda, for instance, or in a different tradition the world-evoking poems of Paul Celan developed a calligraphic economy. If some of Raworth's poems become cryptic and marginal, they depend more on a life off the page than on intertextuality. In this regard they have something in common with Frank O'Hara's more occasional verse and its dependence on a circle of friends and lovers (although O'Hara was attracted additionally to a strain of epic grandeur quite foreign to Raworth).

The penalty of Raworth's errantry however could be a rather unengaging poetry whose operations seem to take place out of the corner of one eye, fully responsive neither to a productive kernel whose mysteries its unfoldings seductively both reveal and hide, nor to declared feelings open to the reader's identifications. It lacks also the dynamics of tension and release, of threatened dissolution followed by resolution. This opens the question of what anyone might want from poetry less than everything. Outside the delimited categories of light verse and children's verse, readers are presumed by critics to demand all of which they are taken to be deprived through their deplorable appetites for consumer goods and lesser artistic forms—in other words poetry would deliver a restored wholeness independent of paternal and maternal orders. How then might this other poetry of vagrant neutrinos interest the reader: isn't it rather thin?

In truth and in performance it is as engaging as poetry could be, if 'engaging' is taken more as an attribute like charm than as the announcement of serious designs on the reader. The everything we want might be better sustained in appetite through feints and glimpses than through possession. Nomads are charmers responding cannily to changing environment as the monads comprising friendship, sexual affairs and marriage change and adapt. For Raworth the environment's primary components are the shifts of light and air, a less cloudy variant on a Shelleyan recipe brought up to date as a unified theory of matter. Light breaks down and reforms across his poems as informational litter, as particular use, whether scanned as sound, as binary data or as language, or organizing for the single but imbued intelligence his or her circumferential world. Slow light becomes music, fast light flashes—or as 'Coda: Songs of the Mask', the work which precedes *Ace* in Raworth's selected poems *Tottering State* and the *Collected Poems*, has it, "time is frozen light" (*CP*, p.201). Such freezing is never a virtue in Raworth's poetry and appears often as the antithesis to light, for instance in the later thin poem *West Wind* whose title is anticipated directly (p.48; *CP*, p.215) and indirectly through numerous gusts of "wind" and pointers "west" in *Ace*, Shelley's great Ode flickering and fleeting behind Raworth's poem, its wave-forms joining and interfering with *Ace*'s or locking together frozen:

> words sleep
> their carapaces
> frost in moonlight
> not one
> tonight
> will wander

*(CP, p.358)*

This light programme (the original name for what is now BBC Radio 2) to which *Ace* refers (p.23; *CP*, p.206) had been announced explicitly in the 1972 publication *Tracking*, an odd melange of already dated beatnik philosophy, Olsonian 'research' notes, stoned notations and shafts of intelligence.[67] Here consciousness and collective unconscious alike are attributed to light's journeys; as is knowledge, as is sex. This ascription to light is associated with a mysticism of presence for which scale is irrelevant, and where any framing becomes arbitrary—merely the contingency of the participant observer and his (in)attention:

> the connections (or connectives) no longer work—so how to build the long poem everyone is straining for? (the synopsis is enough for a quick mind now (result of film?)—you can't pad out the book) (a feature film with multiple branches: you'd never know which version you were going to see). (*Act*, p.43)

This reads to me like a prospectus for the long thin poems, thin not only physically but tested against the expectations of a British reader of poetry. Poetic resource is more often expected, I think, to knit what attention lights upon so as engender out of the fleeting a sense of an inside, integrated and palpable; and out of the insubstantiality of linguistic exchange to stabilize a linguistic stuff so that the unknown corporeal inside becomes re-occupied and restructured by a sustaining linguistic system in whose penumbra of continuing exchange every contingent observation and event becomes richly meaningful. So much for the lyric poem which saves the world. Raworth's poetry offers nothing of this. The knit of the internal barely exists but for warped returns and echoes; there is little or no sense of organized rhythmic, consonantal or vowel patterning, and syntax flickers forward, backward and at times permutationally across parallel columns. With the corporeal and the monumental alike despatched, what this poetry most relies on to deliver its pleasurable rewards is a quicksilver precision of placing "in think," "in mind," "in motion" and "in place" (to return to the poem's subtitles). This poetry is determinedly insubstantial; it acknowledges no substance, only wave-forms travelling and whose lapping, collisions, muddles and persistence down and across the pages might be thought to anticipate chaos theory: "you'd never know which version you were going to see". The self is of negligible account—

    itself same
                    (p.19; *CP*, p.204)

    self
    forged self
                    (p.34; *CP*, p.211)

    cut in
    itself
    not only
    same
    in same
                    (p.82; *CP*, p.225)

—or figured recursively as a status which writing always threatens to confer, while linguistic and feeling exchange elsewhere to this writing protects it from coagulation or freezing.

Here then is the joy of reading *Ace*: that it is ever in motion, ever responsive and contributes a new version on each reading. Its rhythms never lock, pin down and underline but transmit and ripple, an effect which requires more technical skill than immediately apparent, since stops and impediments are intimate with the fraughtness of words' usual reflexivity:

    ace
    i see
    in all
    i am
    not here

may you
have
a small
foundation
of changes
shift
if that's
a glowing face

(pp.59–60; *CP*, p.220)

Here too are deployed some of the paradoxes implicit in Raworth's mysticism of presence—that the presence of the world to the observer requires her reduction or his sidelining both here and not-here; that the light and "the winds | of changes" make so present the world that it is apprehensible only in the most particular and smallest detail; that the foundation of presence relies on an incessant bracketing and leaving brackets open so the subsidiary, the dependent, sweeps forward and then gives way again . . . The relationship here between lyric presence in a romantic sense and fugitive bracketings and glissades exactly parallels the relationship between familial presence and nomadism; Raworth's poetry is deeply reliant on both poetic and social tradition to buoy and make confidant what otherwise might drift helplessly.

Would it be possible to start again and assert that although *Ace* is a thin poem it makes for a fat book for so few words, or to read *Ace* against Tom Raworth's performance so that it winds down to an inordinately slow poem for the number of words? Yes, that might be allowable as a perverse test, but *Ace*'s light verse would emit less energy and its productivity would falter. This verse's smeary blends and shifts countermand portentousness and give no stay of the sort needed for resonance—such scratching, such improvisation funnels and collapses into the multi-frequency light of now, compacted into restless music, stored and retrieved as through the fitful flashes of memory itself.

## Off the Grid: Lyric and Politics in Andrea Brady's Embrace

The most intellectually ambitious collective poetic endeavour in Britain during the second half of the twentieth century has mutated a remarkable and quite new strain of politically engaged writing. This might surprise British readers inclined to believe the routine dismissal by conservative critics of 'Cambridge poetry' as a donnish pastime, or to those who have followed the careers of individual writers. For American readers the entire history of this writing remains occluded, despite the efforts of the critics Keith Tuma and Romana Huk.[68] Therefore the first half of this essay is devoted to a back story, highly selective inasmuch as it discusses styles of political engagement within the history of one poetic group. Since literary influence resembles an urban freeway system more than a royal succession, such an account is liable to be irksome to all concerned, especially the writers to whom the second part of the essay is dedicated. The modest aim is to situate the strategies of these younger writers (and especially Andrea Brady) in their reinvention of the political lyric. A particular question is how they reconcile the lyric turn towards multiple ambiguity and a horizon of indescribable plenitude with the felt necessity to light a path towards an identifiable and attainable political objective (whatever the delay, whatever the conditionals).

### I

'Cambridge poetry' begins with *The English Intelligencer*, a near-legendary worksheet edited by Andrew Crozier and Peter Riley between 1966 and

1968. Along with the *Intelligencer*'s urgent format, the historical resonance of those dates flags an interventionist leftist politics; but there are
further points to be made about this matrix. The first is that the small
group of about thirty participants was as much a Newcastle group as a
Cambridge one, and included the aggressively working-class poets Barry
MacSweeney and Tom Pickard. Nor should it go unnoticed that William
S. Burroughs (then living in London) and J.G. Ballard were of the
number, anticipating the later Cambridge association of the novelists
Peter Ackroyd and Iain Sinclair. As geography and career paths sepa-
rated the Newcastle and Cambridge groups, the so-called Cambridge
School itself resolved into two wings, the Northern branch around
*Grosseteste Review* and the Southern around Ferry Press. At that time, the
*Grosseteste* homes of Leeds and Derbyshire yielded nothing to Newcastle
in grittiness.

In its origins, the *Intelligencer* was a Black Mountain/Buffalo outgrowth, a product of the Olsonian force-field. It reproduced the odd
combination in Olson's thought of high modernism, deep history, and
phenomenology, which in J.H. Prynne's *Kitchen Poems* and *The White
Stones* achieved its too-magisterial synthesis, even as *The Maximus Poems*
were collapsing into archival fragments and phallic flourishes. The
Northern wing stayed largely faithful to the *Intelligencer*'s founding
moment, its Poundian right finding a religious haven (John Riley in
Russian Orthodoxy), while Peter Riley, a Northern poet although resident in Cambridge, elaborated out of sixties phenomenology an ethics
and a poetics of responsiveness testable against geological time, cultural
displacement, and musical improvisation. According with general
British cultural geography, the Southern poets, including Prynne,
showed a greater urbanity, becoming aligned with a Gramscian New
Left more exercised by cultural and sexual politics than with the
entrenched oppositions of labour and business or of industry and
pastoral. Some even were so unorthodox as to be women.

The period from 1969 to 1971 saw Prynne's break with Olson poetically and politically. *Brass* (1971) is the book with which a new British
poetics influenced by European dialectical lyric (especially Trakl, Celan,
and Ungaretti) is inaugurated, and is a work of such power that all ambitious British poets continue to work in its shadow, knowingly or not. Its
materialist poetics are the basis of a continuing distinction between
British and American understanding of what a materialist poetics might
entail. The materialism of *Brass* works at several levels. The first is epis-
temological. Prynne's writing drew on multiple ways of knowing, a

characteristic fated to be misread as postmodern discursive relativism. In reality it was a truth-seeking by way of poetry, reconnected with the ambitions of Wordsworth and Coleridge. The second is political, refusing easy sentiment, disdaining spirituality, rooted in economics and biology, and intensely interested in the everyday signs of capitalist depredation. *Brass*'s poems focus insistently on money and sex, and on neither score are they remotely idealist. Every step will cost, every step will hurt. The third dimension is linguistic, but quite unlike the hedonistic liberationism of some American open-field poetics. Language's materialism is asserted at every turn through its historical and social thickness; efforts to warp the expression of humanity must reckon with the deep resources as well as the resistances of this stuff.

What needs asserting here is that in Britain, 'theory' in its full institutional guise arrived after the inauguration of the materialist poetics represented by *Brass*. This primacy of poetics is marked not only in Cambridge writing, but startlingly in the work of Tom Raworth, a poet with a genius for being ahead of the game, and in the sadly neglected formalist inventions of Andrew Crozier (for instance, *Pleats* (1975) and *Duets* (1976)). Even when theory arrived with the successor Cambridge generation of Denise Riley, Ian Patterson, Martin Thom, and Nick Totton, the poetical working-through of sexual politics by these writers was associated with activism rather than academicism. Far from donnish, this was a generation of dissident and anti-institutional intellectuals surviving on the economic margins until very recently. Although Denise Riley's work came to exemplify a convergence of poetics and theory, it was not until Drew Milne and D.S. Marriott, poetically active since the end of the 1980s, that an accord more characteristic of the American institutional avant-garde was attained—and the disdain of the *Intelligencer* generation for manifestos, explication, even for reviewing each other's works, came to be challenged.[69]

*Brass* opened the way to a remarkably various political poetry. Its vehement disgust at a Conservative government's attacks on the British postwar democratic settlement set a rhetorical standard Prynne was exercised to exceed once the main course of Thatcherism and monetarist economics followed the sallies of the early 1970s. In the book's wake can be found not only Prynne's continuing critique of the capitalist simulacrum of the natural world and its revenge on the social world; but also John James's late-1970s neo-creole arraignments of imperialism, tongue-lashing the lords of language; Denise Riley's exacting lyric unpicking and retracing of her relationship with "the category of woman"; and more recently Drew Milne's diamond edged bits and burrs driven through ideological formations.

The poetry discussed in the second part of this essay might seem the due result of the collision of this literary inheritance with the political circumstances of the present day; but in fact it represents a break and a reconnection, a dialectical remobilisation.

These forebears offer no direct prescription for the twenty-first century poet, because in different ways each of them encountered dire problems reconciling the demands, seductions, and waywardnesses of lyric poetry with the urgent need to bear witness against and actively challenge oppression. Denise Riley's writing career could form the basis of a study of love and impatience with lyric poetry, which at the time of writing she seems to have forsaken for a meditative prose that writes its way into, through, and past social-linguistic intensities that call for a poetic response she declines or feels unable to give.[70] It is as though poetry teases her mercilessly for the intricate reflexiveness of her dealings. John James appears to have separated his political activism from any continuing poetic impulses, little more than fizzles, and his greatest poetry remains the product of a fleeting time when the Communist Party in the UK discovered a progressive force in youth culture and decided style was important. J.H. Prynne sometimes looks to have written himself into a corner where every burst of memory, feeling, and will is recognised as coded by Big Biotech. For Prynne only that recognition itself and its attendant pain might loosen the grip of malign economic interests, were not any temptation to individual or group exceptionalism vitiated by shame:

> All are disfigured. I saw a hole in my chest, feel
> ashamed to plead for your own life it is utter crass
> from a hole in the face word vomit lost for them, hurt
> stain so much disowned. You hear what you say over
> to get off and by right in a mutilation outburst, for
> any life at all stand-in to be shameful in a news
> flesh grease trap. [71]

Drew Milne's various modes, including poems that holiday in lyric sportiveness, densely imbricated poems with a fierce syllable-by-syllable focus, and poems sniffing the air of the open field, suggest a similar struggle with the disposition to lyric and the penalty that might be incurred for succumbing to it. In a 2006 radio interview with Charles

Bernstein, Milne discounted the possibility of politically-effective lyric poetry. He argued that lyric could only influence conditions within which critique might take place and deplored poetry committed to political intervention as "illusory escapism" that substituted for "messy pragmatic struggle".[72] This position is not so far from W.H. Auden's when he contemplated the poetic attitudinising of his youth.

Meanwhile the most prevalent poetic practice on both sides of the Atlantic remains impotently self-expressive. Contemporary accounts of lyric as genre tend to transmute the sublime into the useless (not so difficult an alchemy)—a process nicely matched to English Departments' self-image as holdouts against the utilitarianism of modern universities.

So can political poetry have any function beyond "illusory escapism", a self-exculpation on the part of the poet, or an application for club membership? How potent can poetry's categorical uselessness be against the insatiable convertors of life into measurable value? The question answers itself, and so by imperceptible degrees uselessness elides with spirit, for only uselessness is in hailing distance of The Other, that all-purpose, shape-changing, post-everything justification for poetry, sadomasochistic sex, high-minded tourism, back-door Catholicism—*mon semblable, mon frère*.

Such questions mightily troubled Douglas Oliver (1937–2000), an *English Intelligencer* contributor of a restless disposition in art as in life. Oliver was a moralist in the broadest sense, and more concerned with the instrumentality of his work than any British contemporary. His commitment to lyric was conscientiously provisional, although it is clear that he regarded lyric poetry as possessing unique cognitive attributes, more readily accessible through inherited forms than through high modernism's organised echoes.[73] Three longer works, *The Infant and the Pearl* (1985), *Penniless Politics* (1991), and *A Salvo for Africa* (2000), bear witness to the intensity and integrity of his struggle, each veering between exposition and fantasy, gorgeously-cadenced poetic exploration and clunky versification, assured comedy and unconscious foolishness. Oliver's inconsistency was Blakean in its impatience and unselfconsciousness, and akin to Blake in its passionate morality. Most extraordinary was Oliver's willingness to specify, in half-humorous but prescriptive terms, the constitution of a New Jerusalem, while the European high lyric convention (as in Prynne's poetry after the European turn of *Brass*) has been to evoke only a trembling horizon of possibility.

Denise Riley's writing is much more reflexive than Oliver's, but she also has declined to serve at the altar of lyric poetry as such. Riley is disposed to question the claims to lyric's surpassing value implied by its exclusive pursuit. The same goes for D.S. Marriott, whose critical and poetical strands of work likewise belong to a single political project, centred on black masculinity.[74] It may be symptomatic that these three poets whose writing has been most deeply engaged politically show a lesser degree of fidelity to lyric poetry than the others discussed.

Evidently these poets are sceptical of the use of art's vaunted uselessness. As lyric has become specialised and distinguished from other linguistic usages, its saving grace has been perceived from every angle as connected with its resistance to profit, instrumentality, and material progress—a perception that echoes all the way from conservative humanism to socialist melioralism, from religious authority to new theology, from formalist traditionalism to post-theory, Language-influenced poetics. Analogies could be drawn in the visual arts, where the later-embarrassing sublimity of a Rothko or Barnett Newman was succeeded by the elegant wresting of objects from their use-world, and in high-art music which is especially anxious to achieve distance from any vulgar physical stimulation. Uselessness is art's use.

The more art's uselessness has figured as an exalted reduction, the more lyric poetry has been drawn towards prosodic movement as primary, with analysis and argument conducted under the aegis of this last-ditch spirit—spirit now lodged in the ruts of lineation and the angles of enjambment. For uselessness is merely a status, while spirit is its working afflatus. About the spiritual mist, the dawn horizon trembles and shines, or as Allen Grossman has put it: "In the outlook of the lyric person the horizon has ceased to be a precinct and has become a vortex."[75] Uselessness gives rise to spirit and spirit to the tentative sublime. In the United States this recension can be frankly religious, in the work of serious poets as different as Fanny Howe and John Peck; or the sublime can be reinstated in the material by way of the body and its voice. Did someone say textuality? The MP3 file is the new poetic eucharist.

How radically do such poetic practices differ from a more debased lyric currency, which not without poignancy offers a set of signposts to the poet's untestable and external authenticity? These seemingly opposed practices may be less different than first appears, for the unknowable is their common resort. Gesturing towards the nub of self-hood may look preposterous as long as the reader resists the solicited identification. But however disingenuous its installation of self may be, this ultimate resort of self-expressive writing, like those poetic modes that would oppose it, yearns for transcendence in the communal. How much more admirable, how different the solicitations of the polysemous blaze as it primps for numinous effect? But then, what of the danger of paralysis when confronted by real offence, or when writing under the hyper-critical sway of critical theory? Go for God, or shout the house down and kick the rubble gleefully? Or concede ruefully with Drew Milne that poetry's exactions reserve it as a separate pursuit?

For the British left, Blair's alliance with Bush and the neocons under the Thatcherite banner of No Alternative announced that freedom would be limited strictly to the choice on the shelf, and that as all other commons had been auctioned, the sense of belonging to a free people, the *air* of freedom had been sold. This is physically obvious to a population under closer electronic surveillance than any other in the world.

A cellular politics of cultural resistance has re-emerged through the anti-war movement and in response to restrictions on mass assembly, circumstances that make ideological purity look narcissistic. Younger poets are ignoring fault-lines opened up by previous disputes, including those separating Cambridge poetry from Language poetry; the struggle against US hegemony has accelerated détente with the US cultural opposition. The process began with Drew Milne and Simon Jarvis's journal *Parataxis* in the early 1990s, but the exchange became more intense with Keston Sutherland's journal *QUID* and Andrea Brady and Keston Sutherland's press Barque. Meanwhile as teachers in Cambridge, Milne and Jarvis were deeply influential, initiating a move from scholastic theory into a reenergised engagement with critique in the tradition of Hegel, Marx, and Adorno, a shift paralleled among post-Language poets of their generation in the US. Yet for all the strenuous critical and political prose accommodated by *QUID* and its entire lack of embarrassment with manifestos, a fierce attachment to lyric poetry as a declaratively political practice, persists as the only mode of writing able to ward off its own corruption.

This preamble introduces Andrea Brady, a British-based poet whose recent book *Embrace* prompts such thoughts, as well as Keston Sutherland's recent *Neocosis*.[76] Intellectually, technically, and emotionally both books make most contemporary poetry in English look trivial. Their different strategies in advancing political lyric, configure the terms of this introduction: they make art that exalts uselessness look exhausted, and its fortuitous mimesis—blank plenitude—seem repellent. Lyric expansiveness, which is the exquisite afflatus of uselessness, slides too easily into more or less disguised forms of transcendence. The bind of what Lefebvre calls hyper-criticism—the rigour of thought that paralyses effective action—overshadows the possibility of resolving this predicament, and may be responsible for Sutherland's extreme linguistic violence as well as others' resort to religion. Andrea Brady's *Embrace* is fully cognisant of this situation, and writes in the teeth of it.

## II

At the start *Embrace* retails a shocking outlook, maybe even a theory. The articulations of Lynndie England, fall-guy for the Bush administration's policy of torture in Iraq, are here staged as commensurate with the poet's own bodily and intellectual syntax, from its duties in the academic workplace to shopping in North London to orgasm. Andrea Brady has become English. In *Embrace*'s last poem, 'Saw Fit', England's body undergoes syntactical stuttering and breaks continuously re-piecing her status as abused and abuser—in the familial, social, and political sense. Lynndie England's articulations show how both an American girl and the country of England have been shafted, and how both are complicit in rape.

Brady affords little wriggle-room for self-determination, wilful deviance, chance, or mishap. The most insistently recurrent images of this book, beginning with the first stanza of the first poem ("every paper fed | head-side up down into slits") are of papers and objects being fitted into slots and other pre-formed receptors—second poem, neck-brace, third poem, stirrup, fourth poem, dish racks, and so forth. Most strikingly in 'Hymn on the Nativity', "a sliding hatch clicked eight times", and in 'Ammonia Crisps the Air', "my heart | slipped like a marble into the slot | toddles there even now in a cup of magnets." Elsewhere "the trap clicks through each of its twelve stations" and elsewhere again lies "each 'safe for human' interstice." This is more than a compulsive trope in a poetic rhetoric; it is compulsion felt at a very deep level. Far from being the last redoubt of integrity, the body—and centrally its sexuality, its slits and slots and dark declivities—has become the most sensitive register of abuse; the white doll, the "girl lip", evoke Hans Belmer's puppets and the staged prostitutes of *American Psycho*.

Where is the poetic power to transfigure or at least to mitigate such cruelty? Here and in this book, a great poetic power undoubtedly exists. But transcendence, to call it by its usual name, is by no means the object to which Brady's unforgiving *Embrace* is turned. Brady's management

of verse is expert, and her expertise is marshalled to defeat false hopes
and sentimentality through procedures so well-honed that any tentative
dawn shrinks back beneath the covers, blushing at its own political
naïvety. Her poems comprise stanzas made most often from extended
expository sentences—this is how things are, and this is how and why
things happen—held to their authoritative course by a tirelessly precise,
even-toned, and intelligent lineation. For each poem the achieved
assembly presents itself as the only possible arrangement. Enjambment
can sound unremittingly clever:

> She was docked a time
> out by her father, she's been taking
> snaps by rule to develop in a red light
> tears to the eye Adders set on us
> in the cot, stags blocking the
> stairwell, what chance do we have
> a go at the fair bruiser on his stiff coil,
> asking for more with that apple-red cheek.
>                    ('How Much To Have A Go')

Brady's wit is of an unusual and maybe original kind. Since one
annoying trick in contemporary poetry is the persistent ironical recontextualising of vernacular phrases (everyone does it—new formalist, wild
analyst, whatever) it might appear as though this is what Brady is up to.
But there is zero self-regard in Brady's poetry, an astonishing quality for
lyric. It is as though the machinery of phrasal conversion flattens all
irony, and phraseology is paid out by strips into a system of heartless
consumption, construction, and exchange. The impression is reinforced
by a robotically exact and polished metrics:

> It was easier for the mouth than laughing better
> exercise for the temporarium,
> though planks got stuck and exhaled drafts
> and soaped now, with the unbuttoning of your skin.
>                    ('Building Site')

The suppression of the comma in the first line extrudes a plank of
language, each plank fed through the saw-mill at constant rate—and
rare indeed that any knot or syllable should get stuck. What this
amounts to is a lyric brilliance that quashes the lyric horizon that
Brady's resourcefulness would promise to evoke. The reconstituted

bodies of these poems always betray the perverse interests that have denied—have even smashed—the corporeal integrity from whose splintered limbs their MDF has been compressed. Not merely are these interests revealed, but their contrivances are flaunted in sets of machined traps and arrays of blades. Hence *Embrace* presents poetry that announces the end of the possibility of lyric poetry: for lyric stands displayed as a particular late-consumerist articulate mode expressed through meat and mind, of a cognitive order determining a range of socially-prescribed behaviour—at best another mode to set alongside work, lust, and leisure.

How then does a blatant love poem like 'To Be Continued' accord with this account? Surely behind these lines the generosity of John Donne is audible:

> Having weighed the alternatives, what does it
> matter spilling out of an overfed barrow
> if this explicit and unmistaking you
> for anyone else is less than perfect, cannot be
> there at the receiving end, this calibrated instrument
> still shuddering with the alert notice; not too heavy,
> not too individuated, your face the sun up
> ends the world with racing stripes
> run north to south like a tie to countries
> and to all imperfect people we might still be.

The poem ends with a wonderfully suspended and ambiguous figure, "so gorgeous | a hush falls down | the fault of language" recalling "the calibrated instrument" related in a previous line to language and to the now-conventional figuring of language in terms of grids and matrices. Language consists of a system of faults, powerfully apparent in the faults of enjambment, and at the poem's end, here in the cadence of ellipsis. The "fault of language" becomes the blessing of language, felt at its fullest when it fails, both yielding and yielding to the plenitude of love and of the poem. This extraordinary meshing, whereby the artifice of presence is allowed to dilate, even if its expression implies a bracketed theoretical distance, is related too to John Donne's 'Break of Day' aubade and its lewdness, its description of love-making upon waking. Brady is never shy of the quasi-pornographic, the edge where the loving and the explicit touch; faultiness and fullness meet in the structure of erotics. But whatever the final hushing's involutions, the tone is strikingly and, so far as this book is concerned, unprecedentedly affirmative.

But not so fast. The ominously-titled poem placed after 'To Be Continued' is 'Caught', and 'Caught' closes with the line "love all over the grid", and even worse, a few lines beforehand the splendour visible from a squalid Greyhound station has been revealed as another illusion whose dazzle half-blinds our poet, leaving her winded when she careens into the penned crowd awaiting their bus:

> Behind a new panel slid in from the channel
> opens a window: the keyhole cut reveals not
> aligned nerve I see nothing
> but a blaze of pure gold At this rare
> appearance the turnstile
> puckers in its chest: that we are caught behind
> and blinking, when our lives together could swarm
> love all over the grid.

Perhaps the glimmers of love once acknowledged can never quite be extinguished, and the desired transmutation of the grid into a full comb of honey lingers like an ache, even if by this point in the book the word "could" demands the rejoinder: 'under what circumstances, given the grid's comprehension and anticipation of every move, thought and feeling?' Certainly the following pages, a framed prose text beginning and ending with '*Montani Semper Liberi*', the state motto of West Virginia, present only a negative answer to that question. The text, which draws on guides to the state where Lynndie England was raised, reads like a sour mash of precious Niedecker moments, folk history, tourist-board boosterism, brutal mining interests, genocide, racism, and patriarchal secret societies.

'*Montana Semper Liberi*' constitutes a bridge whose two-way traffic between 'Caught' and 'Saw Fit' troubles both poems. Can "our lives together" in 'Caught', the preceding poem, then be read as signifying anything beyond the redoubt of coupledom, even if these lines in their amplitude of cadence had for a moment embraced a possible throng? Is any 'us' possible? And if it is not, if the first person plural were always as fundamentally illegitimate as '*Montana Semper Liberi*' would imply, then could the deictics which seduce the reader into Brady's traps function any more collectively than to tap out an assurance that there is life in the next prison cell? But Brady will not allow the reader what has become a conventional exit route; for 'we' is too often permissible when it is raised as 'them'—they who know no better on account of the collectivity which claims them. So far as 'we' are concerned, there is the freedom to contest deictic claims, but the likes of Lynndie England are relegated to nothing more than a likeness. On all sides the first person plural pronoun has an agenda.

Through such critical precision and from its title to its final page, *Embrace* bracingly defies the central claims of the academically influential poetics developed by Allen Grossman and Susan Stewart, and it does so with unequalled rigour, resistant to the vortex chuntering at the horizon of the most materially scrupulous lyric—even Prynne's and Sutherland's. In summary Stewart claims:

> Grossman has written that "poetry means, to put it crudely, the context-independence of the person, whose right of presence is not a contingency of history alone, and is in many respects inimical to life itself." Poetry is inimical to life in this sense because it frees us from life's transient dependence on context-bound meaning and because it takes a stance against death—against death's contingent, and monumental, claim to the significance of our individuality.[77]

Leave aside the fact that Stewart's own readings often substitute for vulgar contingency the most fantastic transcultural and transhistorical contextuality, and succumbing for only a moment to the temptation to mock the phrase "to put it crudely", this reformulation of the lyric poem's access to eternity remains applicable to the explicit or admitted aspirations of most British and American poetry that might be termed lyric. Stewart is over-literal in her interpretation of Grossman; his rabbinical discourse allows that in a characteristic aphorism such as "poems are a version of the destiny of the individual in God", God can legitimately be substituted by "a continuing human community", a community enfolding those who neither read not write poetry, just as the Jewish community (or Catholic) enfolds the non-observant.[78] But eternity as community becomes a compulsory violence in real history. To that extent Stewart must be right in reading every line of lyric as choral in the broadest sense, as accompanied by every 'singer' who ever lived. Hitherto the only bulwarks against such nightmare plangency, a tabernacle choir which absorbs every poet from Homer to Bruce Andrews, have been ignorance—hence the advantage of youth in lyric practice—or a violent refusal to play, which has itself become another adhesive tradition, post-Dada.

Furthermore, even in its most affirmative mode, the turn to community performs the same magic that the turn from uselessness to spirit accomplishes; the most isolated and most isolating of linguistic practices is transfigured into the very guarantor of collective humanity and its historical destiny. The useless work, the useless person, are revealed as no less than the World Spirit.

Implacably *Embrace* announces the auto-cancelling lyric. By this strategy Brady's work diverges even from late Prynne, and here I dissent from an impassioned but wayward review of *Embrace* by Marianne Morris, another transatlantic poet working in the UK.[79] Morris refers to

> younger poets writing out of Cambridge who take the practically indecipherable late work of J.H. Prynne as their cue, creating a poetic effect that is almost sculptural, layering cut images and hints of phrases over one another to create anti-linear and viscous hints of experience

and suggests that Brady's poetry escapes this condition "through the medium of desire". 'Desire' is always a problematical term, but the type of the Cambridge poet here seems defined by the construction of poetic counterfactuals whose relationship to social contingency is hard to discern despite an advertised political radicalism. This invents a 'Cambridge poem' to set alongside a 'Language poem'. Such work (if we grant it exists) might be consistent with Stewart's view that poetry "frees us from life's transient dependence on context-bound meaning," although Prynne's recently-published discourse in Guangzhou on the corruptions of contingent language suggests he would contest any idea that the way to truth lies through decontextualisation, while recognising with Brady the unprecedented insidiousness of the forces arrayed against poetic truth.[80] Mendacity cannot be conjured away, any more than metaphysics can disguise the reality of life's transience.

The workings of desire in Brady's poetry are more severely constrained than Morris suggests, and it is instructive to compare where *Embrace* ends up with the final lines of *Neocosis*, a recent chapbook by Keston Sutherland with whom Brady is associated as co-publisher of Barque. First Brady:

> parts not taken to the cleaners with her lovers
> taken to Bragg for abuse
> of alcohol and sexual abandon her own
> performance for her boys with a multitude of different
> stressed out by a tiger team Madonna of the spectacle
> Shit-boy watches through a pair of her smalls
> the CO gives them England's Victoria's Secret

catalogues to loosen them up skeletal ladies
her lewd face in the Lynch mirror the rough side her mouth
    opens
again England has no high intelligence value She cannot say
"I am a survivor" oop oop she'll make her money back
get more out of the birth above her, men, hooded
leave no paper trail through the wreckage

Next, Sutherland:

Papa zero aleppe: none of this is always what
you eat to survive, surviving to sing
a new tune all about having none of it: something
understood not fit to be wasted on understanding,
not brittle in the crammed mouth sick of air
but instead flatly indisintegrable, banished by love
and its sweetest decree to the fringes of red anti-gut,
where love alone shines in beauty, and the liver
waits agape on brass for its flame, and is licked
forever by that flame like a mirror by your eyelids.

Following on a cut-and-pasted catalogue of sparklers and their product codes and prices, the lyric rejoinder of Sutherland's final lines might be music to Susan Stewart's ears; they conjure up a responsive descant across the ages from George Herbert and Lord Byron, while in the contour of its swoop and re-ascent this finale also tickles the off-screen spot where the cadences of Prynne's poems arrived prior to the mid-1990s. Stewart's assignment of all lyric poetry to Operation Eternity is far indeed from the furiously-driven contingent detail of neoconservative conspiracy which packs Sutherland's astonishingly active verse paragraphs—research as a release of high-pressure information recaptured in insect swarms. It is far also from the material and intractably reticulated truths of Prynne's more recent verse.

But while Sutherland's deployment of neo-romantic cadences comes packaged with corrosive agents and bitterly parodic disavowals, the affective potency of the cod finale exemplifies just what anyone is up against when dealing with social-mnemonic concentrations of linguistic affectivity, be they Biblical and hymnal prosody or the long gasps of romantic aspiration. These lines, which so intricately cross-cut neoconservative idealism, Old Testament sacrifice, and eschatology with a descent into the gut of empire, figure a particular constraint on the reach of lyric poetry. The problem is that the lyric surge operates at a

level which can overwhelm or obliterate any counterflows at the semantic level. These lines thus problematically conclude the poem and the
book—the curtains falling into pregnant silence—with a triumphal
cadence and with a suppression of punctuation permitting a reading
whereby the world is flooded with "love alone" and all other properties
derive from its indisintegrable unity. Love is the only vocabulary available once language falls away.

It is true that the previous poems in *Neocosis* have closed brutally with
such decisively dismissive phrases as: "And in any case you should get
out more" and: "Larkin in the air, the net curtains nailed down"—
phrases whose arbitrariness feels imposed. But endings present
difficulties for Sutherland. The reference to Larkin seems oddly
parochial in the circumstances; this swipe from an anachronistic British
literary politics could be thought to exemplify the risks involved in
confusing stale prosody with social restrictiveness, as well in taking
Larkin seriously. After all, Sutherland's blistering, hectic, prolific,
scabrous, and stinging poems could hardly be held, as a *per contra*, to
justify Fox News. The danger here lies in too little mediated a relationship between poetic discourse and social-economic structures of authority, which in turn suggests the poet's exceptionalism as well as his
instrumentality.

By contrast Brady's book finishes with her crudest, bitterest, and most
tabloid-contingent of lines; she ends by defiling the elegance of her own
prosody, loosening its stays, while challenging the reader to detect the
paper trail of patriarchal authority even in this alienated poetry. The
extent of her risk is shown by Morris's response, where in a tone of
more-sorrow-than-anger she deplores the poem's collusiveness with a
viciously sexist pillorying of Lynndie England. The riposte to Morris's
increasingly agitated criticism is precisely that the poem—and the poet—
knows well that its loathing is shadowed by collusion, just as every act
or thought of political resistance throughout this book has been antici-
pated or even scripted by the interests it opposes. Actually this discomfort has been widely shared on the left where the Lynndie England case
is concerned—see for instance in addition to material cited by Morris
herself, Richard Goldstein's article in *The Village Voice* of 10 May 2004:

> offer an image of a woman grinning at the humiliation of men and you
> allay any homosexual anxiety while tapping into the permissible kitten-
> with-a-whip fantasy. You can blame her for being unnatural even as you
> project yourself into her gaze. By fostering this reverie, the press helps to
> transform a horrible story into a source of pleasure. That's where Lynndie

England comes in. She's not just the face of Torturegate; she's the dominatrix of the American dream.[81]

The point is that Brady's "whip kitten" (a term Brady handles with kid gloves given its position in italicised and indented material separated from the body of the poem) struts her stuff at the close of a book where the very idea of a subjectivity that might voluntarily resign from its shaping by capital, patriarchy, imperialism, and every force of darkness, has been rendered untenable. Who on earth is not collusive in their thoughts and deeds? That question is what Brady in her unbearable high truthfulness will not let go. She refuses to masquerade as a privileged exception, by any means whatever, whether theoretical, poetical, or physical.

Even Brady's most affirmative moments, as in the love poem 'To Be Continued' with its hush and all of its generous faults, offer the narrowest margin of possibility, of an outside and a beyond that she demands but cannot expect from sexual love ("north to south like a tie to countries | and to all imperfect people we might still be"). Meanwhile for Sutherland, the inside of the body is that penetralium where air and the living water are processed for circulation, the liver being transformative where the heart is only a pump. Despite the bravura of this twist on a powerful trope, and a play with the symbols of baroque Catholicism that transform the inside into a David Lynch-like theatre, Sutherland's lines sound a last post's combination of triumph and loss to an otherwise frantically distressed and distressing group of poems, their echoes summoned and dying away. The control exercised by Sutherland in this parody of a Mahlerian moment is what ultimately installs the triumph of cadence above all reservations and attacks, because its bravura could only be achieved by a poet who commands his materials and is himself therefore released from constraint.

Such a move could not be ventured by Brady, whose yearning for the hush of plenitude, the vortex she resists but whose pull she feels powerfully, cannot leave behind the accompanying thought that she has been enlisted in the choir under compulsion. What her liver deals with minute by minute is suspiciously sweet or intoxicating, and the celebration of a sexuality freed from the exercise of power, however subtle or professedly playful, is delusory.

Nonetheless, such implacable recognitions cannot be enough to sustain an art—or a tolerable life for that matter. So the womb is a matrix, so love is a by-product of the national grid, so sex and critical theory are alike puppetry. Gasping for any respite, a first faint protest might be to point to the poems Andrea Brady has made in this impossible vice, this embrace. There are poems in this book of a peculiar beauty: 'To Be Continued' has been discussed, and 'Hymn on the Nativity' is appropriately miraculous in its reworking of something very like sexual disgust into a kinship extending beyond the human. Next, these beautiful poems could indeed be held to "take a stance against death" without yielding to sublimity or transcendence. Within a general bleakness what they offer is a hint of warmth, and how they produce this merits some consideration since Brady's predicament is shared, whether or not it is understood. The predicament is *ours*, emphasising the pronoun in keeping with the acknowledgement of possessives in the two poems, most of all in the wonderful last stanza of 'Hymn on the Nativity':

> Yours is like no life I have ever lived, and now
> steams through the dismantled grate a poultice of ginger.
> What do I really need, my old seasonal question,
> lives together flexing the temper even trees skirted.
> Tuck cold behind a sheaf of rubber, tuck your chest
> under feather, and myself sleeps in your mouth.
> All I have incurred so much more I have
> to say before they lower their heads, all yours.

This is terrific poetry. Its achievement entails the poet rendering unto you what is due unto *you*; this makes it possible for her to dismantle the grate elsewhere so rigidly deterministic. It is a simple move in some ways, where suspicion of ourselves and the feelings, needs and memories which make up those selves, has come to separate us from others even as we track the internal depredations of intricately abstracted forces of otherness. To worry about the capacity to love (which entails inevitably an unattainably high standard and valuation for love) can too lightly suspend *your* integrity, which "is like no life I have ever lived." There is a truth here extending beyond sexual love. Prating of community on the part of those representing interests ready to destroy communities at a trice when outsourcing decimates 'overheads' (the makers of things being 'overheads'), or of those nostalgic for bowling clubs and single-sex colleges, has done much to discredit any talk of community. It has become easier to speak of global commons than what might be held in common locally. Still, this time feels like the beginning of a new dark ages, again under the auspices of a warped religiosity, and it may be strategic to forgo the higher ground in forming cells of resistance.

The logic of Brady's position is hard to gainsay, even if sometimes one might wish her to be less rigorous. Here is a writer with all the talents, one of the most impressive lyric poets writing now in English. If her poems can be dispiriting in their cumulative effect, this is because Brady is that rarest thing, a truthful poet. The traps of this *Embrace* do not feel personal, and the personal scarcely survives the book as a viable category. Still, Andrea Brady is an American who has lived and worked in the UK since the mid-1990s. She lived through the delusory rejoicing at the liberation heralded by the end of Tory rule, when people reassured each other that Blair and his cabal did not mean what they said, that it was a stratagem to reassure a fearful electorate, to reassure the powerful press, to reassure the IMF, to reassure American allies, to reassure the banks. These interests were reassured and were not stupid. Further down the road American liberals were to suffer a similar education, more directly brutal. Political commentary might suggest that the tide of reaction has reached its furthest exhausted limit, but the intellectual and motivational helplessness of oppositions tells a different story. The percolation of salt and sterile water into every cranny of civic life continues insidiously, killing hopes, toxic with unfettered exploitation and the assertions of social responsibility, with an increasingly unapologetic authoritarianism and aggressive professions of religious charity.

News relies upon a rhythm of tidal advance and retreat, and two-party political systems are perfectly adapted to this pattern—a pattern so deeply embedded in the social psyche that the truth that since the end of the 1970s the tide has run all in one direction has been slow in recognition. Both fact and denial have been devastating in personal and political life. Hope has become intolerable, a self- generated electro-convulsive therapy that with each spasm damages memory and reduces the initiative toward change. At work, only a gag prevents the tongue from being bitten off. For those living in the ever-enlarging shoestring economies of major post-industrial powers, self-arraignment, self-damage, and self-medication with various opiates including millenarian beliefs have become prevalent. It is right to be deeply thankful for *Embrace*, for it is absolutely clear-eyed, a precise register of the present situation. Other poets may prattle of the spirit, rage obscenely, tend their gardens or seek tenure, but Brady's poems are true.

The chinks of light discernible in 'To be Continued' and 'Hymn on the Nativity' are therefore precious. Here, however swiftly foreclosed by a rigorous judgement, beauty, desire, and truthfulness are married, and this gives reason to believe that Andrea Brady will fight free of her grids and grates, as a poetic ancestor who silently has haunted this response to *Embrace* found herself unable. Her name is Laura (Riding) Jackson, or at least that was one way she identified herself, and to read her poems of the late 1930s is to encounter a self-critical spirit every bit as unvenal as Brady's. Immediately the reader must be struck by the physical resemblance of her poems to Brady's; there is the same shaping of the stanza around expository paragraphs. Yet more remarkable are the sounds of blades engaging and traps locking. Here are final three lines of two successive poems in the 1980 edition of *The Poems of Laura Riding*:[82]

> The lone defiance blossoms failure,
> But risk of all by all beguiles
> Fate's wreckage into similar smiles.
>                     ('Doom in Bloom')

> And fingers stem closely from brain,
> Tight on the plenitudes of pain
> That from the reach of heart remain.
>                     ('Seizure of the World')

There is a bitter tone here unusual in Brady except in 'Saw Fit'. (Riding) Jackson's idea of Truth in poetry is very different—"the journey to the meeting-point where beings have a debt to pay to Being in true words spoken of themselves to one another."[83] Rhetorically however they arrive at a similar place, since both energetically contest or even cancel the seductions exercised by the propensities of their own verse. Although (Riding) Jackson disavows an anti-capitalist intent, her description of "our treacherous time" in the Notes to her extended essay, *The Telling*, echoes uncannily the predicament best confronted in our own treacherous time by Andrea Brady, a truthful poet:

> The time is an end-of-world time, an end of time. We are moving in it, it is not moving. Or, if there is movement, it is a racing in the track of former movement; its forwardness is an infinity of repetition; our progress is an ingrowing into ourselves; our "new" is engulfed in history as we launch it—no future issues from our time to invite, and receive, the new; our future is a distillation of old futures, and the new we present to it is an improvisation on all the once-new that drifts still life-like in history.

Laura (Riding) Jackson demanded a separation from the world of history and entry into a world of truth; poetry would be too hopelessly compromised and contaminated for such a venture. But it is poetry's contamination—the *touch* at the Latin root of contamination—that helps *me* to recognise *you* and to cease "ingrowing into ourselves" through an urgently needed distortion into the quickening of hope.[84]

Contamination returns this thinking to an earlier moment. What can be inferred for Andrea Brady's work and for politically engaged poetry more generally from the introductory discussion of her immediate poetic forebears? Assuming, that is, she will not in her truthfulness suffer (Riding) Jackson's fate of loquaciously-attested silence nor succumb to the metaphysical vortex. There appear to be two possibilities, both acknowledging the dilemma faced by (Riding) Jackson and now by Andrea Brady. One is the division recommended and performed by Drew Milne, whereby the infinitely productive sport of lyric poetry is given its head in a demarcated domain while political activity occurs elsewhere. The other is signalled by the examples of Douglas Oliver, Denise Riley, and D.S. Marriott, whereby lyric poetry is effectively dethroned and brought into association with a more contingent discursive and experienced world. Keston Sutherland's writing oscillates between these alternatives, driven by an enthusiastic temperament as honourable as Shelley's. Brady has internalised the condition of hyper-criticism to a greater extent, but I cannot imagine she will retreat from what her poetry touches. The brilliance of her published criticism permits the expectation that her various work will ever more forcibly oppose its deep contaminations, its lyric touch, to any metaphysics however tempting or compelling.

# 2: Poetics

# *Cadence*[85]

The narcissism of the individual writer may be such that to write the future takes its place within that expansiveness, as the material world is thought to aspire to solace in his or her material. But the transitive verb deployed in *Writing the Future* should cause discomfort; it smacks of that *development* promoted by the disconnected elites of small, poor countries on whose pavements people starve; while *we* write the future, there are others who barely live in the present, but who live *in* it, or below its aegis.

The writing of the future incurs the same necessary ambiguity as does *the writing of a poem* against *writing a poem*. The possessiveness becomes a two-way thing; the arrogance of Writing the Future is dissolved in a double ambiguity. Not only does the future have its writing which is exercised upon us since it is located in our past, to which we may be too frightened or infatuated, or too flattened to obtain access, more, writing is put in its proper place as possessed as much as possessing, quite as castigated as castigating. This is salutary, since the most self-cancelling, ideological of critiques tends to become as hollowly sufficient as fibreglass, when in concert with such a catchphrase as was brandished over our proceedings. Liberated as we are from 'human nature' and such speciousness, then chat of 'writing the future' while repressing the loud and clear and evident pronoun. But enough—or hardly so.

The productive points for the writing of a poem lie deep in an inadmissible past; across the depressive adaptations of the present day, pulses that love- and death-tempo, which snarled and hooked but ever resuming and urgently, becomes felt as cadence, projecting forward to organise the actual and tenderly enveloping day which never will break.

For it is the pathos of lyric poetry that the surface on which these points subtend, is as provisional as the actual future reader for whom in turn they offer always a fullness which is unknowable, ever-deferred. By what then can their future best be best underwritten; I think that is possible of a debt to be incurred, rather than the prepaid promise *writing the future* flaunts and crackles.

Thereby every writer does of course believe in human nature, given a few sets of quotation marks. It is not through kinship with the writer separated by centuries and continents, but because his or her individual past does become an unrealisable but a motive future, where writing is strictly cadenced. Our nature is my greatest privacy, and this is the sustaining and silly paradox, that the most idiosyncratic and inadmissible is the most deeply shared. In other words, the continued future bearing of, to take a tendentious example, Blake's 'The Sick Rose', would seem to be located in the tension between deeply personal, unnegotiable points and their erotically destructive transitivity, on the one hand, and the trips and stoppages incurred in their tangle with the semantics of complex actuality; this is the cadent way. Blake, of course, was also *overjoyed*. But I am thinking how the orotundity of the opening immediately runs into the stop of "sick", to be followed by an insistent and incremental pulse, tripping at the last into the equivocation of "joy" and "destroy", not merely in the obvious semantic opposition and the deeper identity enjoined by rhyme, but in the vowel sounds themselves, whose pitch is strangely unascertainable—indeed, it is difficult to know whether the rhyme termination is a long or a short vowel-sound, an abrupt stop or a resonance.

When I have talked of human nature, and my choice has been deliberate—I am no longer sure if the deconstruction of such a term is not mere complicity with cash-flow—what I mean is, I suppose, to make a cursive and ahistorical claim for the unconscious drives. I don't think the history of clinical symptoms begins to put that claim in question. When I say 'inexplicable', and I almost have, I don't mean categorically so, but poetry does ride just what formal literary analysis has found quite unreadable, for all its irritable reaching. Some psychoanalysts have followed the cadent way also. "Freud said that he had to 'blind myself artificially to focus all the light on one dark spot'", wrote W.R. Bion, continuing "By rendering oneself 'artificially blind' through the exclusion of memory and desire, one achieves F; the piercing shaft of darkness can be directed on the dark features of the analytic situation." Just so the dark features of the poem become manifest in a reading which is

neither an extrapolation to the personal nor an exercise of unpresent-
ing; the moment of *obtuse* presence must be accepted to tolerate its
erotic slippage.

This displacement is indeed the arch into a future, but not one of
inert and utopian integration, or achieved personhood; it is the earnest
of an individuality which is truly unachievable, even more when every
wild lunge in that direction is marketed as a style, and where every
person is the prosthetic 'man who was used up'. In reading the poem
cadently we become impersonal, and only from that impersonality can
individuality be glimpsed, and true self-fulfilment; we can be wrenched
from the time of surplus value, and in that judgment find our corrupt
and dying organs restored. As corrupt and dying organs.

The sorry liability, as much avant-gardism attests, is that with deeper
implication into the impersonal of the most personal, a compensatory
movement occurs, and atop the magma of grossly accelerated, fissile
desire—all radioactive fallout—a tendency is asserted towards the
hollow, posturing figure of the adventuring writer, a frozen romantic
tableau, a rhetoric akin to that of freedom as present. The best can bob
like foolish cork over the radical speciousness which is their true
achievement—I'm thinking of John Wieners, the Boston poet whose
later work often splits between these components, a detraction over-
emphasised by the penchant of his *Selected Poems* for the overtly 'poetic'.
(But in the great achievement if his 1975 book *Behind the State Capitol* can
be heard the dead-urgent as nowhere else, crossed and thwarted by the
politics of his daily life as a campaigning 'faggot' and a hospitalised
mental patient, and by a wild and joyous humour.)

This particular split is fairly recent, since paternalistic authority
structures have informed by a quite different fashion, that the writing
of the future could operate by a dethroning. Credible thrones are few,
with even the evidently wicked regime supported by the fissile rush, a
reckless, trivial and destructive saturation, foreign finance capital. The
erection of a paper pope over and against this can seem kindly, and
hence also that nostalgia for thrones which afflicts the cultural sermons
of a Christopher Lasch; oh where is daddy, stern and generous, to give us
the backbone to boot him down? This was prophesied by Paul Celan in
*Meridian*, his commentary on Büchner, admiring the cry "God Save the
King" at the revolutionary moment.

For sure I recognise in myself a drive to write to keep my delusions
worthy, rather than a mere bloated counterweight or a protective mechanism. On almost every score such an idea as 'humanity' is impugnable,

but to make it a true promise instead of a slick assumption or a slogan—
that may be a morally tolerable relation of writing to the future. So writing must never be cathartic or an achieved circle of reassurance or
recognition; but neither should it just open the sluices to what dwin-
dles to the mimetic of a current social awfulness, a storm of part-objects
as consumer durables. We as readers must always feel unsatisfied, but
not so easily so as with a new stack-system, the more unsatisfied the
better we are touched and discredited, yet through it promised
ourselves if only we turn away, unhooked.

And indeed it is correct that at most we underwrite the promissory
document of a past and as near as we're able to the present, and say to
the future, refer to drawer who's past accounting but whose heirs are
with you.

But terms such as 'humanity', however dislocated and estranged,
remain no more than totems if uncarried and unsustained through
integrative cadence, tensed against a viscous or obdurate semantics—
inconsistent and impure in diction also. The vocabulary for describing
cadence is embarrassingly inadequate; I understand cadence as the relation between a particular body of syntactic gesture in the writer's work,
and the involuntary but acknowledged participations in the larger and
more impersonal careers of death and love, so cadence would both rein-
corporate and is tensed against the depressive complexities of the local.
What Lyotard calls the intensity and surges of the death drive, and of
the erotic, seeks to invest the humane and the adaptive; so they become
translated into the poem's ambition.

The danger, I repeat, is the separation enjoined by an inherited literary body, neatly disposed on the stainless table in autoptic witness;
where cadence becomes the frozen gesture of the misunderstood, the
truly tedious figure of the poète maudit. Post-mortem life is also the way
both of a soured modernism, and the distinctive agoraphobia of much
admired English verse.

But who would subscribe to the tenders floated beneath my name,
how could I imagine? I accept my father's, a nineteenth century ratio-
nalist, as a taker out of patents for machines so useful they snarled in
their own mechanisms' complexity. This materialism of the soul is what
I am weaned and gagged on both; it is the movement between a futile
self-assertiveness and the cogs and wheels and sledgehammered ceram-
ics that spill from the shiny cabinet. There is a distinction to be made
from the theories of schiz-flow; this is closer to the empirical reality of
schizophrenic language, is more interrupted and governed by sedimented

gesture than there fancied; from these points the launch is made towards the investment of unbearable contingency.

Hence this diction, this language of fits and starts. To be left with the unconscious as transhistorical guarantor, this is swampy ground, and there are those who would cut away even this, historicise and relativise the unconscious. Despite the glamour of their anarchic rationalism, following cadence teaches me, both in poetry and in therapeutic attention, that it would lead to moral cachexia. What I call integrative cadence, at least proposes for poetry an ethical future; so to write is an endless forward cast. Of course there is nothing subversive here, I present for the first time my superversive manifesto, the half-arch, the rainbow bridge of cadence!

# The Metastases of Poetry[86]

The sense of completing a poem is little connected to reception, antici-pated or actual. Favourable response may prove a pleasure, critical response may serve as a goad to further writing, but the poem can achieve completion without circulation or publication, a phenomenon sharply indicative of the disjunction of the aesthetic domain from ordi-nary human commerce. For the poem is answerable discursively to its poetic context, in one's own work as part of a continuing argument, however obscure to oneself before its completion,—so whether it pushes out from what has gone before and achieves a separate identity or merely smells of one's too-familiar stylistic mannerisms, these will determine whether its completion is successful. It is answerable by virtue of the coherence of its internal organisation; and answerable in respect of those writings a poet considers contemporaneous, which may be historically and culturally diverse. Apart from signifying the relative autonomy of the aesthetic domain, this state of affairs also indicates the fragmentation of that domain. The development of the poetic book, as opposed to the collection, has been a marked feature of British and American late modernist writing, much as the series has characterised modernist painting; the reader is to be inducted into the language, or as I would prefer, the gestural repertoire of the sequential work.

This opens a number of questions: why the absence or the inadequacy of the second-order writing which surrounds such poetry (I'll try to distinguish the poetry I'm talking about from other sorts of poetry); and what is the relationship between the reading of poetry publicly and late modernist verse? It should be said at once, that there are kinds of poetry which rest within a sociological determination and require public read-ings to a specific constituency for their completion. But it seems to me remarkable that poets traipse the country reading from their work and fidgeting while others read, while the institution of the poetry reading remains little discussed. I shan't attempt any grand theoretical account of the critical or the reading activity, but offer some decidedly personal observations.

The kind of poetic adventure in which I'm engaged has found itself suddenly the object of critical attention both gratifying and troubling from *fragmente*, *Parataxis*, and *Angel Exhaust*, journals which sprung up simultaneously about three years ago. These journals were inaugurated with editorial animadversions on the silence which has surrounded such writing, going so far as to arraign the poets, many of whom are professional academics, for their reluctance publicly to promote and criticise such work. This was read largely as a failure of moral nerve, without consideration of the relationship between the poetry and its surrounding silence, although Drew Milne in *Parataxis* 3 identified four contributory factors: the conspiracy of expertise; an embarrassment with direct statement; a hostility to traditional criticism and literary theory; and the 'tap at the window' syndrome of futurity, the implicit appeal to a future dispensation in which the merits of the writing will be self-evident.

A hostile explanation might be that such writing is so solipsistic that even those who believe themselves engaged in a common adventure actually travel on parallel lines, without interest in intersection. But the degree to which, for instance, the rebarbative poems of J.H. Prynne have influenced others gesturally and lexically—and one could cite several other examples of a rash of gestural exchange—suggests that like DJs, poets at least needle-drop each others' grooves. The response, though, is to be sought in the mix rather than a direct accounting which would contextualise impact. Writing about a poem yields rewards quite different from an affectively-open attention, a poetic rather than interpretative response.

The poetry which engages me can be taken as a continuing postscript to modernism, if modernism is characterised by the advent of an autonomous aesthetic domain, most painfully apparent in the visual arts (the pain is blatant in the contortions of artists seeking to close the rift). It regards the temptations of postmodernism warily, as driven by an utopian metaphorical confusion between aesthetic practice and social action—a confusion exemplified in a promiscuous and unstable use of the term 'text'. The People of the Book supposed that freeing the signifiers would free their readers, while ludically and ludicrously complicit with the commodity delirium which characterises late American capitalism.

Writers of what I would call late-modernist as opposed to post-modernist poems, have not remained content with a categorical separation between the aesthetic and other domains of human thought and activity, but neither have they rejoiced in rodent pollution, schiz-flow or any other post-industrial solvent / board-wiper / blood-thinner. In his writing on J.H. Prynne, Neil Reeve has been concerned to demonstrate that Prynne's focus upon subjective particularity strives to reinvent a *political* domain,—a reminder that the suppression of the political and the expulsion of the aesthetic occupy the same historical moment. Several British poets, particularly Barry MacSweeney, Douglas Oliver and Denise Riley, are struggling in different ways against this categorical separation and suppression, without becoming spokespersons for sociological constituencies; Oliver through closed-system satires, which go so far as to propose and embody precepts for right conduct politically; MacSweeney through a fierce interrogation of his lone-wolf poetical persona which understands the hinge between such a position and the social structures, for instance marriage, which sustain it; and Riley through a scrupulous attention to the details of her ceaseless becoming, her lyrical teetering towards and refraction of an enjoined narcissistic identification. There are much-recited dangers in an aestheticised politics, and it has been suggested that the dismal and domesticated countenance of post-war British poetry has been influenced by contemplating the fate of Pound. Extrapolation to the fallen realm of public governance, whether carried out by poet or reader, crosses to a domain where politics simply dissolves and poetry becomes a fabrication. For these poets, however, politics and poetics are conjoined in a meaning making which balks at edict. Even Oliver's precepts are negotiated within a model of neighbourhood activism which is poetic rather than poeticised and political rather than regulated.

Critical attention has unusual difficulty with this writing, which is not amenable to a traditional moralised reading, nor to a cultural studies approach. Common strategies either refer the writing to the pathology of the poet, which is the tendency of the organs of official culture—MacSweeney's most recent book was dismissed in a few lines by the *T.L.S.* as simply barmy,—or accommodate it to the theoretical preoccupations of the critic, where typically the minimal quotation provided from texts unavailable to the likely reader, appears as mere flotsam on the waves of high-octane prose. Committed and enthusiastic readings of specific poems tend to become highly involved exegeses of localised language-strategies, staggering under the weight of information derived from their recontextualising of the range of specialised discourses in the poetry.

As for the silence of the poets themselves, the relative autonomy of the poetic enterprise is compromised by the directedness, the need for completion in reception, of second-order writing. For the completing audience, poems may become mere exemplars of a programme conceived ideologically or sociologically—and this applies too to writing about kindred poets, where the temptation is to interpret such writing for its bearing upon the poet's own intentions. I have found the only way round this is to become so absorbed in another's writing as to achieve a sort of reckless ventriloquism. Therefore I advocate the risk of reading enthusiastically, a kind of seepage of the aesthetic into the discursive.

I would like now to turn to the public reading of poetry. In *Mop Mop Georgette*, Denise Riley has a poem which starts:

> Who anyone is or I am is nothing to the work. The writer
> properly should be the last person that the reader or the listener
>     need think about
> yet the poet with her signature stands trembling, grateful,
>     mortally embarrassed
> and especially embarrassing to herself, patting her hair and
>     twittering. If, if only
> I need not have a physical appearance! To be sheer air and
>     mousseline!

Riley expresses nicely the dilemma of the contemporary lyric poet, conscious of the familial, gendered, racial and class construction of that place from which her lyric need arises ('the poet with her signature'), deprecating the reference of what is recited to her physical presence; but trapped in her poetic practice, as the final lines of the poem illuminate, between textual producer and lyric creator:

> so take me or leave me. No, wait, I didn't mean leave
> me, wait, just *don't*—or don't flick and skim to the foot of a page
>     and then get
>                                         up to go—

As ever, this poet is stringent in addressing the mirror-mockery of her practice. In the public reading it is the lyric person that is put on trial, and this will traduce the poetic text; and the more the text is de-centred, the more webbed and implicated it is, the further does the lyric cadence depart from the textual business, even as it represents to the audience the true ground of the text, its underlying necessity. (This smuggles in a distinction between poetic text and lyric which parallels that between interpretation and attention.) A characteristic of contemporary lyric writing is the severe tension between lyric necessity and a radical antinomianism in textual practice, disputing the necessity in its very impulse, performing forensics on the urgent self. But even lyric affect is traduced in the public reading; the poet intoxicated by the lyric strain in public reading, reduces lyric to pathos—so this is the more or less unattractive body to which lyric returns and where it will die—just as the antinomian poetic text becomes a perpetual motion machine, our equivalent of the Elizabethan memorial, eternally productive rather than sculpted for all time.

The poetic text read in solitude yields a lyric cadence which is a promise of full meaning ever deferred; in the public reading, the full-ness stands in the suffering or ridiculous or ingratiating poet—or worst of all, may be referred to a member of the audience, as when a poet insists on pointing out the excruciated recipient of a poem of sexual desire.

Listening to public readings I can rarely take in much beyond the spectacle of the poet and his or her particular cadences, the gestural repertoire intimate with the lyric persona. The textual details pass me by. As a public reader, I have been less troubled by this than is Denise Riley, but readers of Riley's feminist heretical work, *Am I That Name?* will understand that this is a writer for whom any categorical definition poses a narcissistic as well as a directly political trap. Rather, I have enjoyed confounding what I have understood readers to anticipate of the poetic genre to which my writing is referred (the nosology cannot be gainsaid); so I gather to my bemusement that the writing is a kind of free-standing production process, set up by writers whose erudition is deployed sadistically against the reader. Of course, this merely accom-modated the writing to ideas which were much in the air in the late 70s and the 80s, and any 'difficult' writing tended to be read as an extrusion of signifiers. Public readings help to challenge that view, but carry other dangers: the powerful folk archetype of the skinless suffering poet retains its hold through a kind of truth.

My reading style has always been confrontational, which is down to nervousness as well as to a wish to present the poetry unframed. I have foregrounded lyric effect, or have thought I was doing so, but the impactedness of the poetic text can be received as aggressive by listeners, the take-it-or-leave-it approach as an assertion of the audience's inadequacy. Failure to explicate implies that only rhythm and cadence can be accessible. On the other hand, I have been troubled by poets reading who have been anxious to frame an otherwise highly recalcitrant poetic text, whose recalcitrance is a necessary and specific departure from the language of information and advertising, out of kindness for the audience or fear of rejection. Good-bloke poets seems always to be making reparation for their poems' demands. By contrast, the poets whose readings I have most admired have tended to become depersonalised; listeners learn to tolerate not-knowing in a referential sense through the poet's toleration of a space of not-interpreting about the poems. To seek forgiveness for the poems is to diminish them.

Before this talk I chose to read 'Facing Port Talbot' because it was the most recent poem I have finished. This has a particular bearing; recently-written poems remain undetached as text, and closer to lyric urgency. There is a risk involved in this—it is only when reading just-completed poems that I have come to grief, that some smart-ass strategy, some preening little bit of text which conceit wouldn't allow me to modify, has thrown me entirely off-cadence, off-truth, and my mouth has thickened with ash. By contrast, poems from some years ago become primarily texts, to be reinterpreted through reading, and whose lyric specificity has to be rediscovered in a tentative way; there is a kind of recent history whose poems I can't read at all, because they represent a still-active past which I still recognise and am subjecting to revision. You could say there is a becoming self and a not-self, and between these a self in the process of dissolution.

There is a difficulty in register, in talking after reading a poem. Speaking like this supposes that I have joined in a continuing discourse, and this follows hard on an act which was a kind of aggressive self-effacement as a subject within the seminar's discourse. The only way to reconcile these positions will be to talk a little about the poem with which I began.

You may have recognised in my reading a rhythmic insistence which suggests that impurity of diction—a use of a range of rarely-associated specialised languages—is not always a matter of calculated exercises in throwing the reader off-track. It's more, to use a favourite image, a kind of shanty construction, grabbing whatever materials press on me in reading, in watching the television, in daily life. These constructions are as provisional as a shanty, they never result in anything I can continue to occupy as a satisfactory place. I'm not willing, and I'm unable, to try to explain such a poem, but what I can do is point out a principle of organisation which I call metastatic. I tend to work across a number of poems simultaneously, and in a long poem like this, across its various parts simultaneously. What gives the poems such coherence as they exhibit is not a metaphorical development, but a set of linked and trans- forming entities, which can be syntactical gestures, vowel and conso- nant patterning, imagistic or discursive modes. 'Metastasis' is a term in rhetoric, but my use derives from a brief experience of nursing in a cancer hospice, the way metastatic tumours echo about the body and these nodes define the shape of the body subjectively, through pain. Of course, the location of the primary tumour is outside the poem's realm; the poem develops around the metastatic nodes, and these gestures come to evoke its physical lineaments. The reticence of the primary helps guard against a reductive essentialism in approaching the poem, that it is *about* such-and-such—in fact, there will be a number of extrin- sic primaries. Too many indeed for amenability.

Since imagistic nodes are the easiest to demonstrate without becom- ing bogged down in local exegesis, I shall glance at one group in this poem, which revolves around the torus which is also the life-saving ring, the lobster-pot, the body, and the starry envelope echoed by the bedcov- ers. The torus—an organisation of eternity—is the key to all these, and I'd hoped to present a computer simulation showing its transformation through morphing techniques, the donut which becomes a trap which becomes a passage. Another morphology takes in the barrow or burial- chamber, which at Parc le Breos is like a great cowry of rubble spilling in towards the inner trench or mouth—but a cowry would have been exotic to Swansea Bay.

What relates this group of images is the outside turning to form the inside. The torus is all lip, at every point on its surface. In the case of the lobster-pot, the torus morphs into a trap. One of the advantages of composing in the metastatic echo-chamber is its serendipitous range—frequently the connectives remain obscure to the writer until stumbled across at a late stage in writing. Rather as what we receive of stars is old light and old radio transmissions, the poem reveals itself as a map of radiant traces. The torus range of metastases in this poem provides a vivid example; my wife was given for Christmas a popular account of the cosmological discoveries of the past six decades, and there I discovered I had been playing all unwittingly with competing cosmological models, with a fidelity which takes me aback. There is a model of space-time manifolds or envelopes, where space-time curves about mass like a starry envelope bent by gravity: here are my bedcovers, here are the stars pulled down like a coverlet at the end of the poem within the bleak otherwise flat and steady-state spread of Swansea Bay. That bay incidentally is another donut, if we can annex Devonshire, where I was brought up—so Swansea, Port Talbot and Devonshire, with their lighthouses, refineries and reflections in the water, trace my speaking lip. The observer in bed is the centre of gravity about which space-time or eternity curves, conformably. And the most pessimistic of the dynamic models of the universe was described by the cosmological author as conforming to the inner lip of a trumpet, with the galaxies rushing in through an infinitely extended plughole—this inner lip conforming nicely to my lobster-pot funnel and trap.

One might then rejoin that the poem is about something after all, although in a sense other than being about a flower, say. Metastases are the scattered receptor sites of a primary memory process, retrievable only in such faint traces. These cosmologies may be the lyric traces of a primary event, a Big Bang, but I do not believe in the cosmological eschatology which returns to basic creation in the Big Shrink, and no more am I offering you an encapsulation of the poem. I have been pointing only to one metastatic cluster, pulling out a particular and rather grand theme. This cluster also has a literary association, a reference to Vaughan's poem which begins 'I saw eternity the other night'. I love Vaughan's bizarrely comfortable relationship with eternity, and the poem runs a parodic cosmology of crumbs and fleas in the bed as a way of taking things down a peg; I don't have Miltonic aspirations. I might add that the torus as such came late in the poem's composition—the figure was there from early on, but it was only as I was completing the poem that news came of one of the now perennial breakthroughs in nuclear fusion, carried out in a torus mapped by a dense interweaving of magnetic fields.

Re-reading the poem in preparation for this talk, I was startled at its play with cosmological models, and with what seems an intent to make the interstellar spaces—which we now know have mass, they are dark matter rather than emptiness—something humanly habitable. This discovery is a good example of the uncertainty principle—the particles arrange themselves according to the quality of attention brought to bear, and their specificity is indeed called into being through attention.

That Negative Capability should have become a precept in particle physics and in psychoanalysis (through the work of Wilfred Bion) as well as a precept for poets, suggests that metastasis—or what a heretical biologist, Rupert Sheldrake, calls morphic resonance—has a remarkable reach. This is a nicely sceptical thought on which to end a talk to professional interpreters.

# Too-Close Reading: Poetry and Schizophrenia

My opening discussion of two poems by John Wieners aims to identify some of the contradictions inherent in the term 'schizophrenic poetry', and to distinguish his writing from modernist and postmodernist verse which exhibits schizoid mannerisms. This will form the basis for some thoughts on the conduct of poetry.

**Billie**

He was as a god,
stepped out of eternal dream
along the boardwalk.

He looked at my girl,
a dream to herself and
that was the end of them.

They disappeared beside the sea
at Revere Beach as
I aint seen them since.

If you find anyone
answering their description
please let me know. I need them

to carry the weight of my life
The old gods are gone. What lives on
in my heart

is their flesh
like a wound,
a tomb, a bomb.[87]

The poem starts in the theatre of memory, that "eternal dream" which is repetition, where at last to forget is to make loss possible and real and to be restored to the flesh. This poet's reverie has spun him off as a god, promoted him as a girl, but while each has ontological priority over the residual self, we know they are cultural archetypes too—the god may have his feet on the ground but the ground is symbolic language. Who is it says "my girl"? Because the boardwalk, the ground on which the god steps, has been appropriated from popular song where such gods live, we can hear "my girl" as another fragment ("Talkin' bout my girl")—the first person is inauthentic, the speaker insecurely located, in god and girl or nowhere.

Both god and girl become dreams to themselves in the look, in the stare; in meeting together they encounter their own inauthenticity and indeed their destiny, since "that was the end of them" means not only their disappearance but the end to which boy-meets-girl always tends in this story. They are indeed the parents as well as the products of that speaking voice marked in the vernacular of "I aint seen them since", the bridge line of the poem in its return to the poet's self whilst still shadowed by the typicality of what goes before. "I" is born of the disappearance of the eternal figures which had conveyed it forth and time is restored.

This is why the final stanza of the poem has its uncanny effect, where the speaking voice is enucleated from the body in a rush, and the flesh which is contemplated from outside is the flesh of the dream-creatures. The dream-creatures are the matrix from which the self has been born, but that recognition is made through the violence of its repression—what is missing and denied and undeniably present in "a wound, | a tomb, a bomb" is none other than the womb.

The poem courts and resists and flirts with schizophrenia, and in that lies its uncanniness; the poet's later schizophrenia might have been an identity-choice. The force of the poem arises from the tension between the exercise of an insistent control and the workings of its productive genera; what makes the poem could also unmake it as a poem, requiring such resourcefulness to keep it within bounds.

How well do I listen? The uncanniness I sense through close reading relies on my reading practice for its completion. Doesn't the poem's care depend on a pre-detachment, a camp displacing of affect into exemplary figures of suffering open to this linguistic investment and for which the title—which probably alludes to Billie Holliday—should sign an alert? Can I take the "eternal dream" seriously? To read a poem in English from another culture and time facilitates my own projections; it may be I enact a paranoid apprehension of the poem as holy writ. But the poem is a gift, and if I am re-made by it I re-make it and its giver too; it answers my description.

. . .

What would a schizophrenic poem look like?

**February**
   Cornhill Life
   *Art News*

Textual exercises are examples to
reward proof that theatre pieces pertain to
human growth. Like for instance jewelry
in German jewry contain erotic imagery, see

Causeways provoke plantagenet gripes
as Richard the Lion-hearted's New York Times
in Londonderry Commonwealth bureau Town
from the Fire-escape to opera stars Boers.[88]

How does this measure against the technical attributes of schizophrenic language as identified by Louis A. Sass—desocialization, automization and impoverishment? Desocialization is apposite to the second stanza: "…language may sound telegraphic, as if a great deal of meaning were being condensed into words or phrases that remain obscure because the speaker does not provide the background information and sense of context the listener needs to understand." The string of nouns and proper names following the verb "provoke" is telegraphic. Automization is as strongly present in those "…tendencies for language to lose its transparent and subordinate status and to emerge instead as an independent focus of attention or autonomous source of control over speech or understanding". "Jewelry" produces or by its variant spelling anticipates 'jewry,' and it is hard to account for "Boers" except by association from jewellery to De Beers, the world's largest diamond dealers, and South African. The poem in its entirety might be a paste brooch, remembered out of February's theatrical experiences. Finally, impoverishment, "… the single most distinctive feature of schizophrenic language, often manifest[ing] itself in utterances that sound, to many listeners, like "empty philosophizing", "fruitless intellectualizing" or "pseudo-abstract reasoning", is marked in the poem's opening flourish, which for all its grandiosity might say little more than 'this poem shows what the theatre has meant to me'.

But "pseudo-abstract" reasoning may be hard to distinguish from abstract reasoning; Freud granted as much at the close of his essay 'The Unconscious', writing: "...it must be confessed that the expression and content of our philosophizing...begins to acquire an unwelcome resemblance to the mode of operation of schizophrenics."[89] Returning with this in mind, I note how "proof" and "pieces" prepare for jewellery, and that the apposition of "textual exercises" and the cold hardness of jewels gives poignancy to the assertion of their significance for "human growth".

So it may be legitimate to read the pell-mell names of the second stanza, a plain instance of words attaining a priority over their signifying function, as not so much a pathological symptom as indicative of the difficult relationship between "textual exercises" and "human growth". Epithets such as "Plantagenet" and "Lion-hearted" are adornments directing human growth—they must be lived up to, as must a commonwealth. These are the causeways of development. The relationship is ambiguous, for human growth may also be thwarted or compromised by names; after all the poem arrives under the sponsorship of the assurance company Cornhill Life and the journal of the fine art industry, *Art News*. Names may be erotically productive or sterile, as indeed "human growth" may be reified as an objective of artistic practice or psychotherapy, or assume the dynamics of a political project. Or the poem may be making sardonic play with the pretensions that surround artistic products such as Shakespeare or grand opera, with the opening clauses being deliberately pompous in their claim for art and the second stanza providing an example of the brilliant tawdriness of memory's constructs; what is retained may not be so spiritually improving as incidental to a social milieu—a gala evening reported in the *New York Times*; bejewelled dowagers. Such emphasis on what straight bourgeois culture regards as incidental is seriously camp; seriously so because it occasions the art of this poem and because in its love of illusion it is radically disillusioned, clear-sighted as to the commercial and social sponsorship. Even eroticism is subordinate as imagery in this scheme of things.

If nothing were known of the writer would this poem appear pathological or as a modernist literary work? Or is this a false binarism; could it be both? And what does it mean to describe language as "an autonomous source of control over speech or understanding" when what is being considered is a poem rather than speech? Is not to make a poem and to see it into print, to assert control over language? And how does the language of this poem sit with the preoccupations of Wieners' earlier verse?

Schizophrenia names a pathological process rather than a state of being, and just as in any act of poetical writing different levels of consciousness are involved, it is possible that in 'February' Wieners is deploying the language of his madness under conscious control, and for calculated literary purpose. There is evidence this may be so in the history of his extraordinary book *Behind The State Capitol: Or Cincinnati Pike* (1975) where poems as formally achieved as 'Billie' in their earlier magazine publication are flooded and swathed in schizoid language revelatory of the political, cultural and sexual matrix in which the poems had been conceived, disturbing irrevocably the originatory lyric self. But this visible process of massive decompensation—if that is what it is—may constitute evidence of schizophrenia's inconsistency and the ability of the poet to call on other resources to put any materials to effective poetic use; might not such late poems as 'February' be merely pathological and my reading an instance of misguided ingenuity? For the intentionalist fallacy has been succeeded by the intentionless fallacy, where any textual shard becomes grist to the critic's own hermeneutic compulsion.

What is striking about the late poems is their formal wit. In the poem examined, both vacuous orotundity and telegraphese, those first-rank linguistic symptoms, are reconciled in brief compass. What of the formal control, the stanzaic patterning, the skilled sound-fabric? Are these to be regarded as the sad relics of the decades of previous work, behavioural automatism carrying away evacuated pathological matter in neat parcels? Or to turn away from the positive markers of schizophrenic language, what do the late poems of Wieners lack by comparison with 'Billie'?

In schizophrenia speech is textualised, and in text the written word disjoined from speech and the situated body. A similar disjunction is evident in the languages of business and bureaucracy. Competence in a formulaic language erasing the situatedness of the writer is a core skill for manager and academic alike; anyone who has worked for a large business organisation will know the expenditure of time on checking and revising written communication to expunge all trace of individual origin. The divorce of language from bodily speech leads to a flattening in tonal range as characteristic of the informational universe generally as of mandarin artistic practices. This applies also to the amateur and popular practice of poetry, where the formulaic determinants of what constitutes poetry tend to overcome the felt necessity for personal expression which impels people to write poetry. The irony is that play with a formulaic repertoire by a person with schizophrenia may be more controlled by intention than the formulaic verse of the amateur poet.

What is striking in 'February' is its poetically non-formulaic quality. The Wieners poem is the unmistakable product of a particular gay literary milieu, the Boston of John Wheelwright and Stephen Jonas as well as Wieners; and what would appear to mark the poem as schizophrenic could be referred to an idiolect—the poem could be 'transparent' to some readers, playing off shared cultural referents. The perils of misdiagnosis of schizophrenia through ignorance of a patient's cultural and linguistic matrix are well-known, as is the ingenuity of the oppressed in linguistic resistance.

Poems which are demonstrative of schizophrenic language may be written by poets who, like Wieners, have suffered a psychotic illness, but by virtue of their individual artistry cannot therefore be considered schizophrenic products. This would not apply to transcribed speech as with some sections of *Behind the State Capitol*; but the control exercised by the poet over the selection of passages of transcribed speech and their disposition within the book as a whole, introduces an artistic purposiveness which also cannot be called schizophrenic. Hence, the language of schizophrenia in poetic use could be consistent with the absence of schizophrenic process, whilst the absence of the language of schizophrenia and the deployment of an excessively conventional—which is to say, an anachronistic—repertoire of poetic phraseology may indicate active psychosis. The empty phrases into which the amateur poet invests his or her feeling are difficult to distinguish from the machine poems of the psychotic—except by their relative linguistic inertia, the dearth of twist or pun.

There is a possible diagnostic explanation for Wieners' manipulation of schizophrenic language and its alliance with camp, in the choice of a schizophrenic career by some severely hysterical individuals, especially men. Wieners works amidst the detritus of popular culture, the film and gossip journals which are exhausted before publication, a formulaic flux of a kind that the conventions of high art—such as the white page—simply disavow. To invest serious feeling into such material may be camp if it holds to the mythological figures; once the investment is made into names, identity may become distributed; the prosthetic star dissolves into the warp of the star-map.

Those sophisticated writers who are romantically inclined towards madness as a patent of excessive feeling are mistaken; rather, a hyper-trophic self-consciousness characterises the language-games the schizo-phrenic plays at more than one remove with the conventional signifiers of excessive feeling. Those who would be dissolute in their language are not writing on the edge of madness but within a secure genre, either flirting with what is no more likely to harm them than ecstasy or follow-ing a strictly literary programme with conscious design to 'subvert' the assumptions of ordinary speech or text. As ever with such designs, they tend to be more complicit with the culture with which they take adver-sarial issue than is apparent to their authors or their readership. The eradication of the author in the mass media or in commercial texts is so far normative, that the assertion of strongly marked personality in newspaper columns has become another factitious construct which the readership knows to be no more expressive of an individual than inti-mate lifestyle features on the famous. Commerce killed the author long ago: who writes Joan Collins?

The further paradox is that what may touch most movingly is that writing which does not presume to share, which like the Wieners poem 'Billie' is of so perilous and personal an anticipation of dissolution. In the informational universe, communication starts with resistance. The impersonality of such poems is achieved by way of an almost unreach-able innerness, become impersonal in the reader's connection with it. It does not set out to be unconventional or subversive, but is driven by a need as much for self-preservation as for expression, and in seeking self-preservation makes unbearable pain or joy impersonal and poetic. Such poetry is always stepping back from madness, and bringing away from madness the materials it requires and which it struggles to accommo-date to the uses of a poem, seeks to make them less harmful. This is a very different motive from the gleeful wish to do harm to the reader (a sadistic fantasy which yearns for forgiveness and reconstitution) or to enjoin the reader in a giddy *folie à deux*, where the readers are connois-seurs of such strategies and subsume the text readily into the categories of those literary theories they espouse.

After Ashbery much accomplished American poetry of the eighties sounded and looked like the epic of hypertrophic consciousness. It was schizoid in its blank control, but also relaxed, sampling and processing its own vagaries with amusement and relish of its extraordinary skill, its look-at-me negotiations; it had access to all areas and consumed indifferently. Revelling in the detachment of consciousness from the body and from coherent subjectivity, its tonal range from touristic to hedonistic was notably restricted. Like commerce talking to itself it was radically unsituated, but like commerce again required niche-marketing to make its readers feel special: there were variants for race, geography, sexual orientation but these were textual hooks; readers were reminded repeatedly and ingeniously that bodies and their activities are linguistically constructed, but did not the advertising industry know that long before poets? Because the 'I' is nowhere situated it is absolutely everywhere, not so much solipsistic as all-inclusive. Consider these recent lines by Charles Bernstein:

> My bread has some nerve. No
> sooner does it come out of the oven
> than I have to slap it for being
> so fresh. My head has some
> curve. No sooner does it run for
> the patio than the lights begin
> to jam, the commotion dies down
> in the corridor outside the
> farm administration building.
> Randy & Billy & Bob grab a Diet
> Lite with a side of slope,
> the nerve doctors convene for
> an all-night session on breaking
> the self-help habit. I'm okay
> you're not worth the paper you're
> printed on, or I'm in deep
> trouble but you never came up
> to the surface after that dive,
> lo these many years ago.
> —Boy that makes me mad. Madder
> than a scratched eel at a
> Crossing-Guard kettle-shoot, tireder
> than a Bel Paese cheese at a
> [...etc.][90]

Where to stop quoting when each line lends itself to a purpose so willing, whilst feigning to disavow purposiveness? Its skippiness is adorable, how jaunty phrase launches jaunty phrase, and its piling-on, its circling round the constellation of slap and slope and curve and dive and nerve, bright and breezy and laughing in the shallows. This Saussurian playground of difference where every phrase is of equivalent value—the same in weight, the same in infra-referentiality—recalls Freud's anticipation of Saussure in his essay on 'The Unconscious': "Moreover, by being linked with words, cathexes can be provided with quality even when they represent only *relations* between presentations of objects and are thus unable to derive any quality from perceptions." What is the poem about but to demonstrate this in a *healthy* way, dissolving the self-construct in an aerobic linguistic workout? There is something of the programmatic schizoid poem about this passage with its head running away and curving; as Freud writes, "Here the schizophrenic utterance exhibits a hypochondriac trait: it has become "*organ-speech*"."[91]

Bernstein's poem is notable for its all-over affective investment, steady tone, and the paradoxical foregrounding of the authorial or the reading self inevitable when referentiality is lifted and attention rests on the self-constitutive operations of language. Everything is then referred back to the constitutive and constituted writer and reader—the first person and the last person, whose pronouns are batted from phrase to phrase in a ping-pong set of reassignments.

There is a long way between what I discover or conceive as the identity perils of Wieners' 'Billie' and the teasing, laid-back lines of Bernstein. 'Billie' is an envelope of semantic anxiety radiating from a point of unbearable tension, torn between concession to "the predominance of what has to do with words over what has to do with things", a catastrophic decompensation, an unhoming which beckons in the final stanza and is resisted in suppression of the word "womb"; and on the other hand the saving knot of experience, however linguistically transformed, which must be integrated and contained that the poem—and the poet—should exist at all.

For me Wieners anticipates a poetry which does not set out with programmatic design but negotiates the torn halves, seeking to mobilise the lyric voice both inaccessibly personal and beyond individuality in full apprehension of the near-fatal fouling of the lyric source by self-consciousness, the felt knowledge of the linguistic constitution of the self, the felt necessity for accepting and making positive a defamed social identity. Writing a determinedly gay, transvestite poetry, publishing in gay journals as well as in the canonical journals and anthologies of postmodernist poetry, Wieners' poetic practice has wrested from the disintegrative attacks of schizophrenia poems of exquisite poise. Lyric poetry unhomes and yearns for home.

But there is no home to which to return; indeed, once to have left home is to see home razed, and to travel linguistically as the gaseous plasma from which physical form is but an evanescent and reactive precipitate. Mass is disposed evenly in linguistic space, cathected into provisional selfhoods, drifting towards coherent texture. The texture of 'the real' is now one of unassimilated knowledge, an overabundance made coherent by the ever-emergent individual's restlessly connective activity across promiscuously assorted domains. Bernstein's poem reminds us by its access to all areas—as does a truly great poem, Stephen Rodefer's *Four Lectures*—that everything does return home to the land of the free. Such poetry may be gold, of a density impenetrable to all but the adept, and script also, of a vapidity unfiltered by intention or for practical use. For if merely contingent and self-replicatory, poetry reduces to exemplars of the act of poeticizing, to the flutterings of the linguistic fabric as it passes through one node, one consciousness, and asserts its ceaseless coming-into-being. Are the only effective skills management and counselling, both of them heedless of the specifics of experience and substituting for conversation and memory—but drained of content and positivistic? Out of unbearable complexity and quantity can one but focus on inputs, activity levels or outcomes? Making gold from air: that is schizophrenic if you like.

Poetry must refuse to acquiesce in this dis-valency. Wieners' poetic practice in despite of schizophrenia has something to teach all who write with and against a schizo-saturated culture. There is a pulse in his arresting lyric poetry between a linguistic productivity, with its straining away from object-perception, and a reintegrative movement which returns to situated identity in the body. The hypertensiveness is registered in a language breathing and physical, which must stay close to the rhythm of exchange in order to not buckle into self-referential incoherence, an extreme of attention to its own processes which would yield to madness.

Identity has become distributed through metaphor. What makes the matter of poetry is connectivity rather than reference; but what charges the connectivity, what cathects the links but forms of identification secured to powerful objects whether of love or of broader social construction? Indeed poetic identity increasingly is composed of multiple pronouns, of part-people whose intersection and interaction develop a populace, deposing both the regal author and the puppet persona. But these figures are not the only alternatives to dissolution; a situated if transcursive reintegration can allow us the sense of a possible instrumentality amongst others.

To read such work is to become entrammeled as though the white noise of information stopped, acquired weight, and it were possible to inhabit it a while and for that to be bearing and bearable and even beautiful. Weltering particularity is re-knit like a bolus, a catch in the throat, restarting the intersubjectivity which produces the world and the traveller through it as preciously, temporarily coherent and inseparable. If unhoming language in its yearning for home tends to be accompanied by sadistic fantasies seeking restoration of belief in the full being of the other, much postmodernist writing could be taken as poignant in its violence on the reader.

I have used these poems unfairly as stalking horses for my self-reproaching and hopes, and just as my close reading of Wieners is facilitated by a studied dyslexia, my reading of Bernstein takes the rhetoric which announced his verse at its word and ignores, for instance, a different filiation from O'Hara which would preclude my typically British moralising. I think my rhetorical hopes describe what has been called identity poetics in the writing of Lyn Hejinian and Lisa Robertson; and Stephen Rodefer's poems are charged with a consciousness of the absurd wager of lyric poetry after the dissolution of the subject, and make it notwithstanding. These are poets who know both lyric control and lyric abandon, the necessary systole and diastole, to be anachronistic, but who work nonetheless by such means in the informational miasma—as programmers say, making choices among local destinies. Being well-spoken I'm hardly one to talk.

# Mouthing Off[92]

In my dream I held a newly-published book, a huge anthology titled *Sexualities*, to which I was the one non-academic contributor—I'd contributed some poems and turned to them after identifying their place in the Contents—there was my name, page 105. But the signatures had been misbound, so pages 105 and following were impossible to track, and pages four hundred and following were where my contribution should have been. So I put aside the book, a little put out. Then returned a little later to find the page sequence had become correct, but my pages were replaced by a bound-in bunch of crude photocopies of almost-obliterated official documents looking much like passports—not even properly aligned, but carelessly skew. So again I put it aside, baffled. But I couldn't resist picking up the book again and turning for a third time to where my contribution should be. There it was, and the poems looked fine—I thought, I must commit these to memory for when I wake. But where my name should have appeared at the head was a blank, and the pages following were poorly inked so whole paragraphs faded out—in fact the entire text looked like sea-waves, with bold and faint shifting incessantly. It occurred to me that what I could read seemed like the writing of another poet—an American poet whose work I've long admired and whose name, John Wieners, resembles mine—and Wieners is not only a gay poet but a drag queen, someone whose identity is spectacularly provisional.

Yet having remarked this I remained proud of these poems, and put down the book intending to copy them with my name added, to the people whose opinion matters to me. This dream points up the anxieties involved in standing before you here in the guise of a poet, close to where I go about my ordinary and respectable life as an National Health Service bureaucrat.

What after all am I to represent? What is the relationship between the poems you may have puzzled over already and my presence? It's only a month or two since I set those poems aside and now I will try to recreate them in a way which differs from the writing relationship—I won't be occupied or surrounded or absorbed, but taking the poems from elsewhere and mouthing them.

They will be narrowed by extrusion through a single voice. That is the conventional account, beyond the separate category of performance poetry—that my standing before you here has reduced the poems before I recite them. There was probably little mistaking my gender or ethnicity when reading the poems as *texts*, but my age, my voice, my respectability—these may be at once reassuring and disappointing.

I think though that translation from text into poem may need to be helped by vocal performance and that this is so especially when it comes to poems which have the appearance of complex texts. The principle of their integration is far harder to discern than are their various discourses to tease apart—for you surely, since students of English feel more comfortable with textuality than with oral hedonism. In fact there's hardly a language to talk about their integration except that of prosody, which most discussion doesn't even recognise as concerned with delivering a unity while incorporating difference—and there isn't a language of prosody which is much help with most contemporary poetry. I find myself reduced to vague talk of *cadence* or corporeality, but the latter has become an exercise-yard for theorists. All I want to do now, by reading these poems, is to ask you to consider their oral unity or incoherence, although that might mean listening out beyond my old-fashioned well-spokenness.

So here are the poems you read in advance, but now replaced within a sector of the galaxy of poems to which they belong. I'm trying to avoid the term 'sequence' which to me sounds too goal-directed and why I don't like goal-directedness will emerge in what I will say after reading.[93]

These poems have their temporal origins in jottings prompted by news reports from Bosnia. Maybe I wanted to say something about nationalism and constructions of identity, but in poetry you tend to discover what you're about or what your poems are about some way down the line, and instrumental intent tends to be frustrated and even quite derailed by the language's collateral creativity. I neglected my jottings, and returning to them after a year or two reflected how pointless it had been to have any point in view for the poems. If a poem has a point, for its author it's often at the point of its greatest opacity, since transparency returns the poem to décor, a recital of the known and familiar. In which case why trouble with all that absurd attention to language's undertones and grace-notes, unless, that is, you have a waiting audience eager to share pain or celebrate membership?

The period of swarming vacancy which commuting to work affords, ravels on my electronic organiser a scroll of observations, erotic musing, and shreds and tags of language. These are never quite random—they have a way of accretion, not so much like a growing crystal as like a hermit crab's assembly of its provisional shell, perhaps. They may also be assemblies or remainders such as tors or middens, which start to map out a wider field. But a few fragments of this and that began to adhere to my Bosnian jottings. And others configured themselves elsewhere—usually there are two or three such adherences or plottings or programmes under way in parallel. That doesn't preclude a different kind of writing where a poem might arrive all at once, but I think that kind of arrival is dependent on its landing-strip having been marked out in the way I describe.

It occurred to me as I pushed around these particular bits and pieces and others, that an interesting proposition would be to generate a work out of a private and inexplicit, an unstated obsession—to generate a work that was beside the point and all round the point, a point which would never be spelt out and might resist identification. The poems would be side-effects, grown fetishistically—impelled by what they looked aside from. And that's the way I went about *Dew on the Knuckle, Due on the Nail*. It differs from the way I've found such clusters to emerge previously, in that rather than simply losing sight of a starting point I insisted it remained apparent to me during the process of writing; repeatedly the linear advance of the poems was bent inward and pleached about the invisible idol.

So these are poems which are *about* something, and what they're about doesn't really matter—and what that would deliver, I hoped, might be poems with the compulsion and compellingness of referentiality but the ranginess of collateral creativity. Or to use a more physical analogy, the poems would be held together by metastases of a primary growth which itself would be difficult if not impossible to locate.

So this full and empty point, this cynosure and repeated distraction, began to appear and not-appear across the field of these poems.

Points lie on or describe lines, especially in poems, and lines three-dimensionally meet to form figures. Soon I found these poems to be preoccupied with boxes and bags. The boxes I associate with the boxes of the American sculptor Don Judd, whose work I'd found discussed in a book by the art critic and intriguingly peculiar poet Marjorie Welish—many years ago I saw black-&-white reproductions of Judd's work and it astonished me now to learn these grey boxes (again reproduced in black-&-white in Welish's book) actually were saturated with colour. Then I saw a Judd at Tate Modern and went right out to buy a book reproducing his work in colour—these are colour sinks or tanks rather than boxes.

So the boxes in my poems don't stand simply for a sort of bad rationalism or formal projection of the points and their lines; they refer also to enclosures like Judd's which are seductive and gorgeous. Equally the bags aren't just a fashionable gesture towards chaos theory (I mean, describe the shape of a used bag) and they aren't invariably attractive because sometimes they clothe someone attractive (in my poems that is)—they also bear crass company logos or can be shoddy and messy.

Anyway, these poems have their fill of points and boxes and bags. And they're at once baggy and boxy—most of them look like boxes and are rather intricately constructed, but they're a bit bumpy too, and some poems sag into string bags and gloop and fluffballs. These also tend to be the poems that arrived almost whole, organic rather than constructed.

Now that's one constellation that might be discerned amidst the poems. One thing that makes my poems hard to negotiate in an a-leads-to-b kind of way is that usually there are quite a few such constellations traceable—but this can allow a relaxed view too. If you deliberately pull back from focus as you might when looking at the stars in order to achieve the gestalt of a constellation, that's not a bad opening strategy with a problematic poem. If you start by looking too hard, there's just too much or many. Poems are not written necessarily for a practice of close reading which can mop up all semantic spillage as it goes, although I do think close reading is the essential skill for enjoying poems of the modern western literary tradition. It's just that we need to be realistic about the conditions for close reading. We are always distracted by the light-pollution of our preconceptions and social assemblies, and by our partiality and laziness.

But more than that, the conditions for close reading are difficult to contrive for those who are not given to it professionally. Attention which is neither immediately goal-directed nor a distracting background nor the reception of what arrives at once acceptably, does not merely require protected time—as protected as the analytic hour in psychoanalysis; but requires a break from habitual and inculcated modes of attention. It is hard to break from the habit of scanning for the sociological symptom, or for information your job will demand you have available, or to be sure the kids are safe.

In reality there must be an intermediate stage in reading poems which recognises that there are far too many poems about. A serious reading of poets as different at George Herbert, P.B. Shelley and Frank O'Hara—to confine the range to dead white males—raises the question of how anyone could read anything else in a lifetime, giving those poets due attention. I have no solution to this. When it comes to complex contemporary poetry, you have to develop a scanning mechanism which enables you to determine that this or that poem might be worth the effort, might be better than going to the movies.

For me some of what decides that is rhythmic, some is about a partiality for what I regard as poetic process—that is, that the poem is driven by a necessity that is marked in the poem through a kind of relay between figuration such as metaphor and conceptual thought, and that this in turn is engaged in a relay with sound-pattern and rhythm. That's a poor exposition, but among what it excludes might be:

- Poems which are self-sealing—title frames, last line wraps up, nothing left.
- Poems which are programmatic—tendentiously refuse to deliver, on the assumption that capitalism will be brought to its knees by disrupted syntax in a poem published in an edition of 200.
- Poems which advertise the poet's travel opportunities or presence at great opera performances.
- Poems which are designed principally to convey green, feminist or anti-racist messages. Poems will register these commitments if they're important to the writer; but look at me, what a good person I am, makes for poor poems.

Your needs and desires will be different, and they change over time and from time to time for any of us. A taste for the unassignable, for the unaccountable, is a minority one. For many, language which doesn't put all the cards on the table or which hurls down all the cards at once, is truly offensive—and that's one reason why there's not a living to be made from writing poetry.

Having made a provocative and somewhat spurious distinction between a text and a poem, there's one more thing I'd like to say about poems which is that a peculiarity of some kinds of poetry—and not just the kind I write but perhaps especially so—is that things and feelings and ideas and so-called images are difficult to separate. The *arguments* of my writing are difficult to distinguish from the relationships between words as objects. I have an intuition that a primitive kind of orality is involved here, with these mouthed objects and words.

Alongside this primitive, lalling usage, language continues to operate symbolically and relationally—that is, to recognise relational networks and an external range of reference which doesn't point chiefly to the author. When I suggest what boxes and bags might have come to mean in these poems, that indicates that linguistic usage is not confined to the psychotic or hysterical. So the tensions and liaisons between primary process and conscious shaping, between the power of infrastructure and the power of reference, contribute to that relay effect between sound chains (that is, words as objects), metaphorical chains and conceptual chains—characteristic of Shelley for example.

As with any artistic practice, writing poetry is a curse to its practitioner as much as a blessing. The curse lies in the exactions of the linguistic field once set in play. I mean the way in this set of poems the points, bags and boxes seized my not-quite-inner life—I don't think artists have inner lives, their innerness is diverted into the materials they manipulate and combine—or chew over. There were many times I wanted to punch my way out of this bag—for months on end I would be unfaithful, following any new sprite, and then be lured back into the prison under construction or constriction. Since finishing I've been writing funk lyrics for a friend's band in a liberating play with genre. Though there's a new bind—I'm kept awake at night by rhyme schemes. Which at least is a change from what I may have neglected at work. Because I tend to be asked about it, I want to take that cue and finish by saying something about the relationship between poetry and what I do for a living, which is trying to improve mental health services in East London.

My work life is governed, harried, by instrumental reason. This is a familiar lot, as much so for someone working as I do in mental health as for an academic teaching English Literature, and in each case is similarly and infuriatingly perverse. The evidence for effectiveness of particular interventions in mental health remains a site of ideological conflict as least as strenuous as anything in critical theory and of rather more acute consequence for their objects—a word I use advisedly. Few could describe themselves as survivors of literary criticism with the moral legitimacy of survivors of psychiatry.

All my acts must be goal-directed; it is expected I should be clear regarding their aims—or indeed 'my' aims which also are 'our' aims because they are presumed to be incontestable and self-evident—; my acts should produce measurable outcomes, which is to say identifiable and predictable effects. Predictability is paramount, and this is the prevailing characteristic of a managerialism which saturates our lives. 'Our' indeed, for managerialism does not only 'impact' as we say on the lives of managers or even those formally occupied in work or as students, but increasingly on the lives of the most socially marginalized (as we say also)—the margin being defined by its distance from a social text which has been formulated for consistency like a Starbuck's latte.

For example, government social initiatives focus on key predictors of disorderly conduct; the child of a single mother on a sink estate in Tower Hamlets will be subject to a range of programmes from the cradle into late adolescence in the interests of his or her social inclusion, in the interests of diverting his or her environmentally predictable course into a course predicted by well-researched social programmes.

- And this is what we shall do
- But it is only through partnership
- We can deliver. We make no excuses
- For asking for a clear return
- On the hard-earned money people
- Like you and me contribute

And so on.

As the managerial discourses come to pervade the institutions of personal development, health, social improvement and education, irruptions of a range of older political and developmental discourses become increasingly embarrassing. This does not apply simply to the language of those who subscribe still to the grand narratives of modernism, Marxist or Freudian, but to any language evidently delivering an excess or leaving a remnant. *Evidently* since despite progress in promoting a bleached and instrumental prose—this government's official documents are consistent in style with Blair's speeches—language always says more than its authors intend; even its impoverishment has something additional to say. When the Department of Health sets up a High Security Oversight Group, the oversight that can allow such a name is telling of a failure to think of how others listen, betraying arrogance as well as a lack of humour.

The language of determinable output and the extraction of the last pound of surplus value and an unmitigated, censorious moralism (whose difference from morality is clear in, for a recent instance, our government's denial of the Armenian holocaust or persistence in sanctions against Iraq), these seem to me to be connected intimately. What will this or that act or act of speech produce? For acts to be accountable, their side-effects must be controlled rigorously. For their side-effects to be controlled, the latitude of their performers must be ever more constricted. Against this it remains important to assert that the journey matters more than the arrival, for the arrival is at best disappointing and at its most predictable, deadly. To feel alive means to say, I went looking for this or that which I thought I wanted, and instead I found something which mattered to me far more.

For me poetry is exemplary in that respect, and these remarks followed from my asking myself: What does it mean to be ashamed to write poetry? For an audience to be embarrassed for the poet? To be ashamed to acknowledge 'being a poet'? (The poet Denise Riley writes about linguistic unease, something wider, but I doubt that John le Carré feels embarrassed to acknowledge he's a writer.) I've come to believe that shame attaches increasingly to ways of being which resist final translation into objects *out there* and their manipulation. Poems have a status as objects which seems to me peculiarly provisional by comparison with other written products, because they work where the outside obtrudes as air and food and where the inside runs its current and sets out its stall against the palate. Shame resides in the remnant, what we have been unable to leave behind or to consume cleanly. Embarrassment is felt in excess, in supplying too much. Which I think is where I should stop.

# Frostwork and The Mud Vision[94]

Published initially in the United States, Keith Tuma's 940-page *Anthology of Twentieth-Century British and Irish Poetry* brings a thoroughly revisionist assessment of twentieth century British and Irish poetry into uneasy cohabitation with a more conventional lineage. The volume's revisionism has two principal aspects. One consists of acts of retrieval of modernist and late modernist poems, implying a neglected or suppressed history, but without disrupting significantly the outlines of the story familiar from earlier anthologies. Chronologically this approach extends approximately from Thomas Hardy to Geoffrey Hill.

But just beyond the extensive selection from Hill will lie terra incognito so far as most previous anthologies and critical accounts go. The sequence which leads up to Seamus Heaney runs as follows: John Riley, Tom Raworth, R.F. Langley, Carlyle Reedy, E.A. Markham, John James, Lee Harwood. Hitherto these poets have been represented chiefly in anthologies which seek to map 'alternative' poetries, notably Michael Horowitz's *Children of Albion* (1969), Andrew Crozier and Tim Longville's *A Various Art* (1987), the 1988 Paladin anthology *The New British Poetry* and Iain Sinclair's 1996 *Conductors of Chaos*. From this point forward therefore, Tuma's book engineers a confluence between the 'alternative' and the 'mainstream' anthologies of the past, but one where the power lies decidedly with the previously marginalised, sweeping away (for instance) the present laureate, an established name like Peter Porter, and much-publicised younger writers such as Glyn Maxwell.

The retrieval aspect of Tuma's dual revisionism might discomfort one already initiated into the twitchers' world of rare pamphlets servicing an avant-garde avid for historical legitimacy. Amidst the massy and sometimes mossy monuments which previously had occluded their poems are glimpses now for a wider readership of the work of Mina Loy, Mary Butts, John Rodker, Lynette Roberts, J.G. Macleod, Nicholas Moore and Rosemary Tonks. How far do these glimpses persuade of a full body of light in the individual case, or reveal a secret and persistent modernist flame, often guttering but effulgent in the late 1960s from the work of such poets as Raworth and James?

There may be a largely harmless inclination to overvalue what has required patience, money and the right contacts to acquire; but prior to the editions of Rodker and Moore edited recently by the poets Andrew Crozier and Peter Riley there has seemed a reluctance to share these recondite enthusiasms.[95] The pleasures of Masonic secrecy and recognition may have been influential, but the reluctance has extended to a reticence in self- and group promotion among those who claim the heritage, compounded of a post-1960s revulsion from the marketplace and a reluctance to imply any inadequacy in the specifically poetic discourse and exchange through framing it by critical discourse.[96]

How such qualms would be estimated by Simon Armitage and Robert Crawford requires no speculation. The introduction to their *Penguin Book of Poetry from Britain and Ireland since 1945*, entitled 'The Democratic Voice', acclaims the sweeping away of 'the mandarin tone', the classical allusions, the public-school-coded speech, with an anti-establishment and anti-intellectual zeal more Thatcherite than socialist. Armitage and Crawford would approve the lack of reliance on academic discourse, but in favour of poetry which clearly addresses 'issues' and reflects 'diversity' while demonstrating that 'the right words need to be in the right order'. This indeed is the diversity of the marketplace and operative within tight limits; the verse of their favoured contemporaries has reached its apotheosis among advertisements for cashmere in *The New Yorker*—a product placement which relies on the assumption that we can recognise a poem and can read unproblematically within the conventions of magazine-browsing.

This assumption of a common reader for poetry has become ever more improbable—and for new poetry is probably nothing but wishful thinking. The primacy of a 'mainstream' continues only in myth which serves both those poets whose work is reviewed alongside new novels, and those who define their work in perky opposition to such an emblem of complacency, whether from a literary avant-garde or from a feminist, queer or ethnically specific angle. To this extent Armitage and Crawford's principle of diversity is sensible; such an anthology should allow a pulpit to each of a hundred sects. The disappointment is the narrowness of a diversity which depends on the fantasy of a common reader and a common practice of reading, and where difference adds no more than a novel flavouring to the noodle pot.

Still, the suspicion of brand snobbery attends the retrieval of pamphlets as much as that of rare soul singles; and with time the passion for the obscure can be stalked by a troubling affection for the most despised chart successes. To reach for a comparison: is the work of the Welsh modernist poet Lynette Roberts (b.1909) more interesting or more valuable than the work of the more linguistically conservative Welsh poet R.S. Thomas (b.1913), the former being the exclusive choice of Tuma and the latter the exclusive choice of Armitage and Crawford? A reader's answer to this question will say much about where she conceives value in poetry to lie.

> These men have brothers,
> Are wived. And in dredging buckets of steam
> Through stable-showers, men sway with the slush,
> Dreamwhile teeming out cables and rope
> Stretch barb wire tight across the crimped moon.
>
> Wringing out moisture from mind and mouth,
> Pulverizing a haze to gauze their contorted feature,
> Inebriate mouths cratered: others with lime fresh
> On briared cheeks cut Easter Island shadows, elongating
> Into weathered struts that strain all clouds for height.
>
> [Lynette Roberts, 'Gods with Stainless Ears', IV, 59–68]


> Iago Prytherch his name, though, be it allowed,
> Just an ordinary man of the Welsh hills,
> Who pens a few sheep in a gap of cloud.
> Docking mangels, chopping the green skin
> From the yellow bones with a half-witted grin
> Of satisfaction, or churning the crude earth
> To a stiff sea of clouds that glint in the wind—
> So are his days spent, his spittled mirth
>
> Rare than the sun that cracks the cheeks
> Of the gaunt sky perhaps once in a week.
>
> [R.S. Thomas, 'A Peasant', stanza 1 of 2]

The second excerpt exemplifies the requirement that all words should be in the right order. Its few polysyllables unravel from the mocked name: "Iago Prytherch" (the 'y' has a short 'a' sounding in Welsh), "ordinary man", "docking mangels", "satisfaction"". Masculine, monosyllabic (although irregular) rhymes pinion the verse's human object, much as he is produced and pinioned by the ungenerous landscape. The position of the poet is one of command, of thoroughly exercised disposition.

The first excerpt is from a long poem published by Faber in 1951 and long unobtainable in its full text.[97] This poetry is at once more sociable and more abstract, with labour here represented both as a jostlingly close group activity and as dominating the landscape through its distorted representation in lunar and poetic shadows. Similarly the relationship between the verse and what it represents is "dreamwhile"—it attends but exaggerates, distorts, overreaches, over-condenses and diverts. A strong preference for one or the other verse excerpt will indicate reliably whether a reader will in general prefer Tuma's revisionist canon or one or another account of the longer-established canon. In passing it might be observed that a judgment on the more 'democratic voice' between the modernist Roberts and the relatively plain-spoken Thomas is far from an obvious call.

While a taste for Roberts or for Thomas may be symptomatic, not all of Tuma's choices between retrieval of the obscure and acknowledgment of earlier taste are so discriminating (whichever side of the discrimination one finds the more attractive). Is Nicholas Moore a more considerable poet than George Barker, or even a more interesting one? Not on the evidence of the poems presented by Tuma, floppy variants of Wallace Stevens and the already floppy enough English surrealists, although Armitage and Crawford's feeble selection from Barker might leave the otherwise unacquainted reader indifferent. But this is perhaps to ask the wrong question, for the glimpse of light afforded by—to take a perfect instance of the slender corpus—the poetry of Clere Parsons (b.1908) does indeed exercise an extraordinary and poignant power after the pages of Louis MacNeice (b.1907) which it follows, simply by virtue of its nimbleness. Here, in poems written during the early 1930s, was a turn not taken (Parsons died at the age of 23) which connects back to the sprightly Mina Loy writing in the early 1920s, and forward to little enough in British and Irish poetry—perhaps to the early writing of the younger Black Mountain poets in the Unites States during the mid-1950s, with the delicacy of lyrics by Edward Dorn and John Wieners?

Tuma's diligence encourages such musing rather, perhaps, than estimates of worthiness.

This points to a difference in the manner of reading enjoined by each of the three anthologies. Armitage and Crawford's is a dipping anthology for a reader whose time is pressed; one principle of selection appears to have been that the poems should not require footnoting to make them readily accessible. Brief headnotes are supplied for each poet, but the information is confined to short biographies and there is no ambition to represent the work of a poet. Since one poem is the ration of the majority of poets, even their biographical paragraphs seem redundant, especially as the failure to date poems means there may be a fifty-year span of uncertainty as to the time and the particular experience on which a poem draws.

Edna Longley's contemporary Bloodaxe anthology focuses on "intense lyrics", as her introduction announces, and certainly can be used for dipping; it also is free of footnotes except to translate a few dialect words. The headnotes, however, amount to short essays on the poets, each of whose work is represented generously; read across the anthology they amount to a highly partisan account and evaluation of twentieth-century British and Irish poetry. The number of poets she selects is relatively small, and the essay introductions encourage reading and appreciating one poet's work at a time. An advantage of Longley's approach is its implicit acknowledgment that reading poetry differs from other forms of reading and, what is more, that there may be different sets of poetic conventions requiring a reader to discover how best to read the work of a particular poet or group of poets.

Tuma's anthology is more academic in two senses. In the first sense it is a teaching resource, providing extensive headnotes together with footnotes (some amusingly misleading) of a manic pertinacity which reduces the Norton anthologies to also-rans.[98] Each poem is dated both by date of composition (where known) and first publication. The only deficiency from a teacher's perspective is the absence of a bibliography or a list of recommended reading. It is academic in a different sense in being an anthology for researchers, poets and oddball enthusiasts, best appreciated by those who already know the main literary-historical features of its terrain. Unwieldily, for such a readership this vast anthology will come into its own if read consecutively from cover to cover.

For the joy of the Tuma book lies in its conjunctions; not just the shaft of light afforded by Parsons after the trudge through MacNeice, but the straightforward arrangement by date of poet's birth also places

Tony Harrison (b.1937, Leeds, glittering career with the National Theatre, pioneer of the televised long poem) alongside John Riley (b.1937, Leeds, and murdered there in 1978), the former writing in a vigorous and often obscene Leeds demotic and the latter celebrating his Russian Orthodox belief in a precise and aestheticised Poundian lightscape. Who could have anticipated that Bob Cobbing, the visual/sound poet for whom the Cabaret Voltaire never shut its doors, would afford some disturbance in the chronological space between Keith Douglas and Philip Larkin?

Such pleasures are less pronounced in the post-Geoffrey Hill part of the book since there the polemical pitch becomes more evident; where the 'diversity' celebrated by Armitage and Crawford is sociological, Tuma is drawn to diversity of linguistic procedure in a way which smacks of an unconsidered modernist progressivism. Tuma's preferences could be better characterised as late modernist than post-modernist; after all, an historically and nationally-organised anthology could hardly be post-modernist, even if the art of retrieval and re-reading opens such mischievous questions as whether Drew Milne (b.1964) might not have invented Mina Loy (b.1882), or Veronica Forrest-Thomson (b.1947) have invented William Empson (b.1906)? There is a tension here connected with the geographical boundary; that retained, it might have been valuable (for example) to wrest the sometimes excellent John Burnside from the clutches of Armitage and Crawford, and to demonstrate a vigorous filiation from the early 'political' Auden through the poetry of James Fenton. Removal of the geographical boundary, consistent with modernist internationalism, might have resulted in an anthology closer to the 'gallery' sections of the invaluable (but often preposterously gung-ho, as another formal constraint falls) two-volume Rothenberg and Joris *Poems for the Millennium*, associating clusters of poets across geographical and national boundaries.[99]

Tuma's compromises seem as much temperamental as contrived. His tastes incline to what might be termed frostwork poets, frostwork being window glass which is semi-opaque through its decoration; that is, poets whose writing exhibits a sustained balance between linguistic surface and reference to an external or internal world, roughly equivalent to the Roberts verse discussed above. Clearer referentiality is mostly eschewed, although an exception is made for black poets—and here it could be argued that for most of Tuma's American readers, his bias towards poems using patois/dub speech and poems where white and black linguistic usage are brought into sharp confrontation ensures a certain opacity. In the other direction, only Caroline Bergvall's extraordinary transcribed mouthings might seem to occlude the windowpane entirely, but it is noteworthy that the selections from Bergvall, Maggie O'Sullivan and chris cheek—perhaps the most 'avant-garde' poets included—are voiced and corporeal in their linguistic procedures rather than textual. This both represents a real difference between North American and British avant-garde poetry (which could be traced back to the qualities which distinguish Basil Bunting from the American Objectivists), and at the same time exaggerates it; for it would have been possible for Tuma to select British poetry displaying stronger affinities with US L=A=N=G=U=A=G=E writing of the 1980s and 1990s.[100]

Consideration of national characteristics in poetry might be focused sharply by reading Edna Longley's tendentious *Bloodaxe Book of 2oth Century Poetry*. The dominant note ideologically is struck in the introduction with the statement that "Country poetry (poetry that turns a particular locality into a microcosm) reflects on older communal meanings in a way that questions modern living." Preambles to selections from individual poets reiterate this point tirelessly; it is one thing (if a little stomach-turningly Blairite) to read that "Hardy's 'Wessex' microcosm turns his personal hauntings into a communal narrative", worse to be subjected to the summary that "[The Waste Land's] literary quotations and jumbled languages…mourn a lost wholeness", tiresome to nod at the assertion that "Lawrence wrote many kinds of poem…including poems (sometimes in dialect) that recreate the Nottinghamshire of his childhood", and quite intolerable to collude in the shrinkage of Auden's "own imaginative landscape" to the limestone of Staffordshire. Longley's other idée fixe is that "…war poetry was a central 2oth century genre". This was fortunate indeed for Isaac Rosenberg, war providing the requisite larks and mud where confinement to the dismal "modern living" of East London might have deprived him of that vital microcosmic stuff. Even Ciaran Carson's "[ultra-] urban poetry gives a new twist to the rural parochial microcosm as developed by Seamus Heaney"—presumably because, since he is Irish, nothing can deprive him of his "wonderfully flexible poetic microcosm" (property of the rather cosmopolitan Paul Muldoon also).

After a tract of this stuff (demeaning to the poetry so recommended) the reader longs for a poetry which questions, mocks or tramples "older communal meanings". But this is not, she is advised, a suitable thing for poetry to do, "modern living" being held accountable for the appalling state of things whereby "'post-modernist' poets are praised for highlighting the instability of language itself. Some of this thinking seems anti-poetic and anti-creative (besides being disproved by 20th century poetry in practice)." Reassuring that twentieth-century poetry 'disproves' anything.

Such Eeyorishness aside, Longley's is an exceptionally artful anthology, constructed so as to channel the reader towards acceptance that the triumvirate of Seamus Heaney, Michael Longley and Derek Mahon stands at the high-water mark of British and Irish twentieth-century poetry. Longley's selection of female poets immediately following this group seems so indifferent that it is impossible to believe her sympathies extend beyond that male, Northern Irish apogee. Her selection justifies her judgement. After the rain and tears of Edward Thomas ("Rain, midnight rain, nothing but the wild rain | On this bleak hut, and solitude, and me | Remembering again that I shall die" etc.) and the obsessional reterritorialising of Geoffrey Hill's verse whose rhyming nails to the Christian cross and stanzas crowd the sacred earth with imbricated history and myth, the controlled mellifluousness of the Northern Irish selection is a grateful pleasure. Neither maundering like Thomas or MacNeice nor stricturing like Hill, in each poem the verse-line threads expertly through a world of objects and feelings, firmly centred and confident. This limits the achievement as well, as a comparison with Andrew Crozier's phenomenologically far more subtle and equally beautiful 'The Veil Poem' (selected by Tuma) helps to demonstrate; a poem such as Mahon's celebrated 'A Disused Shed in Co. Wexford' reads comparatively as though it was already a set text before it was published and adopted.

Seamus Heaney appears in the Longley selection as a poet whose impulses and ambition exceed his convictions, eternally launching and pulling back, and 'The Mud Vision' is a poem which could be read as making a deliberate commitment to reaching 'the clarified place', turning away from the vision which bears "Our one chance to know the incomparable | And dive to a future." Politically and particularly in the Northern Irish setting such a choice is advanced as only responsible, especially for a poet who must know whenever he sets pen to paper that he is seen by many as the embodiment of all that is positive in the province, and that the likes of Edna Longley are determined to box him into his microcosm. This choice of an oddly comfortable disillusion might indeed be a moral necessity if no options were available outside either a totalising, bardic strain or such decently modest humanism. Surely, though, not all doubt, ambiguity and ambivalence need to be

conscientiously picked apart and accounted for in this way, a careful
decision made on the evidence and in the circumstances? Or to use
another of the poem's oppositions, other choices surely exist besides
either 'origin' or 'news'?

Certainly they do, and range from Lynette Roberts' or (closer to the
bardic) Dylan Thomas' lyric shadowing of the natural and social world
through Andrew Crozier's recognition that

> Here at the centre of every intersecting circle
> each infinite yet wholly itself
> whichever way you turn a way is offered
> for you to carry yourself, its knowledge
> will inundate you unless it is held
> along every inch of your skin...

[Andrew Crozier, 'The Veil Poem', ll 77–82]

(leading Crozier later to a strict formalism which Tuma's anthology
unfortunately does not sample), to the *Gesamtkunstwerk* of J.H. Prynne,
wherein human agency is formed and delivered chemically and ethno-
graphically as well as rhetorically.[101] Although Veronica Forrest-
Thomson in *Poetic Artifice* points the finger of blame for English poetic
dullness at Larkin for his "bad naturalism", the combined impression of
the three anthologies suggests first that this is too derogatory of Larkin
(although Forrest-Thomson was writing at the apogee of his influence,
when his sardony was received with solemn literalism), and secondly
that the most influential agent of a middlebrow humanism for which
ease and stability of reception constitutes an ethical good was the BBC
radio producer Louis MacNeice.

Tuma's selection from MacNeice allows nothing published after 1938,
but already in 'Carrickfergus' the characteristic pseudo-elegiac tone of
the later verse is beginning to emerge; this will split into two main variants, one a slightly mocking and superior treatment of popular culture
and its ephemera, and the other reflecting with melancholy on the
poet's own transience as an observer of the ephemeral. His injunction in
'Mayflies'—"Let us too make our time elastic and | Inconsequently dance
above the dazzling wave"—his entire corpus seems determined to abjure
in favour of a self-conscious resignation. Fulfilment of the injunction
might conjure up a very different poet—Frank O'Hara, for instance, so
suggesting a damaging comparison between MacNeice's 'Death of an
Actress' (selected by Longley) and O'Hara's 'The Day Lady Died'. In

MacNeice's opening line "I see from the paper that Florrie Forde is dead" is heard the unmistakeable tone of the old bore at breakfast dismissively shaking The Times; there follows a patronising portrait of a popular singer and her audience "from slum and suburb", progressively sentimentalised as wartime is invoked, before crashing gears into full-blown nostalgia with the final stanza celebrating an innocent "older England". True Florrie Forde was no Billie Holliday, but O'Hara's genuinely democratic spirit, embracing the humblest of bit-part B-movie players, could never have entertained this tone of patrician dismissive appreciation of artiste and audience.

Philip Larkin will at times adopt a similar tone for its comic potential, complete with suspicion of foreigners and fancy-speaking intellectuals. It is a peculiar compulsion in MacNeice's poetic that it should take the reader down a peg or two, insisting that there's nothing new under the sun, nothing so exotic that it can't be made ordinary. You know that bloke Charon?

> We just jogged on, at each request
> Stop there was a crowd of aggressively vacant
> Faces, we just jogged on, eternity
> Gave itself airs in revolving lights…
>
> [Louis MacNeice, 'Charon', ll 9–12]

Of course it is provocatively unfair to blame MacNeice—or any one poet—for the reduced horizons of British and Irish poetry in the second half of the twentieth century, but when from their socio-political perspective Armitage and Crawford celebrate the Butler Education Act of 1944 as laying the ground for a "subtle, accessible and surprising poetry, communicating more directly with a wider public" it is worth asking what the poetry communicated, and whether the imperative to communicate cannot itself injure communication. This is not to propose that some of the more rebarbative poetry selected by Tuma could or should be foisted on a wider constituency; different poetries—like different musics—now address and respond to different constituencies, some very small. Armitage and Crawford's Buskellism takes as definitive the interests of a particular constituency, much as does the common sense of *The Daily Mail*; in their case that particular audience for which the larger British publishers reluctantly supply poetic product. No; what is regrettable is the prevalence of a certain patient, expository, faintly condescending manner which can injure a poem by Seamus Heaney, but also can infect work by the most ambitious late modernist poets of the mid-century, Roy Fisher and Charles Tomlinson.

The rather lowering experience of reading these three anthologies tends to reframe the concern which underlies the Penguin anthology's anxiety to communicate. Can a poetry be conceived—or even identified in these volumes—whose frostwork, meaning a perceptive and productive poetic artifice (to use Forrest-Thomson's term) operative in tension with an imparted reality, delivers condign intellectual, emotional and aesthetic rewards against the effort invested in its negotiation? This would suppose that the artifice cannot be so far the preoccupation of poetic practice that the poems repel all but a small audience of adepts, nor can the imparted reality be so far its object of attention that either there is insufficient artifice to detain the reader—for detaining can be a signal virtue in resistance to consuming—or to throw a new curve, an emotional and intellectual cadence. Or to frame the question in another way: is there a poetry in these volumes which is both as intelligent and moving as the novels of Henry Green or Elizabeth Bowen—or even as invigorating as the best of Martin Amis? For given the effort and the time required to learn the gestural repertoire of any poet's discourse, the rewards must be at least equal to those to be derived from such novels.

A reading of these anthologies proposes a look in the direction of W.S. Graham, a poet who seems oddly isolated in each of them.[102] As increasingly it seems probable that Frank O'Hara will be acclaimed as the greatest American poet of the twentieth century, the virtues of Graham's writing too are becoming more evident. The two poets have some improbably shared characteristics. One of these is contextual; although O'Hara lived in the thick of things in the world's highest-speed and most cosmopolitan city while Graham lived in the small village of Zennor at Land's End, both engaged daily with the work of painters who were at the forefront of their art. This engagement with painting seems especially significant, since for artists both of the New York School and the St Ives School there was nothing scholastic about attention to surface and technique—the relationship with paint and canvas (and other materials to hand) was sensual above all. Neither were the painters of either school as committed as were their critical promoters to 'pure' abstraction or figuration, but they understood that the dynamism of painting was enacted in the tension between surface artifice and referentiality. What they shared also was a powerful ethic of improvisation and discovery as well as tireless practice and preparation, for the latter is the precondition for the structure through which feel-ing can be expressed in the former. It is no accident either that this prescription brings to mind a great jazz improviser such as Charlie Parker—that is, a disciplined improviser referring to an historical body of work, rather than a 'free' improviser.

Connected with this involvement with the painting of disciplined improvisation, and of equal importance, is the poetic mode of address, the greatest poems of both O'Hara and Graham being addressed to friends and lovers. Reading the anthologies, it can feel as though the lyric poetry of the twentieth-century has been harried past endurance by the problem of the first person singular, the lyric 'I', variously by its pomposity, its frailty, its pretensions and its inadequacy. This cannot be evaded by extirpation of the cursed pronoun, for the depersonalised poem tends to then lay claim to an overweening authority. The first person plural tends to a presumption of common cause or sensibility with the smug or wheedling 'I', and the second person singular or plural to arraign the reader or society from the vantage of the arrogant 'I'.

Four lyric poets have produced work which suggests ways out of this dilemma. One is Prynne, through the poetic construction of counter-factual universes.[103] His work may, however, remain inaccessible to all but a few readers.[104] A second is the Portuguese poet Fernando Pessoa through the invention of internally-consistent heteronymic identities. A third, derived from Whitman but with a first person singular splitting, recombining, delirious and transported, is O'Hara. His kinship with Graham lies in the contingency of identity and its sustaining grace being dependent on 'you'. Being more dependent than O'Hara on communication by letter, Graham's full tone is epistolary—it is the love letter to a removed person, whether an artist friend who has died or to his wife sleeping or in the past. The constant sustaining of the speaking self through love, its construction interpersonally, is what makes Graham's 'I' uniquely trustworthy. O'Hara's 'I' on the other hand is highly mercurial, irresistible and enlivening in a way which is charm-ingly promiscuous.

Yet one might look almost in vain for evidence that later poets have learned from Graham; even the work of Tony Lopez, who wrote a pioneering book on Graham, shows no signs of influence. An exception is Denise Riley, although the Tuma selection does not demonstrate this clearly; her speaking self, however, is constructed largely through the hesitancies and gaps of an internal, self-arraigning conversation where the sense of self is always on the edge of collapse. What does sustain it both internally and externally is an affection for the lyric 'I' of popular song, whether Motown or (as in Tuma's selection) Gardner's *The Ballad Minstrelsy of Scotland* (1893), which either is called or comes involuntarily to aid or to deflate the authorial 'I'. As with Graham and O'Hara, this is a highly sophisticated way of having your cake and eating it—of being enabled to employ a direct lyric address while registering its complications. Indeed this is why lyric poetry may continue to be worth someone's time—neither a conundrum nor a tricked-out platitude, but a way, even, of compounding complex thought and feeling through an artifice which is more than adequate to their recognisable demands.

Unlike Longley's, Tuma's anthology does not channel the reader towards a particular poet or group of poets. The advantage it possesses over both Longley and Armitage and Crawford is that its diversity can be recognised to emerge as a delta of possibilities from numerous feeders and subterranean streams, where to identify a main channel becomes plainly a judgment of taste—or in a word, ideological. An instance of the fortuitous in such diversity is the selection from David Dabydeen's 'Turner' alongside Randolph Healy's 'Colonies of Belief'; the black poet's epic historical imagination might suggest to the reader a link to Irish anti-colonialist poetry earlier in the century such as Patrick Kavanagh's 'The Great Hunger', while the younger Irish poet's discourse on colonialism takes the improbable form of a sustained Empsonian scientific conceit. Such linkages frustrate teleology while extending possibilities beyond the presently imaginable, and it is in this that the Tuma anthology's special value may prove to lie.

# The Water-Rail of Tides[105]

In his 2001 *Anthology of Twentieth-Century British and Irish Poetry*, Keith Tuma unveils a jostle of unmitigated modernists, blighted youths, and marginalised women and minorities, all of them fighting for space with the respectable, the canonical, and the representative. Tuma's most valuable recoveries concentrate in the mid-century and testify in several instances to T.S. Eliot's bold generosity as a poetry editor at Faber & Faber. One such recovery is the Argentine-born Welsh poet Lynette Roberts. Tuma publishes two sections from her second volume, a book-length poem titled *Gods with Stainless Ears* that Roberts wrote during the Second World War but did not publish until 1951. In doing so he reintroduces a poet who had seemed doomed to irremediable obscurity.

Roberts, vulnerable to schizophrenia, suffered a breakdown in 1956 and was repeatedly hospitalised thereafter, living in poverty around Carmarthen Bay, near Swansea, until her death in 1994. A 1998 *Collected Poems* from the Welsh publisher Seren was pulped upon issue when her family took offence at its preface. *Gods with Stainless Ears* seemed destined to forever circulate in photocopies among graduate students and poets with a taste for the recondite. Now at last arrives a handsome, elegantly introduced, and tactfully annotated *Collected Poems* from Carcanet, to be followed by a prose collection, both edited by Patrick McGuinness. And now Roberts can finally be recognised as the author of an outstandingly important long poem and a small group of fine lyrics.

From an historical perspective, there are four obvious ways to classify, and thus understand, Roberts: as British, as Welsh, as a woman, and as a war poet. McGuinness's introduction provides a good orientation, though he seems uneasy about her elusiveness and overstates her indebtedness to Pound through Charles Olson. Tuma discerned a link between Roberts and the British New Apocalyptic poets of the 1940s, placing her alongside Dylan Thomas and Edith Sitwell, their Romantic fustian keeping the snug bar warm amidst postwar austerity and social conformism. The young Lynette Roberts was friendly with Sitwell (to whom she dedicated *Gods with Stainless Ears*), sketched by Wyndham Lewis, married to the Welsh nationalist poet Keidrych Rhys, and correspondent to Robert Graves. This matrix fits well with her highly localised modernism, intent on reanimating bodies of tradition to resist a planned and administered world.

The first stanza of "Poem from Llanybri", which opens Roberts's first book, *Poems* (1944), constitutes a short manifesto of her localism. But its idiosyncratic usages (such as "swank" as a transitive verb and the suppression of conventional punctuation) align her poetics more with modernism than with the warmed-over Georgianism still promoted even today in Britain and Ireland:

> *If you come my way that is . . .*
> Between now and then, I will offer you
> A fist full of rock cress fresh from the bank
> The valley tips of garlic red with dew
> Cooler than shallots, a breath you can swank
>
> In the village when you come.

Embodiment of tradition may be linguistic—as is customary in post-chapel, post-socialist Wales, reflected in Roberts's use of Welsh-language epigraphs as well as English-language dialect—or it may be mythological, essentially gendered, or even technological. Roberts's village mix evolved into a radical but conservatively inclined communitarianism, shocked and jolted by electricity, industry, and concentrated bombing.

*Gods with Stainless Ears* is a home-front work that may be set alongside Elizabeth Bowen's wartime short stories and Virginia Woolf's *Between the Acts*, and it stands as Roberts's chief claim to contemporary attention. Unlike her metropolitan contemporaries, Roberts wrote from the hinterland of a provincial city, the port of Swansea, whose incineration reddened the horizon from her Carmarthenshire hamlet of Llanybri. The difference in perspective is yet sharper than this suggests, for Roberts, born in Buenos Aires to a family that had for generations lived in Australia, nonetheless agreed with Welsh nationalists in perceiving Wales as an occupied country. There is no sense in the poem that this is her war; rather, it is the war of "TAWDRY LAIRDS AND JUGGLERS OF

MINT", of "a jingle of Generals | And Cabinet Directors", "those hanker-
ing | After pig standards of gold" whose troops drunkenly tear down the
Welsh flag. The life of conscripts is represented as sheer waste, with men
slopping out their own urinals when not brawling among themselves.
Roberts shared local resentment that children from the slums of East
London had been evacuated to village homes, making it impossible to
take in Welsh children once Swansea became a target of German bombing. For her poem's hero (and it is subtitled "A Heroic Poem"), Roberts
crashes a solitary fighter pilot, an archetypal figure of modernity for
poets of the early 1930s, and makes him Jewish. There is no way she
could have allowed him to be English.

The wartime economy, once sentimentalised for its solidarity and
now for freeing women from housework into industrial jobs, was for
Roberts a trampling of local culture by the mobilised state and the
harbinger of an economy globalised to compete with the Soviet sphere.
Loving couples were torn from each other in the interests of war and
productivity. The poem's dystopian final section, with its vision of
"Chromium Cenotaphs– | Work and pay for all!", sees the figure of
Keidrych Rhys, identified by his military serial number, consigned to a
concentration camp emblazoned with the words "*Mental Home For Poets*".
No wonder, in a country clinging to its wartime mythology as empire and
economic ascendancy slipped away, that Roberts's poem was unwelcome—
as unwelcome as Henry Green's *Concluding* (1948), with its authoritarian
boarding school for girls redolent of similar disenchantment.

Roberts's view of the home front is therefore greatly at odds with a
London perspective. As for gender, Roberts was decidedly not a feminist
in the conventional sense; she regarded childbearing both as biological
destiny and as the focus of human hope for the future, echoing the
general perspective—though not the eugenicism—of Mina Loy, her poetic
forebear. In Part V of the poem, set on a cloud in the fourth dimension,
Roberts elaborates a startling vision of homemaking as female techné.
While her lover pores over "wooden table and glazed chart", she
becomes a kind of cosmic housewife, in

> Sandals and swimsuit lungs naked to the light,
> Sitting on chair of glass with no fixed frame
> Leaned to the swift machine threading over twill:
> 'Singer's' perfect model scrolled with gold,
>
> Chromium wheel and black structure, firm on
> Mahogany plinth. Nails varnished with

Chanel shocking! Ears jewelled: light hand
Tipped with dorcas' silver thimble tracing thin
Aertex edge:

Although horrified by the rational and administrative brand of so-called Fabian British socialism, Roberts treated technology as ideologically neutral; hence, chromium's modern gleam can be either baleful or attractive. Her descriptions of landscapes integrate the organic and mechanical, not just symbolically or through visual confusion, with birds, aeroplanes and angels occupying the same stratum, but with such tight formulations as "sprockets of kale". Like "lime stud | Whitening fields, gulls and stones attending them", these rivets punctuate a text more characterised by flux, whether driven by ambivalence or contradiction. Ambivalence is exemplified in a line repeated variously in Part I: "Into euclydian cubes grid air is planed", "grid air" successively becoming "tempered air" and "carol air". Air's organisation might entail the reduction of the empyrean to plotted air lanes but might also express the tempered and cadenced air of song—and of lyric poetry in its stanzaic blocks and lilt.

But Roberts's prosody insists on her work being read as more than an historical document, and it needs a clearer context than either Patrick McGuinness or Keith Tuma provides. Roberts cites Welsh-language models, and neither editor makes anything of her reference in Part V of *Gods with Stainless Ears* to "Caribbean Crane", which the poet glosses as a reference to Hart Crane. And if her long poem resembles any other, it is surely Crane's *The Bridge*. *The Bridge* plainly anticipates Roberts in its natural and mechanical hybridity ("Invisible valves of the sea"), in its curious mixture of abstraction and visual detail ("Down Wall, from girder into street noon leaks, | A rip-tooth of the sky's acetylene"), and in its cosmic architecture ("abysmal cupolas of space"). The resemblance extends to construction, both poems being tensed between forward impetus and the drag exercised by involuted stanzas. Roberts also picks up Crane's cinematographic scrolling, announcing in her preface that "scenes and visions ran before me like a newsreel", and in the sci-fi Part V (first published as "Cwmcelyn" in *Poems*) she anticipates Powell and Pressburger's 1946 film *A Matter of Life and Death*, both in its theme and its swooping galactic takes. Consider the following stanzas from Part I:

In fear of fate, flying into land Orcadian birds pair
And peal away like praying hands; bare
Aluminium beak to clinic air; frame

Soldier lonely whistling in full corridor train,
Ishmaelites wailing through the windowpane,

O the cut of it, woe sharp on the day
Scaled in blood, the ten-toed woodpecker,
A dragon of wings 1 6 2 0 B 6
4 punctuates machine-gun from the quarry pits:
Soldiers, tanks, lorry make siege on the bay.

Freedom to boot. CONCLAMATION. COMPUNCTION.
Kom-pungk'-shun: discomforts of the mind deride
Their mood. Birds on the stirrups of the waterbride
Flush up, and out of time a tintinnabulation
Of voice and feather fall in and out of the ocean sky.

On one level "frame" and "cut" work as film directions, but these stanzas energise levels as shifting layers, giving rise to meteorological circulation. Precise observation is caught up in dynamic metaphor reminiscent of Percy Bysshe Shelley, then surpassing any realistic imagery with such a phrase as "the stirrups of the waterbride". This imaginative move anticipates the counterfactual poetics of Paul Celan or J.H. Prynne. While rhyme shapes inventions like "waterbride", punning produces the deeply sardonic "freedom to boot", associating "freedom" with conscription and violence. Every verbal and visual element interacts so that the woodpecker fades into a dragon—the symbol of Welsh nationhood—which in turn fades into a helicopter. The Cranian capitalisation, in its assertive textuality, receives mocking enunciation, like a sergeant major taunting an intellectual.

Anglo-American literary modernism, which challenges realism through its attention to perceptual process, has descended through two main channels. One has led to the decadent lyric of personal authenticity, which relates all to a self whose model trustworthiness is supported by mention of parents and children and by tireless re-enactments of infantile and adolescent trauma. Another has led to the varieties of social and linguistic constructivism that embrace structuralism, poststructuralism, postcolonialism, certain strands of feminism, and queer theory. Beside these channels stand blocked capillaries, which might expand to receive some of the force now channelled into self-authenticating or Language poetry. If they did, conceivably one might pulse with sociolinguistic intensities—that is, language as it occupies subjects and subjects as they occupy language. Through its clenching but still mobile stanzas, *Gods with Stainless Ears* incorporates Roberts's hyper-responsiveness to the languages that impinged on her.

For Roberts, such intensities might be found in village dialect, in the idiolects of physical intimacy, and in the jargons of chemistry and technology. A poetry of intensities consistent with her communitarianism demanded a respect for repetition and persistence, while gathering new intensive folds of its own. In *Gods with Stainless Ears,* Roberts achieves this formally through "the water-rail of tides", the combing motion of "parallel nerves" and "hurting lines" whose propulsion is peristaltic, immutably in place while also pressing forward. The poem's archetypal couple, evidently Lynette and Keidrych, produces a child through her forcefully described contractions. By such deep wave motions the poem holds; it is *slatched,* to use a characteristic Roberts word-retrieval signifying the dips between wave crests. Such force drives a lyricism neither sentimentally individualist nor carcerally constructivist. It is worthy of emulation and extension.

But *Gods with Stainless Ears* is not the sum of Lynette Roberts's achievement. *Collected Poems* rescues from an unpublished third book a few short lyrics of a distressing exigency, as we see in "Englyn":

> Where poverty strikes the pavement—there is found
>   No cripple like contentment
> Which stultifies all statement
> Of bright thought from the brain's tent.

Through its obtrusive use of rhyme as a semantic motor, this writing anticipates uncannily the manner of John Wieners, the great Boston poet of the second half of the 20th century, and especially his 1970 book *Nerves*. It is intriguing that Roberts's rhyming hews to the Welsh form of *Englyn unodl union* to accommodate an effect that in both poets recalls 'clang association', a linking together of words by sound that psychiatry regards as symptomatic of schizophrenia. Such deeply embedded affinities across time and culture suggest that lyric feeds on a biological substrate. By the same token, modernist poets can never resist the importuning of traditional modes, often seemingly more wayward than Roberts's local attentiveness.

Lynette Roberts's writing faltered not only for personal reasons, but because in postwar Britain there was no one to hear it. Tradition came to mean a common-sense parochialism, and modernism became academic.

# Following the Poem

## or, Misty Thoughts on Winnicott, Celan, and Shelley

One kind of writing about contemporary poetry is preoccupied with the meaning of difficulty, and how texts whose difficulty appears programmatic rather than incompetent or pathological, might most adequately be accounted for. Such writing has become frustrating for anyone recognising that 'difficulty' usually refers to a barrier we wish a critic to help us across rather than contemplate as an object in itself. The preliminaries to reading start to feel too self-protective of the critic: you want to insist that a poem isn't a cache of live ammunition, and the worst that can happen is that through a missed allusion, a dreadful ignorance of *The Tempest* might be exposed.

This essay limbers up towards a reading of some recent and heroically intractable poetry, but doesn't arrive, being detained by broad questions of how to follow a poem, and thinking through them with the help of some quite canonical examples. What might be found intractable is of course historically contingent and particular to a readership; widely accessible poems can become as problematic as those apt to advertise their difficulty. In a recent *London Review of Books* Adam Phillips wrote about the poems of Dylan Thomas, arguing that the pleasures of reading Thomas bypass the extraction of purified meaning which academic reading has often meant—the poems make sense in another way.[106] Oddly, in reviewing the collected *Poems* of J.H. Prynne, the most infamously difficult of British poets, Phillips relied on the same suggestion.[107] Oddly, because Dylan Thomas is a rare instance of a poet whose writing has influenced popular culture, and whose lines are familiar to many with no idea of their provenance — people feel his lines *say something* as the phrase goes, in a way they might not feel of Swinburne's poems, let alone John Ashbery's.

The argument here is that through following a poem (not just any poem), a reader can become involved in the evocation and enactment of a radical hybridity, pulling together ways of thinking about the world modernity has categorically but falsely separated; but such reading takes place in time, so continuously a reader unpicks and re-integrates elements of the poem in a felt motion which can restore a healed and full being in the world, involving in its fullness and as a condition of it, the detours, the lapses and the breaks in his or her journey. In music an analogy might be *stretto*, a squeezing-together in canon form at the end of a fugue, the compression or overlapping of musical material, in German 'Engführung'—the title of a poem by Paul Celan whose reading by Peter Szondi is this paper's starting point, since Szondi sought to trace exactly such a following of the poem.[108]

In approaching Paul Celan's 'Engführung' through Szondi's reading, this essay discerns an analogy with the British psychoanalyst D.W. Winnicott's efforts to describe how what he calls a transitional object leads towards the use of an object socially.[109] It is suggested that both Szondi and Winnicott experience great difficulty in staying true to the hybridity or transitional status of their objects: that while drawn towards a dense edge-world of intersubjectivity, each writer repeatedly reverts to a binarism exemplified by the subject/object divide. It is argued that 'Engführung' resists the more reductive moments of Szondi's reading, and a comparative example shows how a reduction of George Herbert's 'The Pulley' to the confines of a conceit, fails to take account of the intricate hybridity of Herbert's poem.

A diversion into Song dynasty China shows how even a court poetry contrived for reductive decoding, escaped such limits through its politically subversive use at the time, and subsequently through the obscuring of its intentions.

A phenomenological theory of prosody as cognition is then introduced, modified to provide a dynamic model of prosody as oscillating between inner object and external object, between rupture and integration—a model which marries well with Szondi's and Winnicott's dynamics of reading and individual development respectively. The essay finishes with a close reading of a passage from Shelley's 'Prometheus Unbound', showing the dynamics of its prosody.

Drawing on prosodic work by Simon Jarvis and Keston Sutherland, it is suggested that one way towards a substantial reality lies *through* a prosody, its materialising of the world,—not the *other side* of prosody, whereby a meaning residue is delivered, sense carefully dissected from sound. Prosody as cognition requires and enables the reader to follow the poem, cleaving to it as transitional. Such a journey is complex but need not be complicated: it can be accomplished joyfully, as with the poems of Frank O'Hara or of W.S. Graham, as well as in the powerfully engaging thinking-through enjoined by the poems of Paul Celan or of William Wordsworth. The journey connects a reader with a dense, inter-subjective world entirely distinct from postmodern filminess. Since some of the most compelling journeys of prosody as cognition can be embarked on through the poems of Percy Bysshe Shelley, the present excursion will lead us as far as the rock of Prometheus, with the present-day world just visible on the horizon, whelping its many exclusionary totalities—science here, spirit there with the scented candles.

...

Many people may share an unconsidered assumption that the imaginary or, in another context, poetic language represents a deviation from ordinary reality and ordinary language. They assume, that is, that ordinary reality and ordinary language represent and enact an instrumental relationship between human beings and their worlds, which poetry and the imaginary disrupt, pleasurably or less so.

Otherwise however is suggested by two remarkable essays, D.W. Winnicott's 'The Use of an Object and Relating though Identifications' and Peter Szondi's following of a poem by Paul Celan, 'Reading "Engführung"'.[110] In different ways they imply that a relationship with reality is hard-won, in poetic practice as in the world of the infant and then the adult.

Winnicott's writing was founded in a tension between his theoretical adherence to the work of Melanie Klein with its terrifying account of the inner life of the infant as driven by implacable greed and homicidal envy, and his work as a paediatrician interested in socialisation. How does a child develop from a furious, chewing and excreting bundle of fantasies into a more or less tolerable human being? Klein's account of the depressive position implies that the best we can achieve is a kind of lifelong sulk, nourished by more ingenious forms of psychic appropriation. On a large scale this doesn't seem so improbable: the way we live in the West sustains us in an infantilism of extracting greedily and spewing copiously. This is a kind of use which never knows its objects except as flows of commodities and rapid-disposal waste, and is based on relationships with objects (such as human beings, rivers and DVDs) rather than engagement with reality.

Taken together, Winnicott's and Szondi's essays suggest that the 'poetic' in the widest sense, whereby people contrive a world and its contents including those around them, might support (but does not at all guarantee) an edge-world materialised between a primary greed and a world of hallucinated and exploited objects. A prosody can continuously reunite and break the inner object from and to the outside, creating a thick, impure, and hybrid incorporation, a porous skinscape which is neither objective nor subjective. This zone may be termed hybrid not only because it is neither inside nor inside, but because it is at once cognitive and sensual.

Should this be true, poetry might offer the best-advantaged sites for work that journeys towards a reality beyond the exploitation of objects expelled from the edge-world; this is what Szondi struggles to undertake through or with Celan's poem "Engführung"; and the difficulty of the undertaking is demonstrated in the way his reading lurches between hailing now a linguistic autonomy and now an historical fidelity, only to concede their inseparability. Szondi wrestles constantly to determine the domain of reality to which "Engführung" pertains, while the journey of his reading exposes the poem's hybrid character. Similarly for Winnicott the *use* of an object requires that the transitional object, the found tatter a baby creates for himself from what is already there, has to be assigned a distinct domain ("part of shared reality") to then become available individually and socially. Such faltering in both the literary and psychoanalytical adventures is symptomatic of an underlying adherence to sets of binaries. These traduce Celan's poem in Szondi's reading towards this-side or that-side despite Szondi's best efforts, and leave Winnicott with a usable object out-there and a destructible but surviving object in-here while asserting simultaneously that "the object develops its own autonomy and life" through surviving destruction in fantasy. Since this fantasy factory is not the object's, even where the object might be a human subject, "autonomy" seems too strong. Both Szondi and Winnicott stimulate through their thinking, dichotomies that militate against the radical integration they seek to comprehend and enact. In practice their thought works in both directions at once.

Consider one passage in "Engführung" which Szondi follows, here translated by John Felsteiner:[111]

Am still the one—

Years.
Years, years, a finger
gropes down and up, gropes
all around:
sutures, palpable, here
it gapes wide open, here
it grew back together—who
covered it up?

The first answer to the poem's question is that a word covered up this caesura, this wound, 'covering up' here being studiedly ambiguous; but even if words are mere opinion or cover-up, a flurry of particles obscuring the wound, silence would be actively poisonous as the poem will later assert:

It was also written that.
Where? We
decked it in silence,
poison-hushed, huge,

Szondi is wonderful on the phenomenology of reading Celan: he describes "a landscape that is not merely the subject of what we are reading—it *is* what we are reading", and we recognise that, for instance, as we grope up and down, all around with this text. And again, "it is not only the words and phrases that must be *read*, but also, and perhaps above all, the relationships created between them by means of repetition, transformation, and contradiction". Less happily he refers to "the caesuras of inner time created within human beings by the past" as though a caesura were an incursion or lapse, a break opposed to continuity, where his argument has prepared us to acknowledge the caesura is as much a meeting point as a break.

This is important because breaks, caesuras, the black and white of writing, the activities of unity and sundering, are what compose this poem, which begins:

TAKEN OFF into
the terrain
with the unmistakable trace:

Grass, written asunder. The stones, white
with the grassblades' shadows:

and finishes:

> Taken off
> into the terrain
> with
> the unmistakable
> trace:
>
> Grass.
> Grass,
> written asunder.)

A flurry, mere linguistic shadows upon the stones, allows the stones to sing, gives the stones the power to mend the breech (these white stones of the poem); it is only through this prosody, this exquisitely meticulous placement, that the ground of being is marked, as its wounding and mending restitches us into a world of use but not of exploitation. Both our bodies and the world are produced through prosody:

> We
> could not let go, stood firm
> in the midst, a
> framework of pores, and
> it came
>
> Came up to us, came
> on through, it mended
> invisibly, mended
> on the final membrane,
> and
> the world, thousandfaced crystal,
> shot out, shot out.

Shot out only to face death by firing squad. And that is what this flurry of particles covers up and mends, and in being relinquished sets the white stones along the path our reading follows.

What leads to the "thousandfaced crystal"? What is the unspeakable "it"? There is a "We" here at the start, "a | framework of pores" — that's a 'we' alright, for the pores proclaim our permeability, and 'we' is the pronoun of exchange for which our pores provide a framework. (The Michael Hamburger translation has "porous building" which disturbs me by summoning breeze-blocks as well as flesh.) When "it" comes the pores are transformed into "the final membrane"—"it", in a strange turn of phrase, mended "on" the final membrane, the point of a decisive change of domain, for this membrane is a division, something mended "on", closed up and sealed, mended, but only to burst asunder. The "thousandfaced crystal" is "shot out" as the obdurate, objectified, separated world. In an astonishing turn, the world crystallises as a reflective, multi-sided otherness at the instant of death. The porous surface of exchange, of incorporation, evacuates the hardest, most gleaming thing imaginable. Maybe the soul which leaves us, restores our transacting world to the 'other side', that is to the world we no longer inhabit. But for Celan's poem to use the word "mends", given the "bullet trap" encountered later in the poem, seems shocking. It means the "we" of the poem do "let go", and we may also discern in the disembodied crystal the horror of the pure, objective and inhuman project.

This passage cannot be resolved so as to send the reader forward with a unified, reconciled and neatly extracted set of meanings. A reading cannot be authoritative because the steps of this poem between pores, frameworks, membranes, crystals and shots depend on its prosody—the poem is thinking, and my recounting can only strive to follow its thought rather than set out its products. But this short passage engages me in acts of exchange which are social, involves me in the porous human universe, reminding that the most alluring and beautiful of objects are deathly, at the last. Our bodies enter the object world when they are corpses. The objects of thought we extract from poems are mere stones until restored to prosody.

But why make such a fuss about subjects and objects? Surely information passes between us and the object-world all the time, more or less reliably, and not just the information we feel indifferent to or mildly interested in or quite excited by; but all that synaptic processing necessary for any personal construction of reality. And what each of us constructs seems to an important degree familiar, or at least we can distinguish strong dissonance from the reality we take for granted—and decide that it's mad or might be art or the birth of a new way of looking. But neuroscience proposes that at a level below or aside from consciousness, self and reality are indeed mutually shaping in ways driven by the survival requirements of the organism. No neat separation can be made between the organism and its environment. The fact that at the biological level our individual and social interests are framed anachronistically, through aggressive acquisitiveness and resource competition, is a reminder that greed and squander can bring consequences more severe than dire poetry, in the despoliation of the surroundings of which we are part. The way we use objects will determine our survival.

When Winnicott talks of the use of an object, he means something as particular as the real which Celan's poetry invents so it then may be recognised. Through following "Engführung" we come to know that a person, animal or thing is neither an object in our world nor an otherness, but can subsist in a relationship of equality, external from us but responsive to our responses. Analysis of this phenomenology has influenced the way we look at painting and in which painting is practised—it's hard to imagine how Jackson Pollock's painting could have been approached outside a climate of reception influenced by Merleau-Ponty's essays on art, cultivating a seeing that oscillates between blur and focus, pull and push. But the written trace of following a poem demands a practice of writing rather than one of dissection or accountancy. Maybe this is why to track a poem through print as Szondi does remains rare, while the literary accountants continue to weigh their meaning residues.

According to Winnicott, in using an object we go beyond talk of relationships—such talk is just about ourselves instead of dealing with reality, he suggests. Getting real involves recognising that what we create *towards* is always there already, although what we create must be a hybrid on the margin of inside and outside, not a division but a securer binding of the transitional object: "the baby creates the object, but the object was there waiting to be created and to become a cathected object". Neither baby nor object then but their hybrid, and use is transformative of baby as well as baby's object.

For a writer "the property of having been there all the time" recognised in the writing, decides that he or she has done something right, as for the lover it means feeling forgiven for what we put on the other because it is received into and towards the wholeness of the recipient. Such a property should be distinguished from the test of "often thought but ne'er so well expressed" applicable in a literary monoculture, that is, relying on idea as categorically separate from expression, and distinguished also from pastiche. Appropriation or coercion damages the object, which at best can have only a twilight existence in a continued dependence on the oppressor. Bare-faced translation of the object into a field demarcated and dominated by the needs of the writer or the lover, turns away from reality.

There's a danger here of conflating the real with the sublime, but the sublime of a painter like Barnett Newman involves a mutual inflation of viewer and object, a fattening of intersubjectivity. Viewers are wowed by the painting that is wowed by their attention. By contrast, the consisting with the real described by Winnicott and performed in Celan's poetry may be closer to love in the Christian rather than the mutually-inflating sense—a love that offers itself for use through accepting trials and death, ensuring continuing life. The sublime entails consisting *in*, the real means consisting *with*—by which latter is meant a mutual shaping rather than inundation. Sublime expansiveness, close to romantic love, contests divisiveness *per se*, as it were abstractly. Such aesthetic oceanic feelings leave the universe undisturbed however, swinging towards the pole of the (super)natural and the unconstructed essence. The real a reader is led towards by Celan's "Engführung" or *stretto* is not for a moment transcendent: Szondi asks:

> "Engführung," stretto, being led through the strait—does this title, which is a name, designate the *strict* manner in which the poet leads the poem? Or the road his reading forces the reader to follow, to retrace? Or even the commemoration of the straits of the "most recent casting out"? He who has learned to "read" Celan's writing knows it isn't a matter of selecting one of several meanings, but of understanding that they do not *differ*, but coincide.[112]

One might go further and assert that "Engführung" knots nature and construction, history and desire, language and materiality and spirit, and that to *follow* the text as Szondi does, entails picking along a strand which subsequently must be recombined in stretto; hence Szondi's categorical location of the real of the poem at one time in historical reference, at another in linguistic materiality.

Celan's knotting can be reduced neither to a sequence of linked metaphors nor to that favourite device of close-reading practice, a conceit. It does however have some kinship with the metaphysical poetry conventionally reduced to conceits, such as George Herbert's poem 'The Pulley' (published in 1633).[113] The successful operation of a conceit requires a prior excess of information then to be accommodated at every point to a supervening (meta-)metaphor, an ideal economy of the poem as simultaneously highly productive and thrifty, and above all waste-free. Measured against the ideal conceit, a writing of dynamic metaphor and categorical transgression such as Shelley's would be judged irresponsible: in the conceit, categories may appear to be confounded but only up to a point—the point at which resolution is achieved and the master meaning clearly sorts figure from ground and performs a hierarchical sorting.

In truth, however, the conceit of 'The Pulley' leaves a considerable surplus. The poem's central play around the word 'rest' leaves much of 'the rest' unaccounted for. In its first stanza the flow from God's "glasse of blessings" passes through "the worlds riches" to "contract into a span", and the span becomes the support necessary for the pulley which will haul his creature back to God. This knotting-together of water (spiritual blessing), earthly riches (nature), span and pulley (human construction), and rest (the linguistic centre of the poem) is designed to ensure that the reader as one of God's creatures shall be forbidden to "rest in Nature, not the God of Nature". The poem exercises a strict tension in this knotting; for instance, God's glass of blessings is whisked away after the third line, and the reader longs for its return. Surely

> If goodnesse leade him not, yet wearinesse
> May tosse him to my breast.

—and there will the reader find again the spiritual draft, the glass? George Herbert found it in the language of Saint Augustine: "Thou awakest us to delight in Thy praise; for Thou madest us for Thyself, and our heart is restless, until it repose in Thee." Herbert's pulley then was textual, but 'The Pulley' pulls in the humanly invented, mechanical world in a stretto with God's blessings and His envy of created nature, exercising such a pull on humankind. As for mechanics, Archimedes' pulley was foundational for Western science and its broadly irreligious course. The supervening 'conceit' would therefore more accurately be termed a stretto—a recapitulation binding elements of the poem but by no means exhaustively and decidedly unnaturally. Similarly in the contemporary poetry of John Donne, emergent objects, ideas, economic forces and religious emotion are mutually implicated so as to exceed what the rhetorical figure can comprehend.

Tracing a poem may indeed require the reader to distinguish elements and purify them; the journey may entail a detour through Saint Augustine or through Archimedes. Readers may vandalise and scar the poem with partial attention and pre-judgement, destroying it in fantasy, finding in 'The Pulley' only the conceit they have been trained to expect: but the poem may remain with them, surviving any such attack. Having followed the poem no matter how clumsily, false steps being part of the journey, a reader may recognise it as both in-here and out-there, the trace of the journey itself has become a knot, no longer an event-sequence but something like an ideogram compacting past, present and future. "In this way a world of shared reality is created which the subject can use and which can feed back other-than-me substance into the subject", concludes Winnicott, in his paper whose subtextual intent is to challenge the narrowness of the Kleinian attention to the whirl of part-objects trafficked between analyst and analysand. Much as Winnicott's transitional objects will in time be categorically replaced in the external world, so for Klein the bizarre objects of the infant's internal world under the sign of the paranoid-schizoid position, monsters of a world preceding the inside-outside binary, must be pushed back inside to enable the depressive acceptance of a social world where the survival of objects becomes ever more unlikely. No need to cite global warming or comet impact: every season clears the decks, this year's black is green, and the loved one wants more varied experience.

Prosody as cognition does mark time's passage, without succumbing to depression; but using the term 'ideogram' implies a wish to poise the poem on a point escaping the time of prosody. This is reminiscent of the poetic artefact asserting fixity within an ephemeral world, self-vaunting and imagined so potently in English-language poetry from Shakespeare to Yeats. But even the intended content of poems written with an eye to their subsequent decoding, notably those written under authoritarian conditions, yields to the paradox that the poem's immortality may depend on the loss of its intended content to obscurity. Court poetry whose coding and decoding confirmed the status of both poet and readership, fostering skills then available to sustain positions of resistance and undercover truth-telling, may have reached its apogee in Song dynasty China, that is about the 10th to 13th centuries. Alfreda Murck in her book *The Subtle Art of Dissent* describes the elaboration of what she calls encoded poetry, where "the uninitiated readers were not privy to the underlying allusions signified by rhyme words. To make the recognition of such sources even more difficult, the author rearranged the selected rhymes and established a new sequence. This allowed the author of the encoded poem to allude to his favourite couplets while constructing his own poetic message, creating two simultaneous and inextricable strands of meaning."[114]

Where might this triumph of encoding be deposited if not within a social domain where meanings shift uneasily and contingently, even within its own epoch, and within court circles? The game of artifice mutated to exploit such contingency, through messages subversive to the Emperor's authority, but which the modern literary historian cannot follow, merely dissects. The modern history of imagism persisting through the 'timeless' moments of *The Cantos* of Ezra Pound, would make a virtue of the perverse fate of the Song dynasty poem, dwelling just where extreme precision becomes mistiness owing to loss or suppression of context. Mistiness itself, conducive to the emergence of forms compiled within a prevalent mood of melancholy and foreboding, is a trope highly familiar to the contemporary reader. Hence poems featuring distinct types of mist, typified in part through bindings performed by rhyme-words, can scarcely avoid travesty in keeping with the impression of Chinese poetry in the West as simultaneously precisely imagistic and vaguely atmospheric. But the literary historian of the Song dynasty asks different questions: does mist here refer to "phenomena that hide natural features" or to "the erroneous thoughts that hide self-nature"? These particular mists seem not too different from our own misty notions. As for clouds representing lying courtiers whose obfuscation prevents the reflected radiance of the loyal minister from being appreciated by the emperor—it would take some learning to infer this from couplets starting "How the flying clouds drift over everything! | See how they suddenly cover up the bright moon!" Mist here is far from representing the growth of individual consciousness through object emergence.

Self-centredness may be the decadent fate of subjectivity in a world of objects, a poor substitute for the 'Prosody as Cognition' which constitutes a radical rejection of traditional metrics.[115] Not only do metrics have an extremely shaky empirical basis, but they start with the nonsensical strategy of adding sense which is "nothing in itself" to sound which is "nothing in itself" and thereby producing "Engführung" or 'Prometheus Unbound'. "Poetry as cognition starts from the core proposition of phenomenology: 'I am my body rather than just having it.' Just as "I am my body," so "the prosodic sense really is" cognition. There is not a cognition belonging to prosody; prosody is cognitive, and vice versa." In other words, we are back in the edge-world of intersubjectivity: to follow a poem cannot entail extracting sense from it as though sense were distinct from prosody. That is not to deny that many poems *solicit* such an operation; but what they yield is fleeting and insubstantial. If you want banal exercises in purification, where sentiment is encapsulated here, and observation of nature displayed here, and God has a place here, and celebration of identity is all over the place, you will receive in abundance and feel under-nourished.

But the statement that 'I am my body' introduces another mystification, a short cut to unity. If life were so simple, anybody might jump straight from the womb to the lecture platform or diving board. Similarly the statement that prosody *is* cognition advances a false unity: prosody is as much transgressive as reconciliatory, a dialectic marked by the device of enjambment in formal verse, introducing a rhythm of breaking and resumption into cognitive prosody. The subject following the poem may journey along a knife-edge, but the subject's survival and sustaining remains critical to prosodic movement: if time were no more than an infinite set of present points, for time too "is nothing in itself," the wake of human being would be digitised across a gaseous field, a "particle flurry" in Celan's phrase. Through breaking and resuming, people know the past and future, "the unmistakable | trace".

These ideas can be tested in reading a passage which makes much of mist, from Shelley's *Prometheus Unbound,* act 2, scene 1.

> The mountain mists, condensing at our voice
> Under the moon, had spread their snowy flakes,
> From the keen ice shielding our linkèd sleep...
> Then two dreams came. One, I remember not.
> But in the other, his pale, wound-worn limbs
> Fell from Prometheus, and the azure night
> Grew radiant with the glory of that form
> Which lives unchanged within, and his voice fell
> Like music which makes giddy the dim brain,
> Faint with intoxication of keen joy:
> 'Sister of her whose footsteps pave the world
> With loveliness—more fair than aught but her
> Whose shadow thou art—lift thine eyes on me!'
> I lifted them: the overpowering light
> Of that immortal shape was shadowed o'er
> By love; which, from his soft and flowing limbs,
> And passion-parted lips, and keen, faint eyes,
> Steamed forth like vaporous fire; an atmosphere
> Which wrapped me in its all-dissolving power,
> As the warm ether of the morning sun
> Wraps ere it drinks some cloud of wandering dew.
> I saw not, heard not, moved not, only felt
> His presence flow and mingle through my blood
> Till it became his life, and his grew mine,
> And I was thus absorbed—until it passed,
> And like the vapours when the sun sinks down,
> Gathered again in drops upon the pines,

And tremulous as they, in the deep night
My being was condensed, and as the rays
Of thought were slowly gathered, I could hear
His voice, whose accents lingered ere they died
Like footsteps of far melody: thy name
Among the many sounds alone I heard
Of what might be articulate; though still
I listened through the night when sound was none.[116]

Characteristically for Shelley, the mountain mists at the opening lead into a detailed if half-parodic meteorology, founded in the physics of cloud formation but rising on that model of watery circulation to articulate a hybrid system of exchange: breath condenses into language and prosody condenses corporeal being—here Panthea (a Shelleyan concoction if suitably Greek) undergoes corporealisation. The first condensing is performed by *our* voice (the voicings of Panthea and her sister Asia, but our voice too who follow this poem and join with them); dialogue is necessary to the vocal shaping of the body and world. Indeed, the isolated second half of line 4, "One, I remember not" lends itself to double meaning, for the physical resolution of being relies on a heard as well as a spoken voice, so, *as* one I would not be capable of remembering. But it seems also that the loss of the twin dream haunts the passage, as though there is always another, an unvoiced consciousness, an inarticulacy which Shelley relegates to an imaginative ether not yet made physical, rather than cloddishness not yet made intellectual. In other words, *dream* is situated as the primal state; and the reality so hard-won in Celan's poem, becomes the voice's task in its dialogue. For both Celan and Shelley the first person plural is a prerequisite which must then be made flesh. To materialise is what voice and prosody are about, as this materialising of the mythological performs.

To distil this passage to extract its meaning residue would belie the way the poetry works. An exegesis of the first three lines could entail a long struggle first to map the bizarre physical process described, and secondly to map the moon's agency—reflection obviously, but how should a reader weigh the information that in Greek mythology Selene, the moon, gave birth to Ersa, that is to dew—and therefore to the circulation whose by-product is an improbably fluffy and protective variety of snow. Nonetheless the stress falling on "Under the moon" scarcely allows the phrase to be passed over. The moon presides over all this passage and governs the following dream, as might be inferred from the phrase "Under the moon" preparing the way sonically for the parallel phrase "Then two dreams came", with the emphatic shift in the second foot from iamb to spondee. As the ninth Orphic Hymn apostrophises Selene, "female and male, with silvery rays you shine, and now full-orbed, now tending to decline"; and this pulse, this waxing and waning, and this bisexuality govern the dream material.

The opening lines solicit a return particularly if the passage is read aloud; it is hard to avoid stumbling over the word "keen" and the oddity of its appearance three times in swift succession. Each time "keen" appears to mean something different. The first encounter is with "the keen ice shielding our linkèd sleep…"; keen here is reconcilable with the dictionary definition of 'cold and penetrating', hence "mountain mists" and "snowy flakes" shield from the ice's penetrating cold, however far such a notion departs from plausible metaphor. So far indeed that the lineation and cadence, separating the line "From the keen ice shielding our linkèd sleep", facilitate an ambiguity which the fitness of a sheet of ice for shielding, only strengthens. The ellipse trailing at the end of the first three lines enacts a threshold syncope leading into dream, prepared by these lines' wrappings and circulations amidst the softness and strange warmth of mist and snow. This hypnogogic state is modulated through the ellipse, gently breaking into sleep. The thread may be broken, but 'our voice' has done its work, composing a landscape governed by scientifically-based transactions but impalpable until voiced; and condensing it into a cradle for dream imaginings, whose voices further condense and disperse into a rhythm of breaking and rejoining, of corporealisation and dissolution. Even dream however is dialogic and social: "our linkèd sleep".

When "keen" next occurs, the "intoxication of keen joy" is associated with "music which makes giddy the dim brain"—such is a sensational keenness adjacent to dissolution through swooning, the characteristic Shelleyan syncope preceding restoration and enacted from line to line of this verse: "and his voice fell" (stop) "Like music" (restoration) but not simply through the device of enjambment, for "Faint with" provides an unexpected continuation of the dying cadence before the abrupter consonant of in*tox*ication initiating a surge up to "keen joy". This keen joy chronologically precedes and determines the 'dim brain' but in the poem's *récit* it launches the evocative restoration performed by Prometheus' speech. *Keen* then is the fainting word, the word of syncope, the feint in both spellings: and seven lines later appear "keen, faint eyes" and if a reader hadn't been drawn up by the strange swings around the prior appearance of "keen", surely "keen, faint eyes" should give pause with its outrageous, bisexual oxymoron, directly following Prometheus' feminisation: "his soft and flowing limbs, | And passion-parted lips".

It would not be difficult to hear behind the enfoldings of Prometheus's speech the mother's murmur shaping the emergence of her baby into the linguistic world. Such a corporeal condensation through language might be read as a journey to ego-resolution. But Shelley's verse makes something only through going nowhere; the physical emerges through breaks and pulses and continuous circulation—poetry constructs as much through its lapses as its propulsion. Consider what happens to Prometheus' limbs, which "pale and wound-worn" "fall away", only to be restored in ideal but highly eroticised and feminine form once he starts to speak. It has been apparent from his first words that not only the body is materialised by voice, but the world on which the body walks; these footsteps are the feet of verse, and if that sounds far-fetched, look ahead to the "footsteps of far melody" which die away once a materialisation has been achieved. This model of creation secularises, in a way perhaps deliberately blasphemous, the opening of Genesis: a human and intensely sexualised calling into being from a kind of cosmic plasma. Panthea dissolves into a coition which seems extraordinary for its *écriture féminine*, a non-penetrative sexual exchange reminding us that this dream emerges in the "linkèd sleep" of Panthea and Asia. But gender under the moon is as changeable as the tide, and even Prometheus yields.

Intersubjectivity is born as words are born. Prometheus solicits Panthea: "lift thine eyes on me!", his limbs and his organs having fallen away and dissolved, and it is only with love's responsive look that his "immortal shape was shadowed o'er | By love" and his body's functions are restored, including his "keen, faint eyes". Keen *and* faint because both light and shadow, radiant dissolution and opacity, must commingle as the ground for being in the world.

Shelley thinks through prosody, and this reading concurs: inner life must be pleated with the outside, social world, to engender the simultaneous connection and disconnection which makes loving and thinking possible (among other things), and prosody is therefore *useful* in Winnicott's terms, it engenders a world for mutual use, it treads it out. For much of the time people are dissolved in their necessary doings or absorbed in themselves—it isn't *simple* to refresh the edge-world and too much conspires to obliterate it. Neither is it possible to go away hugging messages dragged from writing so irreducible, for that residue would be resonant claptrap. The *stretto* of poetry is bound closely with the adventure of prosody as cognition. This is what a reader finds in following in the writing of poets as different as Celan, Shelley, and Frank O'Hara.

Eventually, high-pitched claims and noblest declarations are always founded in someone's most cryptic obsessions. To end, or to snatch away any ending, this essay proclaims truths and discoveries out of following poems only to recoil from the scars it has inflicted on the text—from the scars which even worthy intentions will already have left on the text before the essay starts.[117] The way such an essay can be followed is suggested best by Winnicott's account of the external object: "The fact is that an external object has no being for you or me except in so far as you or I hallucinate it, but being sane we take care not to hallucinate except where we know what to see. Of course when we are tired or it is twilight we may make a few mistakes…"[118] Winnicott went on to worry about this "we", how hallucinating where we know what to see begs the question of the socialising construction of *how* we know what to see—I would say further, how the hallucinated seen can be instated as a real, bound hybridity, the social object, part-object, the spoken and written, the seen and the touched, the theorised and felt, the accepted and held at arms' length. There, I mean *here*, consisting with us, however provisionally, in what feels like an unreeling world. J.H. Prynne's poem, *Biting the Air*, ends with the most tentative possible intimation of such a hope:[119]

> Don't you yet notice
> a shimmer on bad zero, won't you walk there
> and be the shadow unendurably now calibrated.

Just as for Celan a flurry of particles could form a last gasp against silencing, so on the digital walkway our prosody may still cast a shadow, even if our very shadows will be weighed.

# 3: American Poetry

# Chamber Attitudes

The name John Wieners appears in the indexes to many guide books for the Beat movement as well as in memoirs of the New York School and the more pedantic archivism devoted to Black Mountain. His biography does not appear in any of the several directories of gay writers—which is decidedly odd; neither have his *Asylum Poems* or others referring to psychiatric incarceration been reprinted alongside those of Anne Sexton for example. People who follow the available leads, could well be puzzled by the role of a Beat poet lacking all rambunctiousness; a New York poet of exquisite shyness, stranger to the cocktail circuit; and a Black Mountain poet more dedicated to heroin and anonymous gay sex than to diorite and glyph. The place of John Wieners is to be out of place, but admired, even envied for the extremity of his devotion to the poetic art; yet the absence of all reference to its products beyond a side-glance at *The Hotel Wentley Poems* as the most elegant artefact of beatnik aesthetic, begs a biographical explanation: perhaps he sank into a narcotic stupor and wrote nothing further? or cleaned up and abandoned poetry for a sensible career? or his later writing is simply too embarrassing to mention?

John Wieners was born in 1934 in Milton Massachusetts of Irish working class Catholic parents, educated at Boston College, and returned to Boston as its constant though errant bride until his death. He remained true to his poetic vocation through drug abuse and severe mental illness, not that such tribulation precluded political activism in movements associated with gay liberation, mental health system survivors, and local publishing and educational cooperatives and campaigning. Alongside his more temporary or tangential literary affiliations, Wieners belonged to a Boston literary scene where an important mentor for him and contemporaries such as Gerrit Lansing and Joe Dunn was another poet whose work is only now receiving due attention—the Latino, gay Poundian Stephen Jonas (1921–1970), also a resident of Beacon Hill, to whom Wieners paid tribute in his preface to Jonas' first collection *Transmutations* (1966).[120] That Boston scene had an important poetic precursor in John Wheelwright (1897–1940), an aristocratic gay Christian socialist revolutionary, avowedly Bostonian rather than American, although his verse has more in common with Hart Crane than with his Boston contemporaries.[121] A history of Boston poetry would promise to reshape strikingly the present understanding of twentieth-century US poetry, locating Wieners in a literary way as well as literally in his city; just as an history of gay liberation politics in Boston might show (as indeed the thumbnail characterisation of poets above suggests) affiliations at variance with recognisable 'identity politics'.

It is true that Wieners' poetry became embarrassing to some of his admirers and practical supporters; Boston poets such as William Corbett are reputed to have urged him to refrain from publishing *Behind the State Capitol*, and perhaps following the embarrassing impact of that book, earlier poems which had read acceptably enough in the literary politics of the time as *shocking*, belatedly were revealed as embarrassing also. The known literary associations of a poet influence how work is read, especially with our contemporaries; and what looks avant-garde in a readily attributable way may later look either conventional or radical in quite unexpected ways. One factor influencing the reception of Wieners' earlier books was their eccentric publication; after *The Hotel Wentley Poems* none appeared from the house publishers of the US avant-garde. His next major collection, *Ace of Pentacles*, was published by the book dealers James F. Carr and Robert A. Wilson in New York in 1965 as a one-off enterprise; while *Nerves* (1970) and *Selected Poems* (1972) were published in England and consequently little known in the US. (Hence his death at the beginning of March 2002 prompted full newspaper obituaries only in the *Boston Globe* and the London-published *Independent*.) Even this does not account fully for the subsequent lack of attention. That this was to a degree courted is evident from the following response by Wieners in a 1984 interview with his editor Raymond Foye:

> RF: Do you have a theory of poetics?
> WIENERS: I try to write the most embarrassing thing I can think of.[122]

William Burroughs claimed in an interview "I say the most horrible things I can think of", and these two statements of strategy point to affinities between the two writers to be discussed later. Meanwhile *Ace of Pentacles* affords much potential for embarrassment, although it may often be inadvertent. The first few pages run a bewildering stylistic gamut from the exaggeratedly formal:

> Since winter froze your flowing summer sound,
>     And dried your copper ducts of spring and fall,
> You sheltered four have waited, wrapped and bound
>     In ice, for March to loose your muffling shawl. [Etc.]
>         'Ode on a Common Fountain'[123]

—to fin-de-siècle decadent symbolism to apophthegm to surrealism. Other poems include outtakes from *The Hotel Wentley Poems*, several showing evidence of the occultism prevalent in the circle around the Blavatsky-taught San Francisco poet Robert Duncan, and to which Wieners belonged briefly—although Catholic Mariolatry is a more frequent strain. Across all styles, drug use and gay sex are prevalent. The keynote of the sexual episodes is regret and yearning, their characteristic mise-en-scène post-coital; a tone distinct from the gay social round of Frank O'Hara's poetry or the promiscuous abandon of Allen Ginsberg's. Similarly the drug references have little in common with the psychic self-improvement then promoted by Timothy Leary; whilst numerous drugs are name-checked, the romance of heroin, associated with the easing of emotional pain and the courting of death, is all-prevalent. Billie Holliday's name may not appear in this book, but she is everywhere ("Tell me that may not rise again | she sings still in our breath") and she will remain the most constant presence in Wieners' work.

It is difficult to select an *Ace of Pentacles* poem as typical, but 'The Acts of Youth' exemplifies (if not overstates) the typical stance, and opens with these stanzas:

> And with great fear I inhabit the middle of the night
> What wrecks of the mind await me, what drugs
> to dull the senses, what little I have left,
> what more can be taken away?
>
> The fear of travelling, of the future without hope
> or buoy. I must get away from this place and see
> that there is no fear without me: that it is within
> unless it be some sudden act or calamity

to land me in the hospital, a total wreck, without
memory again; or worse still, behind bars. If
I could just get out of the country. Some place
where one can eat the lotus in peace.[124]

The stance is passive yet the verse highly controlled, seeking resolution
in formal grace and in stanzas of classical impersonality, but syntactically threatening always to break the bounds of the verse-form, reducing
it to incoherence. The fear of mental illness and the references to hospital treatment recall the contemporary poems of the Boston writer Anne
Sexton, but Wieners' poetry differs from hers in important respects: his
predicaments are represented as archetypal, rather than ascribed to
damage incurred at the hands of malignly-motivated family members
and psychiatrists. Comparisons could be drawn where the treatment of
the mother is concerned; separation becomes the occasion for tenderness in the exquisitely poignant 'My Mother' in *Ace of Pentacles*,[125] while
alienation in Sexton's contemporary 'Christmas Eve', an elegy for her
mother, becomes the occasion for self-pitying and self-exculpating
identifications. [126] The 'confessional' in Sexton's poems discloses the
personal regardless of—or even so as to court—indignity:

I could admit
that I am only a coward
crying *me me me*
and not mention the little gnats, the moths
forced by circumstance
to suck on the electric bulb.[127]

This passage displays the quality of Sexton's poetry in much the exaggerated way that the passage from 'The Acts of Youth' does that of
Wieners. A moment of acute self-knowledge co-exists with a transcen-
dently egotistical lack of self-knowledge, reducing lesser human beings
to the status of the "little moths, the gnats". Nothing can quite make up
for this, but "to suck on the electric bulb" displays Sexton's strength,
which lies in spots of language of an intensity reducing the surrounding
matter with its endlessly *announced* intensity, to inconsequentiality.
Sexton's poetry is distinguished always by its finish; although she does
not use inherited forms, every poem occupies its boundaries perfectly,
and these boundaries are set by an all-powerful first person singular to
whom language remains subservient as though to atone for the indisci-
pline of human beings. The Wieners passage is driven more by literary

antecedents, particularly a half-buried and Baudelairian voyage trope, and derives its force from rhythmic and semantic accumulation which can ingest the silly pun on "buoy" unruffled, and plays with and against poetic form rather than laying down each line as a self-sufficient semantic unit.[128]

Nevertheless, 'The Acts of Youth' would in 1964 have been and remains now a difficult poem to swallow in its paean to "pain and suffering" as the royal road to "great art" and its completely unironised performance of self-dedication, its yielding to the linguistic exactions which it launches and which then govern it "until the dark hours are done". Reaching back to Baudelaire and to *The City of Dreadful Night* and further back to Beddoes, how anachronistic such writing must have looked to the inheritors of William Carlos Williams, whether Olson or Ginsberg, or to New Yorkers schooled in Dada and after. It says much for the generosity of these poets that so many declared their admiration for Wieners, if more often for his vocation than his achievements. And how unfamiliar such writing appears now; what is its relationship to modernism, to post-modernism, to new formalism, to Language poetry?

∾

The 1970 collection *Nerves* and numerous poems uncollected before Raymond Foye's 1988 work of retrieval, *Cultural Affairs in Boston*, deploy a typology of emotions, fixed and emblematic. This ahistorical and essentialist understanding of human relationships distinguishes Wieners' poetry even more than its adherence to stanzaic form, from that of his Black Mountain mentors and friends; and in so doing, sets it aside from Anglo-American modernism, a defining characteristic of which has been a density of particulars. In *Nerves* Wieners' poetry recapitulates the seventeenth century in the twentieth and with *Behind the State Capitol* will engross the eighteenth, but it is fundamentally pre-romantic in its view of human nature as fallen and as immutably so.

The core vocabulary of *Nerves* is highly restricted and chiefly abstract with the exception of vocabulary drawn from nature (including the cityscape), and of place names evoking nostalgia. The contrast with *The Cantos* or even *The Maximus Poems* is extreme, for in such a comprehensive work the abstract is deployed either with the force of theory (economic or geological, for instance) in order to bind and organise a dense array of particulars, or to throw an occasional line of common humanity to the reader. Tonally though, even the simplest poem in *Nerves* can confound:

*In Public*

Promise you wont forget
each time we met
we kept our clothes on
despite obvious intentions
to take them off,
seldom kissed or even slept,
talked to spend desire,
worn exhausted from regret.

Continue our relationship apart
under surveillance, torture, persecuted
confinement's theft; no must or sudden blows
when embodied spirits mingled
despite fall's knock
we rode the great divide
of falsehood, hunger and last year[129]

As often with Wieners' poems this begins as though a simple—even simple-minded—song lyric in the first two lines, although such perfectly-judged rhythm would be rare to find, before swerving in ll.3–5 towards a comic and prosy deflation; the casualness of the first five lines is visible in the suppression of the apostrophe in "wont" and the absence of punctuation which thereafter marks the progressive inspissation of verbal texture until the unstopped final word. The tonal switch is marked but held within tight control with the transition to ll.6–9, and with their strong echoes of Donne ('embodied spirits mingled' is an epitome of 'The Extasie') then intervening and persisting through the second stanza. The first two lines of the second stanza may seem to veer into the language of paranoia, although both surveillance and torture have their history in metaphysical and recusant verse, and l.12 is bizarre syntactically: could "confinement's theft" be read as 'confinement is theft', does "no" operate as a general negative, meaning 'nothing' when governing "must" and 'no' when governing "sudden blows"? "Embodied spirits mingled" may provide a nice sonic analogue for oral pleasure with its kissing and sucking sounds, but is very strange: the "embodied" is affected by the preceding negative, especially bearing in mind that "we kept our clothes on". Is "we rode the great divide" supposed to be ludicrously sexually suggestive? What of the stepwise bathos of "false-hood, hunger and last year"?

This poem is difficult in a way unlikely to concede much to exegesis. Wieners' own reading of 'In Public' does not sound in the least incoherent; his vocal poise, his timing are reminiscent of the stand-up comic, and the swerves of tone, the sudden accelerations and drawling skids, build to an affective complexity as well as intensity, each moment remaining on the air in a carefully judged relationship. Hear again the perfect punctuation and divide provided by the line "despite fall's knock". Is it possible for a lyric poem to be funny as well as desperate? 'In Public' certainly sounds like both. How can a critic show this without sounding foolish in labouring the obvious, or foolish in constructing a case for what might seem to come a slight bit of campiness? For either the reader gets it or doesn't.

There is a paradox here which 'remaining on the air' contrives to conceal, since effects of delay and punchline are necessarily sequential in time while the poem's assemblage strives for simultaneity—"last year" is comic partly because of the contemporary and strenuous expression of suffering. Similarly, camp can derive from a fixed, heavily knowing standpoint resulting in monotony, but can also dance between positions opportunistically while remaining recognisable. Wieners' delivery sounds both offhand in its overall phrasing and weirdly precise in syllabic enunciation, an effect achieved by unexpected emphasis. Whether heard or read on the page, a combination of extremely localised exactitude with a more general emotional pressure driving towards incoherence and often achieving it, leavened by unhinged humour, will come to characterize Wieners' later poems.

One particular way in which generalisation and precision co-exist is through the exact deployment of abstract phraseology. In the poems of *Behind the State Capitol* tranches of elided abstract nouns come adorned with hundreds of names, chiefly of movie starlets, but certain short poems collected in *Nerves* present the passionate abstract in its neat strength:

*Desperation*

In what mad pursuit, or competition
the marvelous denies object
to what subject melancholy resignation?

drowned exile flight

down what exit, fall's fused endeavor
discharges incessant order

for what crushed languor,
what hapless ascension
rejected entreaties pace

cruel chase, within vain decline?
Annoyed, over-drawn, exempt
to what rest, borrowed dichotomy

unmasks its single purpose.[130]

The exploitation here of sound association can seem troublingly close to the 'clang association' symptomatic of some psychotic states. The lyric's rhythmic tightness, wound up through insistent internal rhyme, keys in place an entirely abstract vocabulary like a drystone wall, yet there is something tumbling, precipitate through its abbreviated lines. Not so much fluent then, since fluency implies urbanity, not so much metaphorical, since metaphor implies concretion, this poem derives from a withheld emblem. This allows the poem its equivocation; its extreme emotional expression is both contrived and genuine; so while it is impossible to believe it, it is difficult to not believe *in* it, and the poem conveys not love so much as being *in* love. Such a state of immanence within love or belief acknowledges an exterior to the envelope, an elsewhere (but by no means an opposite or contradiction). Great passion can be troublingly detached from one possessed by it, and Wieners who regarded himself as a Catholic poet knew this well, that passion is entered into, and also as a gay man with a drag-queen propensity.

The interrogative form which dominates 'Desperation' is characteristic of religious, meditative verse:

> What! nets are quivers too? what need there all
>     These sly devices to betray poor men?
> Dies they not fast enough when thousands fall
>     Before thy dart? what need these engines then?   [and so on...]
>                                       Quarles, *Emblems* Book 2, III, ll.1–4

Wieners' poem is even more strongly reminiscent of Richard Crashaw and might be read in its shared paradoxical extravagance as a response to 'M. Crashaw's Answer for Hope'—as that poem itself responds to Abraham Cowley's 'Against Hope'. Take the first stanza, and think how 'object' becomes the 'subject' of the following clause, how 'subject' shifts from the agent to the dependent, how the subject is subjected and denied its object; the entire stanza is a verbal seesaw where positions are exchanged and whereby "melancholy resignation" does not supersede "mad pursuit" but coexists with it. The state of being unrequitedly in love is exactly where hope coexists with despair, where frenzy accompanies despondency, where adoration shadows furious resentment, even hate. Crashaw speaking for Hope says:

> We are not WHERE nor What we be,
> But WHAT and WHERE we would be. Thus art thou
> Our absent PRESENCE and our future Now.
> Crashaw, 'M. Crashaw's Answer for Hope' ll.37–39

Wieners replies for despair: "dichotomy | unmasks its single purpose." Dichotomy is literally 'cutting in two' which describes the kind of desperation Wieners' poem expresses; moving to its second stanza, the first line is stretched between "drowned" and "flight", flight being cut short rhythmically by the false internal rhyme of "exit". The following phrase delivers multiple puns where, as in "fall's knock" in the poem discussed earlier, 'fall' acquires intense religious overtones—not only Adam's fall from Eden occasioned by the "fused endeavor" of sexual desire, but also the Satanic fall from heaven. Although both poems may well refer to the same love affair and 'fall' may have a particular and personal significance as 'autumn' in addition to 'falling' in love (a usage which reflects a shared ambiguity as to the desirability of such a state), it is the religious senses of 'fall' which elucidate the paradox of line 6 in 'Desperation', for the "incessant order" of God's disposition has relied on sexual discharge; human and Satanic misdeed can only serve the purposes of God's order.

The first two lines of the third stanza proceed out of and reinforce the sexual pun of "discharges" in images of compulsive masturbation where "hapless ascension" is both erection and crucifixion, and its glorious aftermath in the redemption and spilt seed of the poem. The relentless procession of qualified abstracts in counterpoise brings the reader at the seesaw line of "cruel chase" and "vain decline" to a pitch where well-prepared for the final sentence—a death sentence indeed. The intrusion of "annoyed" and "over-drawn" is a true Wieners touch, partly self-referential and self-deflating, but accurate in a twist where the component terms of 'overwrought' and 'overdrawn', both innerly and in poetic construction and no doubt in neglect of life's ordinary business, sketch the exterior of being 'in love'. "Exempt" presumably of any response, any requital, but also through the state of being in love (and commitment to a vocation whose conventions have permitted a Christ-like self-presentation then undercut); nonetheless neither insistent desire nor life's daily annoyances grant respite.

Last, consider the oddity in the penultimate line of "borrowed": in what sense borrowed? "Substantiall shade!", "fair fallacy", "Hapless ascension"; Wieners may indeed borrow such tropes from Crashaw and other seventeenth century poets, but the borrowing goes deeper than this to the sense of lineage, persistence and repetition, primarily of loss bound with sexual love, which pervades *Nerves*:

> 15 years of loving
> men, women and children
> with what result
>
> Another silver Iseult
> joins svelte Tristan
> down a vault of tears
>
> under what insult
> account with draw
> on sorrow's bank
>                          'High Noon'[131]

Such an unshakeable continuity is asserted in the opening of the book, invoking the lost poets of Boston, San Francisco and Long Island as "shining martyrs", and in the many poems commemorating love affairs such as 'High Noon'. A typology of emotions is developed, fixed and emblematic. This ahistorical and essentialist understanding of human relationships distinguishes Wieners' poetry even more than its adherence to stanzaic form, from that of his Black Mountain mentors and friends; and in so doing, sets it aside from Anglo-American modernism, a defining characteristic of which has been a density of particulars. In *Nerves* Wieners' poetry recapitulates the seventeenth century in the twentieth and with *Behind the State Capitol* will engross the eighteenth, but it is fundamentally pre-romantic in its view of human nature as fallen and as immutably so, with salvation obtainable only through grace. The extravagant vision of poetic destiny and the often-adopted stance of suffering poet may indeed be post-romantic as filtered through the Beats—

although utterly devoid of Ginsberg's neo-romantic bardic confidence—
, but such posturing figures either a repudiation or an abasement from
the pretension to world-shaper and transformer of consciousness; it is in
this regard as un-Shelleyan as can imagined.

John Wieners was not the only younger Black Mountain poet whose
writing repudiates such romantic projects implicitly. The most subtle
and integrated rejoinder may be found in the earlier poems of Edward
Dorn: while Olson's heroic Gloucester fishermen farmed the wilderness
with the sea, creating a coast and settlements worthy of a poet's residence only for them to be mucked about by vulgar commerce (echoes of
the arraignment of Usury in Pound), Dorn's understanding of the
impact of capitalist economics on working people was more developed
emotionally and intellectually, informing the remarkable collections
*The North Atlantic Turbine* (1967) and *Geography* (1968).[132] Nonetheless,
Dorn's writing of this period shares the modernist particularity, even if
later he was to resort to formulaic apophthegm, countering slogan with
slogan. A yet more suggestive parallel can be found in the personal,
political and poetic trajectory of LeRoi Jones/ Amiri Baraka; poems
brought together as 'Black Magic' in his 1979 *Selected Poetry* occupy a
position comparable to *Nerves* in Wieners' oeuvre, shifting from
modernist object-particularity towards a discourse of social generality,
which would in turn transit into a poetic discourse akin to rap and
'ebonics' much as Wieners was to draw on faggot speech. In Baraka the
changes are always declared, and here in terms of a commitment reminiscent of 'The Acts of Youth':

> The lovers speak to each other as if they were born
> this second without anything but the world and their vision
> which is a blue image of themselves, on 7th ave drinking, and
> pretending to be the few things of value in the world.
>
> We all need to tighten up. We all need each other. We all
> need to stop lying and lock arms and look at each other
> like black humans struggling with depraved eagles.[133]

The position is more assured than in the Wieners poem, and with the
extended syntax in street speech rhythm seeming to pour effortlessly
into shapely stanzas; the assured position allows scorn, which does not
belong to Wieners' emotional range; and in Wieners the note of stricture
tends to be self-directed. Baraka's divorce from orthodox modernism
was attended by extremist language of a sort which divorce is apt to trig-

ger, although few would give vent to the extent of Baraka's murderous anti-semitism, homophobia and celebrations of rape. Next to this, Wieners' provocations and embarrassments in *Behind the State Capitol* and afterwards are evidently generous and humane.

~

While Charles Olson may have been Wieners' acknowledged poetic father, the matrix from which Wieners was born as a poet was female and decidedly not modernist; through following this clue, the abstract but emotionally overwrought manner of his poems can then be traced further back to metaphysical poetry, and his warped songs to less strenuous models, especially Herrick.[134] In the Foye interview which prefaces *Cultural Affairs in Boston*, Wieners does not hesitate:

> RF: Who are the early influences on your poetry?
> WIENERS: Edna St. Vincent Millay was the first. Later it was Charles Olson.[135]

In an interview a decade earlier with the publisher of The Good Gay Poets and *Fag Rag*, Charley Shively, Wieners is more expansive:

> SHIVELY: I've heard you talk before about your sources. Who were the earliest people that you cared for when you were in college just starting?
>
> WIENERS: I cared for Edna St. Vincent Millay until the man I worked for in the catalogue department at Boston College Library told me Emily Dickinson was a far greater poet; that Edna was a bit too popular, too available, and I found that to be true. By the time I got to be thirty Emily Dickinson had transcended her. But she was my first poet. And then I liked all the women poets: Elinor Wylie, Sara Teasdale and H.D. as well, initially though anthologies.
>
> SHIVELY: [...] It's interesting that you responded first to women poets.
>
> WIENERS: Yes, and to their observations of nature, to their love feeling and to an abbreviation of expression.[136]

It is not difficult to imagine the attraction Millay's name held for the young Wieners; she had been the most glamorous, sexually-dangerous and famous poet since Byron. The heyday of her reading tours lay back in the 1920s when she epitomised female sexual emancipation for the press and her fans, but her decline towards her death in 1950 had a certain Sunset Boulevard glamour too. Faded, half-forgotten female stars were to become a Wieners penchant. Millay anticipates Wieners' antinomianism (as well as, unexpectedly, his use of heroin—in which she exceeded him and almost anyone else but Charlie Parker), and her poems share with his the characteristic of investing abstractions and received images with great emotional force. Millay gained poetic celebrity for her sonnets above all, and her sonnet XXV begins as follows:

> That Love at length should find me out and bring
> This fierce and trivial brow unto the dust,
> Is, after all, I must confess, but just;
> There is a subtle beauty in this thing,
> A wry perfection; wherefore now let sing
> All voices how into my throat is thrust,
> Unwelcome as Death's own, Love's bitter crust....[137]

Millay's poetry is closer to court poetry than Wieners'; it is smartly turned out, deals with eternal themes of human desire, and often conveys an attractive note of drollery. At times though, as in the last couplet above, it gathers itself to memorable effect: after the droll "fierce and trivial" and the self-reflexive "wry perfection", the enactment by poetic form against the current of syntax to produce a violent penetration of the throat by "all voices" against the current of song, a penetration associated with both death and love, and unavoidably a love-making which violates—this exploitation of the hand-me-down to deliver a complex emotional shock is remarkable. The poem's combination of distance marked by knowingness, of faith in the resources of poetic tradition, re-animating the hackneyed and reverberating the flat, of emotional conviction, sexual frankness and post-Freudian frisson, marks it as precisely *unmodernist*; that it to say, it could have been written only out of a critical relationship with poetic modernism, a secession as principled as that of Wieners in favour of charged and historically resonant abstraction.

This is so not only where high emotion is concerned. From a late modernist perspective, the poems of *Nerves* appear most baffling when most disingenuous. Wieners' 'Melancholy' begins:

> Across the deep and brine
> we'll go, Tristan and his lass, a ho,

and sustains this manner to a final couplet of a complex simplicity reminiscent of Blake:

sturdy lass I'll be for there,
and faint-hearted song you'll whisper.[138]

The earlier poems of Edna St. Vincent Millay, especially those collected in *A Few Figs from Thistles* (first complete edition, 1922), are doubtless the source of this manner rather than say, Yeats, and the comparison offered by the following passage could be multiplied:

> Lass, if to sleep you would repair
>     As peaceful as you woke,
> Best not besiege your lover there
>     For just the words he spoke
> To me, that's grown so free from care
>     Since my heart broke![139]

Throughout *A Few Figs from Thistles* Millay twists tropes inherited immediately from W.H. Davies and Walter de la Mare and further back from Herrick and from folk tradition, in the interests of a sexual bouleversement where the female leads in dalliance. Wieners' variant goes further in turning gender-dissolute, and in playing with the figures of tragedy where Millay prefers classical and folk stock figures. Millay's tone is consciously modern if her style is unmodernist, both being bright and clear: 'Melancholy' on the other hand becomes bizarrely scrambled, deploying poetic phrases with little regard to literal meaning ("up the brine, down the glen" suggests Wieners neither knows nor cares what "brine" or "glen" might mean), and more interested in the emotional charge of the obscurely simple which in nursery rhyme presents to children the peculiarity of poetic language.

Such a familiar and strange quality, at once artificially poetic and emotionally pressured, distinguishes unmodernist writing at its most powerful, and corresponds to Wieners' approval of an "abbreviation of expression" in the female poets who influenced him when he started to write—an influence which continued to mark his verse distinctively from Black Mountain and New York contemporaries. In *Nerves* it leads to the extreme elision shown in 'Desperation' and elsewhere, for instance:

> More fierce cunning of the mind
> That invents its own breaking

To seek then resort to blind —[140]

or to the quiet resonance of 'Determination' which describes poetry as:

> Activity of one's own,
> much as Mother's bedroom
> or twilight, Sunday evening
> when one's parents feel old.

Wieners' adherence to the unmodernism of Millay despite his debts to Olson and O'Hara, made possible a sophisticated verse independent of irony, and of disproportionate claims for the social and ideology-shaping efficacy of verse. His writing of this period has therefore represented a significant resource for poets seeking a way forward from the epic adventures of L=A=N=G=U=A=G=E poetry (however inadequate that label) in reconnection with an unmodernist poetic tradition; the finest exponent being Jennifer Moxley:

> The objects have gone quiet. Even old
> Mister Unicorn has run out of words,
> despite his painted red lips. Things inured
> to emptiness continue with their cold
> busyness. And thus the flurry of cash
> around the center silence still appears
> charitable tinsel, bright with the solace
> of distress, the joy of being in arrears
> so much more joyful than other joys [...][141]

"The solace of distress" echoes John Wieners' high lyric style: to emblazon abstractions is a rare facility, which Wieners' own later poetry seems to abjure. The relationship between the highly-charged economy of *Nerves* and the spectacular splurge of *Behind the State Capital*, its vortex of proper names and syllabic strings, must surely then be a first puzzle to contemplate among the many posed by that monstrous and magnificent book.

∾

Wieners wrote emblematically until at least the mid-1970s, at the same time that much of his writing had started to take a very different turn. To recapitulate, the factors most salient for Wieners' lyricism are his Catholicism, his early infatuation with the poetry of Edna St Vincent Millay, and his fraught gay sexual identity. These influences translate into a poetry of deeply felt abstractions and symbols, yearned-for and feared, of nostalgia both for their realisation in transcendental moments and for the fullness of subsequent guilt; then increasingly a poetry of betrayal—betrayal by whatever ameliorates the poet's isolation, whether sex or poetry or the glimpses of glamour in the gossip magazines which became his daily reading material. But even in his most *outré* volume, *Behind the State Capitol*, the poetry of nostalgia and formal grace remains, despite being swathed in seemingly extraneous material.

The poem 'Larders', published as a broadsheet in 1970, is a fine instance of Wieners' combination of formal elegance and control with an urgency threatening to break its banks, handled with more restraint than in 'The Acts of Youth'. An elongating line is characteristic, as though poetic form struggles to encompass the affective build-up. Characteristic too are the smudges on the surface, moments of clumsiness here prominent in the middle two lines of the final stanza, much as in 'The Acts of Youth' the fourth stanza evinces the awkwardness of "those young who would trod". Only in *The Hotel Wentley Poems* did Wieners permit himself to strive for the immaculate, achieving in their revised form a chamber-music of perfect, almost stilted prosody. Elsewhere the smudge on the lyric at once celebrates and deprecates poetic artifice, drawing attention to it while witnessing an authenticity of lived experience exceeding poetic compass—until the category of lived experience itself started to come apart.

Larders

Oh, the night beckons so
as young children sleeping
in another room; the night beckons
so as a dinner party on the floor

up near Columbia in a large apartment
house; the night beckons as a teacher
holding forth on Greek in a house on Long Island
for the weekend; cocktails at lunch.

My favorite feelings; a weekend in the country,

perhaps a long walk by the river, or
adolescent memories of a metropolis, the standard
usage prepared; perhaps Third Avenue in the 50's

where admen go to drink afternoons away and sometimes the
evening; yes the night beckons so as Walt Whitman's
line, what he predicted in San Francisco or New York;
Boston seldom, too many Irish strays to ever cause

a revolution; the night beckons nonetheless and I am
lost within its wilderness with only the brains of friends to
relay, for a way home into the kitchen, where the food is,
but where my parents sit before, guarding the hoard.

'Larders' opens with two beautifully-composed stanzas whose movement is reproduced at greater amplitude in the following three stanzas; the sonic punctuation of "cocktails at lunch" at the end of the second stanza, tacking down the rhythm just after it threatens to fly away in the elongated and enjambed lines "as a teacher | holding forth on Greek in a house on Long Island | for the weekend", is paralleled in the way the final phrase of the poem, "guarding the hoard", reins back the runaway lines immediately preceding it. This prosody proclaims an ambiguity performed by the poem at several levels and consonant with the surface smudging. A first reading of the poem might succumb to the "relay" (to use Wieners' word) performed by desire for the night and an insistent forward impetus, although the ambiguity of the little word "as" tends to snag—does "as" at the start of the second line and thereafter mean 'like' or 'while', a decision which significantly affects the agency of the night? Reading 'like' for "as" would associate the night with the world of normal sociability and family—a yearning often expressed in Wieners' poetry and unaffected by anti-bourgeois posturing: the night would stand for the irrecoverable of the past and the irreproducible in the future, from all of which his poetic vocation has alienated him. In this reading the hinge phrase is one which at first looks like a bizarre interpolation, "the standard | usage prepared". The night forms in the gap of the simile—its beckoning is present while the comparative term is temporally distant. Once this phrase is understood as governing the memories of childhood and early student days, the phrase "My favorite feelings" conjures up a counterfactual autobiography, a John Wieners who developed as his background, education and his country's values of the time would have dictated. The "hoard" then might be understood as the inheritance and nurture which parents guard in both senses—that is, they protect it but they refuse access to it, owing to the familial dynamics of love and alienation.

Reading 'while' for "as" invests the night with more glamour than a status of exclusion necessarily attains—"beckons" now becomes sexualised and regret for normality weakens. The "standard | usage prepared" had been shadowed from early childhood by the alluring night, permitting no promise to be realised, be it personal or social, as the references to Walt Whitman and to revolution betoken; but this destiny now attracts an affirmative cadence, striking its full note across the phrase "and I am | lost within its wilderness". These alternate readings are braided in the poem and govern the position of the first person singular, as the regret and value ascribed to the spilt and the wasted govern Wieners' poems up to the mid-seventies. The night is the shape of the self, the point between the regretted past and the yearned-for future which cannot be realised as the present. That gap is the 'I' at work in these shapely poems, housed in them. 'Larders' yearns for home, for houses, for shaped space to contain the I in its longings.

Another kind of writing by John Wieners rafts the present moment, and the only habitation it can conceive is fugitive, the hotel room, another persona, a snatch of music from a jazz improviser. When in present currency 'I' breaks into transsexual figments, into fantasy hordes, chiefly female figures of glamour and wealth—Barbara Hutton, Jackie Kennedy, numerous movie stars: yet this is not an impersonation, its tendency is at once towards abstraction and hectic in its compulsive adducing of evidence from printed scraps or private associations. The individual unconscious is afforded no play; these poems are animated by a flighty intelligence at work across a social unconscious which sustains it, or in linguistic terms, an individual voice which skitters across textual decoupages and is reshaped incessantly by the surfaces it crosses. The treatment of earlier, shapely verse as material for collage amongst fan-mags, newspaper stories and other stuff, is noteworthy; these agonised, tremulous poems are recycled as material for performance, lent to mockery and distortion, their introspection allowed no privilege. What Wieners lays down is a shifting pavement; lyric shape and body have been flattened into strips or layers, and the proxies for interior space are fantastic tableaux, peopled with part-selves flouncing in the pier-glasses, room service always available. This will-o'-the-wisp self, this stage improviser, escapes despair to revel in transience. The tacky, the ephemeral, the trivial, the self-indulgent release the self from its prison of nostalgia and yearning. Strikingly the poems invent a society-with-a-capital-S, concocting an exclusive society code where Jackie Kennedy's circle intersects with Charles Olson's and it is assumed everyone knows everyone else without introduction.

But there is a different side—collective and political—to the society poems. Essential to a reading of Wieners and to an estimate of his poetry's worth is his vulnerable knowledge of the material substrate to his transcendentalism. In the earlier lyric poems this is allied to a homosexual trope of tenderness in sordidness, exemplified in the novels of Jean Genet and later of John Rechy, and to a self-laceration at the waste of life through use of drugs, a theme pervading the journal published in 1996 as *The Journal of John Wieners is to be called 707 Scott Street for Billie Holiday 1959*. In the later collage poetry this materialism interpolates political and economic facts with society verbiage, relating to Boston's high society and the heiresses tracked by gossip columnists. High society, community, and collective forces in more abstract, conspiratorial depiction, these three pluralities supply the constitutive material for the later writing. This poetry is composed of chains and clang-associations, and holds to templates; it does not encourage reveries in the reader—rather, it shuts down and cools association, bites back the circumstances, and produces its own speaker, a macaronic first person composed of multiple voices and discourses but simultaneously their virtuoso. Something strange happens to these poems when read aloud, or perhaps when written down, for the compositional priority is impossible to determine: the ghosts of old formal poems may be visible behind accretions, or records of performance may have been tidied up for the page. At whatever point in this to-and-fro, when read by Wieners the poems sound improvised, alive in the voice and almost unimaginable without the voice, consistent with the persona of the interviews, quick, smart, wicked and poised. As with William Burroughs' more orderly routines, the texts require an extrinsic presence to mobilise and infuse them, to add tone, to direct the phrase; but this is achieved not through vocal presence as guarantor of authenticity, but through a construction, a caricature personality—Burroughs the crackerbarrel philosopher from St Louis, the plain dealer, and Wieners the drag queen eschewing the illusion of authentic femininity, his drag always a collage of thrift-store oddities tacked onto an evidently male canvas.

∾

In his thrillingly eccentric survey *The Writing of America* Geoff Ward cites as "a deranged masterpiece" John Wieners' 1975 book *Behind the State Capitol or Cincinnati Pike*, going on to describe it as "at one and the same time the capstone of Wieners' career and the book that would sink his reputation."[142] The appearance in 1986 of *Selected Poems 1958–1984* and in 1988 of a collection of previously uncollected work *Cultural Affairs in Boston* suggested a residual buoyancy in Wieners' reputation, although each book required the advocacy of a preface from in the first case Allen Ginsberg and in the second Robert Creeley to assure readers that here was a notable poet, both invoking Keats. In this perhaps unconsciously they betrayed a complicity with the view which their prefaces explicitly reject, that Wieners' finest achievement came with *The Hotel Wentley Poems* published when he was 24, subsequent writing being a sad testimony to the effects of poly- drug misuse and mental frailty. Despite their efforts, in the 28 years since the publication of *Behind the State Capitol*, Ward's has been the first recognition in print of this extraordinary book as a "masterpiece".

Here I wish to explain to myself as much as to any reader why *Behind the State Capitol or Cincinnati Pike* (*Behind the State Capitol* henceforward) has meant so much to me for so long and why it has been so difficult to explain this—or why I might have resisted asking an explanation of myself. This does not imply a lower estimate of earlier Wieners books; in fact I feel the poems collected in *Nerves* to represent the bedrock of any case for Wieners' greatness as a lyric poet. *Behind the State Capitol* is not exactly a collection of poems; a good starting point might be to try to characterise this book which Wieners insisted to Raymond Foye, editor of his *Selected Poems 1958–1984*, had to be considered "a single work—a single *poem*"—the excepts published in *Selected Poems* as discrete poems therefore being in some way traduced.[143]

*Behind the State Capitol* is a chunky book about $8^{1/2} \times 5^{1/2}$ inches of 204 numbered pages. In its regular paperback edition its appearance does not correspond to expectations of a book of poetry. The cover (front, back and spine) consists of a black and white collage of typed correspondence, programs, newsprint and clippings from movie magazines in which Lana Turner features more than once; a young Prince Charles makes an appearance. The reproductive quality is of an indifferent photocopy. Author's name and book title appear in a Broadway stencil typeface on the cover, in lipstick pink, and set with a notable lack of visual taste and technical competence. The spine bears the legend similarly stencilled, JOHN WIENERS 1975. The price is stencilled large on the reverse, with the postal box address of the publisher, Good Gay Poets, next to a curious splotch which might charitably be described as The Good Gay Poets' logo. The rarely seen limited signed hardback edition is bound in a kind of gold lurex, with exactly the same cack-handed typesetting stamped in silver but somehow looking more apt in this format, Odeon-like.

Opening the cover reveals a half-title which is a further warning of what is to come; the legend BEHIND THE STATE CAPITOL OR CINCIN-NATI PIKE features between-letter spacing varying in a manner which seems completely arbitrary. The next page presents a further collage, including an announcement from the Judson Poets' Theatre of *ASPHODEL, in Hell's Despite* (by William Carlos Williams) and mention of Lana Turner (described as "America's former "sweater girl""). The title page features a full-length newspaper photograph of the woman whom Wieners addresses rather formally in the poem 'To Jacqueline Fitzgerald Kennedy Onassis-Richmond' and whose identity he half-assumes else-where in his female role of Jackie Wieners (pp. 69, 161); information is laid over this photograph in clumsily-scissored slips of paper, one of which describes the contents of the book accurately as "cinema decoupages; verses, abbreviated prose insights." A contents list follows; acquaintance with the book reveals several misprints here, the omis-sion of a poem, incorrect page numbers.

The first poem in the book is titled '1952' and its opening stanza runs as follows:

> Beyond this river which I have no desire to cross
> There are mountains which I have no desire to climb
> I am fenced in by mountains and rivers
> And though year's day goes, I feel no loss.[144]

Such an overture may be familiar to the (rare) reader of *Ace of Pentacles*, but to most will seem weirdly out of keeping with its presentation. The conventionality teeters towards the preposterous. How can rivers or mountains be described as *fencing* someone in? Should "year's day" be read as an ellipsis which can be expanded into something sensible? After another three stanzas in similar mode, the reassured (in that these stanzas offer at least the parade of meaning) but perhaps slightly queasy reader might turn the page to read:

> UNDERSTOOD DISBELIEF IN PAGANISM,
> LIES AND HERESY
>
> Prick any literay dichotomy
> sung unrent gibberish from maxim skulls
> west Manchester cemetery

recidivist testimony damned
promulgated post-mortem Harry Ghouls
wills pleasant chicanery hulled

in opposition to queer honesty,
flying hapless good humours
Morphe erroneous untedious mystery[145]

This vein continues for another nine stanzas, introducing a Parsifal muff and a San de Remo cape among other enticing but occult entities. The text is set in a particularly unattractive small sans-serif face whose proper use might be for the small print on a loan application. Further collages and pages ripped from movie magazines and gay porn magazines appear throughout the book. Wildly erratic typesetting is a recurrent feature, with seemingly pointless eruptions of capitalisation, arbitrary line-breaks dividing monosyllabic words (for example 't-o') and overall an impression of the most comprehensive disorder and complete lack of reverence for the text. Indeed the effect is reminiscent of the home publishing and websites of conspiracy theorists for whom the urgency of communicating the threat Prince Philip poses to civilisation outweighs any aesthetic concerns.

Some further general observations might be made of this book: No aesthetic space is cleared for the presentation of the poem. Poems abut on aesthetically unpretentious visual materials, including clumsily ripped movie-star and gay porn mag collages. Economy of means appears to hold no virtue. The classic US poetry chapbook presents poems in a carefully chosen typeface, each buffered from the vulgar world by a substantial spread of expensive, hand-made paper; the poem's presentation announcing the time and consideration invested in each word's selection. *Behind the State Capitol* subjects poems to jostle. Those poems which commence tightly stanzaic, collapse into ribbons and into blocks of prose. Gossip-column prose unexpectedly squeezes out a few lines of verse.

Returning to the verses quoted from the opening two pages, the following observations might be added: Inconsistency appears to be a principle. And even where poetic style is most conventional, it is never, never tasteful. '1952' is likely to be contemporary with its title and with the 'Ode on a Common Fountain' opening *Ace of Pentacles*—that is, written in the poet's late teens and before his encounter with Charles Olson. 'Understood Disbelief' then delivers a shocking stylistic uppercut, although the poem is consistent developmentally with local effects of extreme elision in the poems of *Nerves. Behind the State Capitol* subsequently revisits every period of Wiener's poetic development, and the writing it incorporates can be assigned roughly to its categories, bearing in mind that arrival in this book will have changed them. There are numerous poems from the late 1950s and throughout the 1960s, most of which suffer indignities in the transcription, ranging from brief incursions of star-chat to full transvestism in swathes of gossipy material almost hiding the original hard-edged poem from view. There are poems from the seventies which reflect the transition from the manner of *Nerves* to that epitomised in the stanzas quoted from 'Understood Disbelief'. There are prose pieces either reminiscing about past times, literary or sexual or both, or adopting a breathless gossip-column style or the persona and voice of a movie starlet—but which also are saturated with loss and nostalgia. It is noteworthy, given the timespan of this book, that for all its cultural compendiousness, not a single rock or soul singer is name-checked, any musicians dating back to the glory days of Billie Holiday just as the movie stars date to the Hollywood of the same era.

'Understood Disbelief' is a poem which can induce a feeling of help-lessness, but it is an important statement of principle and method whose outline can be traced readily enough if anxiety at refractory detail can be kept at bay. The "dichotomy" of the first line refers the reader forward to the 'opposition' of line 7 and proclaims Wieners' secession from post-Olsonian poetics in favour of the qualities set out in the third and fourth stanzas:

> wills pleasant chicanery hulled
>
> in opposition to queer honesty,
> flying hapless good humours
> Morphe erroneous untedious mystery,
>
> non-said mistakes; pure levity
> to a method of confused doubt;
> lipping erratic contrary indexd
>
> Brevity;

The poem expresses scorn for a slavish "post-mortem" adherence to Olson's historical and mythological programme, and insists that Maximus lies dead and buried ("maxim skulls"). Instead Wieners will negotiate the dichotomy between "pleasant chicanery" and "queer honesty", offering "pure levity" as well as "confused doubt"; dream and drug-produced "erroneous untedious mystery" are opposed implicitly to the scholarly mysteries expounded by Olsonians (and indeed by Poundians). The espoused dichotomy then is summed up as "lipping erratic contrary indexd/ Brevity"—the "Brevity" subsequently unravelling through an explicit pun on 'breviary' to invoke the mysteries of Catholicism and the cinema as a single complicated melodrama:

> Taught in the text as poor flopped sisters,
> reeked convent blood between pleas
> of gospel purblind drawn melodramas.

"Poor flopped sisters" nicely has the 'poor sisters' at prayer and at textual study while introducing the distractions of sexual passion and the seductions of melodrama, and this offers an apt characterisation of the book which this poem serves to introduce. The poem concludes with two extraordinarily compressed stanzas:

> A viscosity submandered elopes
> deluge senseless colophon
> Forgotten opposition
>
> in the face of negligent monetary
> station or bookstore adherent nation.
> (Debauched, bequeathed goad.)

"Submandered" is a verbal invention which might be parsed as 'subverted by command from below the level of consciousness'; so the "viscosity" of quotidian experience is induced to 'elope', and any conclusive attempt at a "colophon", a final flourish or signature, is rendered "senseless" by its "deluge". A previous line suggests that drugs are helpful agents, or perhaps that adopting the role of "spies" to achieve *impertinence* rather than quotidian vision, produces an effect similar to drugs—in any event, it is suggestive for explaining the dominant presence in the book of Mata Hari whose name, according to The Crime Library internet site which provides a detailed history of her life and times, "has become synonymous with spying, espionage, intrigue, and sensuality".[146]

The senselessness of the colophon is then understood reflexively; that is, the opposition which in its opening the poem articulated in distinguishing its strategies from those of Wieners' literary paternity, also had drawn the line of a colophon; now this in its turn has to be deluged and forgotten in that the Olsonian paternity itself represents a "forgotten opposition" to financial chicanery and the "bookstore adherent nation"—a phrase which recalls an earlier spate of references to 'breviary', 'prayerbook', 'text', 'gospel' and 'hymnal', implying a misplaced trust in textual authority. But as the final parenthesis stipulates, resistance to patriarchal textual authority requires not its disavowal but "good humours" and "levity", the debauching of what has been bequeathed and an understanding of its value as a "goad". Hence not only the continued reverence for the Virgin Mary, Edna St. Vincent Millay, Charles Olson, Robert Creeley, Lana Turner and Mata Hari (to name but a few) but also Wieners' treatment of his own history and texts in this book. The patriarchal line which elsewhere is taken back to one of Olson's literary fathers, the nineteenth-century historian William H. Prescott, endures (as its cultural dominance only deserves) considerably more "submandering", deluging and levity at its expense than the matriarchal, as in the following excerpt from 'Gusta with Madame Simone de Beauvoir' (where GG stands for 'Great Garbo, a.k.a. Gusta'):

> Ariadne either acquits fatally reversed exotic miscreants both rurally benefiting Prescott; desparatedly staunching the body and blood or Her Son, for the supreme act of sacrifice, heard daily in the weekly celebration of The Mass, not upon the federal apronstrings braided as coils from Circe's turret Pike's peak. I consider poetry and problematic philosophy to be *outre* ga u c h e, avowed, regarded skitterish tabulating of worldliness galoshed Southern central juxtaposition to this N o r d de P A R I S visitation, mourned you professionally servant girls upon the
> MANONNAED be-paths of my put-out. POINT—
> ED ingly, plUrally
> GG: *Coquettishly.*[147]

'Understood Disbelief' assists therefore in the understanding of the book which follows, proposing that its disorderliness will be programmatic rather than pathological. It yields enough evidence to the focussed attention to support such a presumption, both semantically and in its sustained if unfamiliar formal discipline; yet is as tonally wayward and difficult to pin down as 'In Public' and—in an odd contradiction characteristic of *Behind the State Capitol*—is simultaneously compressed to the point of Empsonian obscurity, and extremely 'noisy' in the sense of high levels of apparent redundancy. It is unusual to find either such compression or redundancy associated with such a forward drive rhythmically, although an analogy might be drawn with the screwball comedies of Frank Capra and Preston Sturges where complex verbal wit and a bewildering intricacy of incident can never quite be absorbed given the hurtling narrative pace. The kind of reading which unpicks puns meticulously makes a reader feel slow-witted; such writing invites riposte rather than interpretation.

At the same time it is possible to claim too much for the programmatic nature of *Behind the State Capitol*; what emerges out of this book has always been 'taught in the text', and 'Understood Disbelief' was probably a late poem in the book's composition and could be read therefore as a post-hoc programme. This does not make it implausible; this book does seem to me to be driven by the dialectic which the term "Morphe" encodes in the third stanza of 'Understood Disbelief': between Morpheus and morphe, between unconscious process and formal control, between morphine and morphology. Biographically and in regard to compositional process this might reflect a relationship between the products of mental illness or substance misuse and of literary craftsmanship, but not necessarily in the direction of conscious control revising a primary splurge in order to create a distinct, sufficient artefact; as frequently the process subjects the artefact to invasion, and the book as a whole could be regarded as the product of a continual dialectical process—where a prior text, perhaps from the sixties, might become the launchpad for a standup schizoid improvisation then transcribed and further treated in the transcription. Undoubtedly chance comes into it too; the reprinting of certain poems in the *Selected Poems 1958–1984* corrects errors in the transcription from Wieners' typescript. But as a whole, *Behind the State Capitol* sustains and exploits this shifting, dynamic relationship brilliantly and "coquettishly", at times lurching into gloriously paranoid arraignments of government agencies, at times pausing for heartbreaking laments, at times lipping a quip a line. The difficult triumph of keeping this edge becomes evident in looking at the later poems collected in 'She'd Turn On A Dime', the last section of *Selected Poems 1958-1984*, where too often queenish quips perish in inconsequentiality. *Behind the State Capitol* remains endlessly surprising, moving, funny engaged and flip, and its gender indeterminacy, its transvestism in which maleness is not disavowed through the assuming of parodic traits of femininity, permits (for example) a serious regard for manual labour and the materials of building construction as well as for fashion trends—and a headfirst, intoxicated response to glamour to co-exist with a sharp critique of the economic realities of the fashion and film industries and glamour's cost.

Switching directly from this performance to a text from *Behind The State Capitol*—'Signs of the President Machine' chosen with the voting machines of Florida in mind—and applying Wieners' vocal style to an imaginary performance, tightens the score so that it seems to produce its speaker out of the 'terms of language, love and fashion'.

**Signs of the President Machine**

I've got 25¢ coin on the bureau
or maple mahogany table, built out of
magnolia limbs, and a Persian carpet airing in lawn

yard a baby flood, TELVA magazines with my photograph on
the cover as Marilyn Monroe, jack dead mother's nutty sister
saying, *Who Is She*, I'm A Lot of Man, by the late Nancy
                    Cunard of course

that pauvre Rose la Rose, Billie Shakespeare, or was it Sanctity's
                            Holiday drugged as Moynihan across
behind a red lantern, ask Mme Brenda drinking torpid Gloucester
cyan—
ide dutied United States Postmen, plastic transparent basket.

Poor Benedict posing as a Polish sister
I can feel his dope over the Hedges, wintergardening carol form
the Meirovingian corner besides
the master bedroom, the military treason in their acquisition
from accumulation in the United Feds prison of
not only food at Agriculture, but terms of language, love and
fashion.

Pussybile, fresh from black George's suicide at 86 Charles.

Oh. yes, a week of, a month of, two years moving shirts with
Treasury numbers
poor secretaries becoming international thieves, from failure
to absorb

> newly hung curtains, encroaching plants and poisoned burners
> on the stove coiled charcoal sexual yens in the dish dryer.

The poem's first line initiates a notation of the present, to which words offer only an approximate fit—are we talking a bureau or a table, and is it of maple, mahogany or, ridiculously, "magnolia limbs"? The quarter proffered at the beginning might display any option in the presidential and linguistic fruit machine, or operate a callbox or a washing machine or drier. Telva magazines—a Spanish fashion and gossip title—introduce a melange of Wieners' obsessions, ranging from Marilyn Monroe to Jack Kennedy ("jack dead") to Billie Holiday to, rather more buried in the text, Charles Olson—Olson's father was a postman in Gloucester, Mass. and Olson wrote a memoir of him under the title 'The Post Office'. Rose la Rose was a stripper, the owner of a well-known burlesque theatre in Toledo. Mme Brenda may perhaps be a drag queen. But enough: this assembles out of prior texts and the writer's immediate surroundings—"plastic transparent basket" sounds straight from a pocket ad in the Sunday Papers of yesteryear—a text which uncannily parallels 'Larders' in its movement, with "plastic transparent basket" echoing the pause supplied by "cocktails at lunch" in the earlier poem. The hero-worship of earlier poems' references to Olson is replaced by an oblique accusation of poisonous patriarchy, preparing for the poem's second half.

This draws on the literature of right-wing US conspiracy theorists; surfing after 'Merovingian' gives entry to a universe of anti-federalist material dedicated to frustrating the schemes of world government concocted by illuminati, masons, Knights Templar, the worldwide Jewish conspiracy, the Bilderberg Group or whatever. The misspelling of 'Merovingian' as "Meirovingian" may reflect the anti-semitic genotype of this thought, evoking the name of Golda Meir, Israeli prime minister until 1974. Institutionalised treason and theft dominate the world view of the conspiracy theorists—taxation being their particular bogey—and Wieners cross-cuts this material with misogyny, with drug abuse and with "black George's suicide", a constellation reminiscent of William Burroughs in its integration of sexuality and narcotics into systems of capitalist control. As with Burroughs' cutup technique, Wieners' collage mobilises fortuitous effects as proxies for character and subjectivity: Burroughs deploys lay figures and mouthpieces to drive narrative, where Wieners recombines trash to produce faux lyrics complete with subjectivity-effect, their movement invested with a weirdly endogenous compulsion—the "terms of language, love and fashion" being set into a sprightly motion as far removed as imaginable from the turgid screeds of conspiracy theories or the inert ephemera of *Hello* magazine and its international equivalents.

Such paranoid constructions in Burroughs and Wieners invite comparison with Ezra Pound. Pound sought clarification, whether in his stipulations for poetics or in his quest through historical records for the telling detail which would bring to light the structure of a sensibility, or the fundamental error responsible for the ills of the present day. Transcendence typically was expressed in flashes of intense and clear vision of isolated phenomena of the material world, spots of energy discharging entire historical-cultural formations. Such transcendence was achievable only through the poet's will; through scholarship and through craft. The investment of labour was redeemed by moments of evident truth. Refusal in others to acknowledge what was made clear, had to be motivated by ignominious interests which worked through blurring and opacity. Granted, this attitude entailed a continuing struggle with a never-extirpated legacy of *fin-de-siècle* symbolist haze, and the sharp contours of modernism may be exaggerated in the service of academic territory-marking: nonetheless the proclamations are unambiguous.

For both Burroughs and the later Wieners, however, all terms of language, love and fashion embody controlling interests, and moments of transcendence and authenticity are to be mistrusted above all. Since the media of communication, language included, can neither be trusted nor bypassed, and that goes for the syntax whereby we apprehend our own agency, the best recourse for the writer is to relinquish illusions of originality and exceptionalism, splitting and ripping any vaunted integrity to reveal its partiality. But Wieners doubles back, employing trash materials including those of paranoid politics, to recreate lyric performance independent of individual self-contemplation. In 'Signs of the President Machine' the final stanza re-inscribes "the standard | usage prepared" with no interest in inhabiting the gallery of normal snapshots paraded in 'Larders'; looking back at the earlier poem from this vantage, its opening stanzas now present a sequence of publicity stills for a pastiche of life, the poem reverting only in its final stages to something recognisably vehement and painful. The pain pervading 'Signs of the President Machine' radiates through damage to immediate acquaintances, to tragic figures in popular culture, and to wage-slaves, and is inflicted mainly through betrayal. Betrayal might be personal as with Charles Olson, but the personal has been subsumed amidst media exploitation, food hoarding, corruption of workers, "sexual yens", opiate dependency and grand conspiracy. Such a brew may be hellish, but also demonstrates that "terms of language, love and fashion" can be liberated from their prison to enunciate their own lyric—this is detritus singing its own song, and the poet can be only its occasion.

Olson's presence is such that he can emerge, like a supportive or admonitory parent checking around the bedroom door, at any moment; this is a characteristic shared with a gallery of spirits presiding over *Behind the State Capitol*, although where women are concerned Wieners is as likely to assume their costumed identity as to have recourse (as here) with Mme Brenda to a "plastic transparent bucket". This attribute of repeated and locally unaccountable incursion by figures such as Jackie Onassis, Mata Hari (why does "parched imbecilic Mata Hari" appear in 'Toady's Singular', for instance?[148]) and Barbara Hutton not only confirms the necessity of reading *Behind the State Capitol* as a book, but eradicates any distinction between memories founded in first-hand experience and those derived from saturation in movies and glamour magazines—much as compelled watchers of a particular TV soap find their autobiography implicated with the dramas of invented lives. Thus poets become confused with stars:

> Robert Creeley's buttocks disappearing down a path to
> Mountain          Lodge. His beautiful thighs that I touched Once
> through corduroy trousers [...][149]

and stars decidedly become poets, or more particularly, John Wieners assumes the identity of the star who becomes the poet. *Behind the State Capitol* is above all else a commemorative book, where co-memoration brings Stephen Jonas and Jack Spicer into the same assembly as society's A-list.

What after all does it mean to be a drag-queen poet? Simultaneously it is to accept and contest that "accumulation in the United Feds prison of | not only food at Agriculture, but terms of language, love and | fashion" found in "the master bedroom" in 'Signs of the President Machine'. "Terms" here are as much the length of punitive sentences pronounced by fashion dictators and love's law of loss, as the particular discourses of this trinity; but Wieners' poetry insists on the facticity (that is the fact as well as the factitiousness) of a persistence beyond term. No love ever fades, glamour reigns, the most ephemeral printed matter lives forever, even as all recede into a season's sensations; but here is no Shakespearian enduring monument, but a sort of Busby Berkeley memory spectacular where character is not just 'under-developed' but ditched wherever known, and the trappings, the image, the iconographic screen moment achieve immortality. And this is true: it is the biography revealing the man behind the mask, the star behind the make-up, which now reads as closer to fiction than the gossip column. The Feds and "bookstore adherent nation" may seek to exercise the authority of death, but the Queen exercises the power of necromancy.

The articles of Necromancy are set out in the astonishing poem of that name,[150] starting:

> The Queen can grant no mercy, no clemency
> for she is owed permanently too much money

and clambering to the peroration:

> Settling well earned laurels aghast the legal masonry
> Relating of course privately of textual similarity
> beset from arrest, abduction, amnesia, murder and false
>       sentences
> apology as a dear sacrifice out of form in referred harmony.

'Necromancy' offers an irresistibly noteworthy anticipation of a later popular mode, through its mono-rhyme sustained with occasional lapses through 44 lines, and around which the lines hinge, swing and unspool. This extremely impacted writing consequently moves with the unassailable authority of what has since emerged as rap, where rhymes are used for propulsion and to prevent the slackening of invention and audience attention. Rhyme acts both as a stricture and as a demand to say more, to go further; these combined make for the oracular, authoritative style.

A concluding *tour d'horizon* of *Behind the State Capitol* would have to cite the excoriating social realism of 'Children of the Working Class', the most powerful denunciation of the state asylum system ever published, and any number of painfully moving lyrics as well as travelogues such as 'Four Excerpts from *Playboy*' (a trip to the Florida Democratic National Convention in 1972 with a gay liberationist group), letters and several disquisitions on 'The Rich and The Super Rich'. What distinguishes the book across all this range is an affective excess which had once seemed closed down in modernism's appetite for semantic productivity, as though the directedness or comprehensiveness of feeling would inevitably set restrictive terms on indeterminacy; but in *Behind the State Capitol* the ersatz is mobilised by immediately connective joy and pain, and the highly complex driven by affective urgency. Swathes of seemingly redundant information are brought under the spell of eternal verities, religiously charged abstractions, and gather out of the disregarded and disposed-of, a carnival company; this is entirely to be distinguished from the congeries of objects characterising Angle-American modernism, where (as in William Carlos Williams) the object occasions its own unveiling; in Wieners, newspaper reports of a star's appearance at a premier both veil and resurrect The Woman, the memory of a blow-job veils and restores Love. Archetypes are discovered in pulp rather than fine art, and recusancy meets transvestism.

When Wieners refers to "terms of language, love and fashion", fashion refers both to the passing guises of immutable glamour, but also to the fashioning which his poetry performs. Detail, particulars, phrases from an interview are dislodged from fetishism and subordinated to the dictates of the essential. Fashion (*pace* Walter Benjamin[151]) here dislodges the fixed lustre of distraction and makes of it a miasma, a halo for the true "terms" by which Wieners is governed: beauty, love.

∾

The relationship between the early 'As Preface to Transmutations' and the late 'Cultural Affairs in Boston' is analogous to that between 'Larders' and 'Signs of the President Machine'.[152] The verse portion of 'As Preface to Transmutations' was written soon after the first version of *The Hotel Wentley Poems* was published and shares its tone, but this has become mannered—the deftness is a little too arch, the marks of exclusion and election just too hip:

> Those old elms bend over
> the street and form an arch
>    that we walk under.
> Sad priests in the 20th century.

The poem is addressed to the Boston poet Stephen Jonas, and for the student of Boston poetry, has charm as an association piece. Dana was Wieners' lover at the time, and Marshall probably refers to the

Boston poet Edward Marshall, author of the impressive collection *Helan, Helan*. Jonas, by some years older than Wieners, seems to have marked out a path of damage and excess which Wieners determined to emulate—"6 months in Danvers" refers to the Danvers State Insane Asylum, Wieners himself later being detained in Taunton State Asylum, part of the same Massachusetts asylum system. But the poem's professions of loss are unconvincing because damage here figures as initiation, much as in 'The Acts of Youth', and such anointing has become anachronistic; so the final lines on the indifference of the traffic intimate and the subsequent prose section records, with Scollay Square, the centre of the vice trade and the lawless romance of a great but decaying port, shortly to be redeveloped, and with the poetic nucleus dispersed.

But what if the question mark is reinstated at the end of the poem? "What traffic | drowns out | all our notes"?

'Cultural Affairs in Boston' responds to a magazine editor's request for "work" and opens with a riff on the meaning of literary work which articulates directly the rationale for such writing as 'Signs of the President Machine'—that is, to direct the traffic rather than pipe ineffectually on the road shoulder. In his high society guise, noblesse oblige, Wieners remarks "I like to hazard a guaranty a behavior-involvement would reduce the withholding circumstances, attributable to man's position in society. For my servants, after all, the working man is not a dual-motivated hypothesis." Wieners seeks an "unearthing of one's position" in place of the imposition of that precious literary work which denies its community and spuriously asserts its independence from social determinants. The specification is to start from outside rather than within, eventually to unearth yourself as "another human person" by working "outre-contradictionedly to employ yourself towards in words". "Yourself" then is a tool, an occasion, mobilised to provoke the contra-dictionary, while "in words" implies that yourself exists out there linguistically, "repetitiously as a document", needing and available to be brought home to the collective.

The second part of the text instantly contradicts this thesis: "Believe me, you can be nobody else, but who you are." But such contradiction serves the true work: who this writer might be, becomes confused in a whirl of "upperworld restoration", a fantasy of luxury hotel life throwing into relief the conditions of labour and reproduction.

Hotels stage their guests historically and culturally, and as figures of power and influence; for Wieners, hotels also encourage a performative staging of gender. The performances are private, soliciting no applause from others, mobilising outré selves unable to survive off-stage—and for the very rich as well as for actors and actresses, even the way from the limousine to the lobby is canopied. Barbara Hutton required the support of immense invisible labour. In the hotel, scattered magazines compose the social world and demand continual study—'society' as a paranoid system may be abstract and formal but demands an incessant study of detail, as readers of Proust recognise. But for Wieners no detail can be numinous. The particular would allow nostalgia to rush back, as it does at the start of *Du Côté de Chez Swann*; in Wieners' writing details crowd to the point of indecipherability, here and now. Here and now the questions may be: is this fashionable? chic? truly of the moment? But then the world of Barbara Hutton, and here and now the world of, let us say, Jemima Khan née Goldsmith, depend on robbery; fashion, corruption and violence are intimate in Boston and Hollywood, tarnishing the golden dome of the State Capitol, decaying the mask of make-up, turning tawdry the interior décor. But of course not. The commemoration of celebrities precedes them.

These secular churches, chapels of the stars, obliterate all sign of the distasteful workings of life. Their lure for Wieners lies in translation of the bohemianism of poverty into glamour. Hotels are crash-pads for the affluent, anti-domestic, places of assignation and anonymity or a choice of names and identity, "chamber attitudes". The dedication to "unearthing" in the text's first section is guyed in the pronouncement "man can stand just so much exhumation", and writing now becomes a therapeutic delight, "preparing against anxiety". What fascinates Wieners is exactly what must be exposed, what is treacherous but remains desirable, whether poetry, drugs, sex, Hollywood starlets or hotels. All are criminally-implicated, and part two of 'Cultural Affairs' concludes like a crime report filed from the Albion hotel in Miami via A.P. (Associated Press).

The third section of 'Cultural Affairs in Boston' hits the road in a sort of anticipation of *The Adventures of Priscilla, Queen of the Desert*, with a faggot band fleeing the Albion, presumably on a first leg en route to Boston. The notations are bewildering, snatches of high camp dialogue. No matter. Treat this as a road movie; the transitions between set pieces are often hard to follow. Section IV starts as though it will reproduce 'As Preface to Transmutations' but it parodies the original—abbreviated fake reminiscences centre on the glamorous Nico, Warhol superstar, model and musician. Although the capitalised word "CORANDEL" is positioned as a final stop following a European tour in a progress through hotels, "Commodore, Commander, Cambridge", it may allude to Mary Butts's short story 'Brightness Falls' with its character Dr Corandel. John Ashbery's description of Mary Butts's prose makes it sound like 'Cultural Affairs in Boston'—he writes of "her startling ellipses, especially in conversations; her drastic cutting in the cinematic sense; and her technique of collaging bits of poetry and popular song lyrics…into the narratives".

Home leads to the Pantry, the larder where this adventure in reading Wieners began; the larder however is guarded no longer by the poet's parents but releases a mid-century American Pandora's box of middle-brow culture, from Rogers & Hammerstein to the Family Theatre, a long-time TV institution inaugurated and presided over by Father Peyton, a Holy Cross priest from South Bend, Indiana, unctuous interviewer of Rose Kennedy after the death of her two sons. Catholicism lies deep in this mix, compressed into the last word of the poem, "Spencerboy", which conflates Spencer Tracy's name with that of the movie 'Boys Town' where he starred as Father Flanagan alongside the delinquent Mickey Rooney. Another faux lyric, composed of "early Thanksgiving alloy | and silk sitting room for our Virgin Mary", this final passage too rips up personal reminiscences ("Norton Union" is a student residence at SUNY Buffalo where Wieners enrolled in the graduate programme in the mid-60s) and sticks their fragments alongside style magazine cuttings. High society Catholicism is jostled in its gilt and alloy, its "sweet parlor", through the incursion of "vanitate", summoning the object of ascetic renunciation 'De Vanitate Mundi'—and false-rhyming with "imitate". The entire verse passage is propelled by rhyme and false-rhyme which holds together its disparate elements so as to achieve another heterotrophic lyric, fretfully integrated and gratifyingly obscure.

The poetry of John Wieners through its different stages holds promise for a different kind of postmodernist poetry, drawing on the affective power of the post-Romantic lyric but fully implicated in the traffic, linguistic and otherwise, of the human collectivity. Contrary to the dictates of good sense, untainted by epic grandiloquence, unuinter-ested in smart moves—this writing so far exceeds camp that all inverted commas are off, subsumed in memory's theatre where any intake can be held and structured by the deployment of traditional poetic means beyond accepted limits (as in the mono-rhyme of 'Necromancy'), going out gaudily and collapsing though the terms of language, love and fashion liberated from correct usage. At a time when the term 'stereotype' carries a pejorative political meaning and when religious faith seeks justification through immediate social relevance rather than faith, this poetry could not be more out of place—which in truth or in fantasy is where we might desire poetry to take us.

# A Poem for Liars

Could the poem as an enticing untruth, interrupt the poem of everyday life, the poem of everyday life itself having interrupted the poetic diversions of refined sensibility? Could the poem interrupt its attentiveness and the attentiveness it has attracted, in favour of a saving obscurity? When all is about to be brought finally into the light, the evidence produced, could the poem then provide the protective cover of a strange intimacy? The affirmatives are to be found in an early poem by John Wieners, dated 6.16.58 and written in the Hotel Wentley, San Francisco.

A poem for vipers

I sit in Lees. At 11:40 PM with
Jimmy the pusher. He teaches me
Ju Ju. Hot on the table before us
shrimp foo yong, rice and mushroom
chow yuke. Up the street under the wheels
of a strange car is his stash—The ritual.
We make it. And have made it.
For months now together after midnight.
Soon I know the fuzz will
interrupt, will arrest Jimmy and
I shall be placed on probation. The poem
does not lie to us. We lie under
its law, alive in the glamour of this hour
able to enter into the sacred places
of his dark people, who carry secrets
glassed in their eyes and hide words
under the coats of their tongue.

This is the revised 1965 version of the poem; the 1958 printing titled 'A poem for tea heads' ('vipers' was 1920s slang for dope heads) ended with the line "under the roofs of their mouth." The singular of the final word in important in both versions: the sought words will be the provender of the one occulting tongue, as the poem's final sentence, after a double interruption to the nervously fragmented speech at Lees, wraps through the lines and so ordains in liturgical cadence that "We lie under | its law".

At its start the poem anticipates Frank O'Hara's lunch poem style of a year later, and modulates into something closer to Allen Ginsberg's contemporary outlaw romanticism, via a scenario of white-boy transgression which soon would be retailed more widely in the early LPs of The Velvet Underground. And this poem is written during the San Francisco Renaissance. But such timeframing is the work schedule of the literary-historical police: take note of what is on the table, stake out the strange car, record the pattern of comings and goings at Lees. "We have made it" means that you didn't interrupt us, Mr Policeman; but for us to have made it "For months now together after midnight", that has now made for routine. These precisions of the illicit have become the details of accountancy in a trade subject to ritual exchange at Lees, much as the downtown dealmakers gathered over their three-martini lunches. Ritual has become ritualised: "We make it. And have made it." Any restoration of power to ritual now requires ritual's interruption, and an interruption in the language of exchange; what if this poem and the book of *The Hotel Wentley Poems* have rudely interrupted the proprieties of poetry with street speech, the drug trade milieu, the bebop metrical improvisation—the poem is too particular, too available, its outlaw pose already banal. We don't want information, we want the stuff.

The poem cannot lie *to* us because it will not be involved in the language of exchange, instead, the poem lies: and the relationship it demands is that "We lie under | its law". The lies of the poem are not in bad faith; and it would mistake the nature of lyric poetry to hold the poem to account as though its lies were somehow personal. But if we submit to the poem's lying we too may become true liars, and leaving behind the 11:40 routine, find ourselves once more "alive in the glamour of this hour", and participate in a transfiguration. Obscurity is not the same as murkiness or intractability; transparency can be obscure, as with unaccountable glamour, as with "secrets | glassed in their eyes"; and the impenetrable may lie on the surface as an open secret. The truth may be spoken and written and at the same time hidden, through the agency of the interrupting poem whose law lies under "the coats of their tongue"—its words like little packages passed from mouth to mouth during visiting hours.

So there are two possible interruptions which a poem may incur. One is the interruption of the police, who will arrange the appropriate disposal for those involved, and nail the guilty words. The other is interruption as the renewal of ritual, a dive for cover, a plunge into otherness. Yes this poem by John Wieners is somewhat clumsy and its romanticising of the black other a little embarrassing nearly fifty years later, but how astonishing it is that a poetry which introduced into American poetry a new note of fidelity to the experience of the dispossessed—the drug addicts, the prostitutes, the transvestites—should in the same beat have insisted on infidelity to its own occasion, interrupting itself to secure to the reader the endless promise of poetic mendacity, a supply of real stuff.

# Stumbling, Balking, Tacking: Robert Creeley's For Love *and* Mina Loy's Love Songs to Joannes

To stumble and to stammer are cognate, and each such mis-articulation predicts its own righting, an almost-falling resolved into the step forward, the words stabilising as the speaker gets his mouth into gear. In neither case does stumbler or stammerer ordinarily resolve the disturbance through a change of mind, as a stutterer might by substituting a more readily pronounced phrase, or the balker stock-still who decides to adopt a different path; the stutterer and the balker might through steadfast purpose risk failing completely, as the stumbler will not, for he is destined to walk his way out of trouble—since as Laurie Anderson has noted, in a tone of such equanimity that her stammering is unthinkable, falling is itself a component of the complex articulation of walking.[153] Fear of falling might prevent walking, but not so actual falling through stumbling (leave aside such special risk factors as osteoporosis), for even if you stumble and fall you will likely pick yourself up, dust yourself down and continue to walk. You might even make a dance out of such righting, like Fred Astaire, falling with panache and the confidence that the earth will be soft or arms stretch out to catch you.

Should you wish to stumble with panache in poetry, you might study Robert Creeley's lyric poetry, for this is the special thing it does. Following this example, you might discover real advantages in your adept stumbling, for every mistake you made would be rescued by a self-righting mechanism, while your righteousness would be found tolerable because of your openly-acknowledged mistakes. This might be true especially if you were male and your stumbling and stammering occurred in the purview of a woman whose definitive womanliness incorporated that maternal care exercised over a toddler. At once you could be a precocious and loved toddler, and an adorably clumsy, fallible man—and the universe would conform to your arms-out terror and trust, to your longings, being organised about you in a way you could feel more or less responsible for, perhaps even prompting you to reproach or thank a woman.

To bring Mina Loy into conjunction with Robert Creeley may appear anachronistic, but they correlate alongside a patriarchal lineage of modernist poets sharing grand if not grandiose ambition, in Ezra Pound and Charles Olson respectively; poets aspiring to major status and duly granted it academically. Of course, Mina Loy's occlusion has been much the greater, but her sexual assertiveness and prosodic syncopation read against Pound's asserted and acknowledged mastery, is paralleled by Creeley's use of sexual vulnerability and prosodic hesitation read against Olson's dominance over the open field of his poetics. At first acquaintance the poetry of Robert Creeley between 1950 and 1960 collected in *For Love* looks engagingly modest, where the early poetry of Mina Loy in her 'Love Songs to Joannes' (published 1915–1917) looks enjoyably brazen, even exhibitionist. This is especially marked when the two poets write of physical sex, something they both do with a rare and exact descriptiveness. But what I wish to argue in this paper is that Creeley's poetry exhibits a sustained poise in both presented self and in prosody through its hesitancy, tending towards self-regard even when self-doubting, through a circuit requiring the presence of a woman. By contrast, Loy's categorical-sounding starts and stops are driven by internal contradictions at the level of argument or *position*, producing abrupt changes of direction marked prosodically; which in turn encounter new oppositions and tensions, these also subsequently reconsidered although not necessitating any revision or suppression of the prior record. Loy's poems know nothing of time passing; instead they gather their positions and stages in an uneasy coexistence.

On this account it might be tempting to call Loy's poetry dialectical (and it has already been termed 'analytical' by Rachel Blau DuPlessis and Michael Palmer, and as exemplary of 'logopoeia' by Ezra Pound as long ago as 1918[154]), even if this is a curious term to apply to 'love songs,' but then, these are love songs of a very particular time, when relations between the sexes were under the most intense debate and personal negotiation among people associated with progressive politics in the United States and Great Britain. Since this historical context has been treated extensively by Carolyn Burke in her biography of Loy and by other writers, it will not be a major consideration here.[155] Rather, the concern will be with the particularities of internal movement through the configurations of Loy's poems, which are, in Donna Haraway's usage, *situated* as to gender but where situatedness is a continually renewed process rather than a settled fact. The originality of 'Love Songs to Joannes' lies in their phrasal and prosodic sensitivity to a changing situatedness, demanding a linear and relational reorientation. Their lines are as it were incised definitely but run into objections, they refuse and are refused by each acknowledged new configuration, but will not allow of being transfixed; rather, they transgress each other in the argument in which they participate, but do not erase or disfigure. Creeley's poetry of the late 1950s and early 1960s may seem hesitant, but its hesitations occur within a situation never understood as culturally situated in its fundamental configuration—relations between woman and a man being taken as archetypal—nor questioned in its default *balance* of power; for the hesitations, the stumbles, always redound to the advantage of the stumbler even if he may dream betimes of a perfect masculine ease.

To stumble or stammer implies a directedness interrupted, which on resumption will spur consciousness of bodily motivation and impediment both; it is expressive of individual will and of personal embodiment with its attendant fallibility—for while one may stumble over a chance hazard, maybe a broken paving-slab, the obstruction causing one to stumble is not social, and even a stammer is social only by way of a looped self-consciousness, feedback induced by a break in the intersubjectivity of speech. Its correction brings mastery, rather than restoring the *status quo ante*. It is in such terms that Charles Altieri expatiates on three poems by Robert Creeley through a fine-grained reading in his book *The Art of Twentieth-Century American Poetry*, associating Creeley's procedures with a Spinozan view of individuation founded in conativity:

> The goal of expression is not self-knowledge as a concept or image; expressing the self consists simply in an awareness of how "the body's power of activity is increased or diminished, assisted or checked, together with the ideas of these affections." Conativity is the felt power to find reflexive satisfaction within one's capacity to control the physical and imaginative space a being occupies.[156]

Since Altieri is at this point interested in establishing an affiliation between Creeley and Robert Lowell and Adrienne Rich, and in downplaying Creeley's conventional assignation to 'Black Mountain', he neglects to note—a lapse surely tendentious—the kinship between Creeley's conativity and Charles Olson's proprioception, proprioception being the phenomenological expression of conativity. In his essay on the term, Olson riffs on proprioception as "*proprious*-ception | 'one's own'-ception' and as 'the 'body' itself as, by movement of its own tissues, giving the data of, depth."[157] Will and desire (conativity) expressed through the body's reaching and being reached, lead to an ontological position whereby "the extent of longing and desire is both our own extent and the extent of the world around us, and we are at the centre of the world around us by a supreme prerogative."[158] This position is stated stumblingly but assuredly by Creeley at the close of his poem 'The Awakening' dedicated to Charles Olson:

> God is no bone of whitened contention.
> God is not air, nor hair, is not
> a conclusive concluding
> to remote yearnings. He moves
>
> only as I move, you also move to
> the awakening, across long rows, of beds,
> stumble breathlessly, on leg pins and crutch,
> moving at all as all men, because you must.[159]

The final line's "at all" is extremely carefully poised, "at all" implying 'towards all beings and all things' as well as 'in the least'. God then is not an entity to be subject to scholastic argument, nor ubiquitous and general as air, nor arbitrary as "hair" (such slippage carrying over from a flurry in the previous stanza, "err to concur", "the seen, the green green"), nor to be distanced from "yearnings" which can only be located in the body, here both creature and instrument of male will. Male will, because "all men" attains its gender specificity from the poem's earlier allusion to "a woman's impression", whereby a woman not merely is the recipient of impressions rather than a mover by intention, but present only in her absence—the impression perhaps of the woman departed from the bed; perhaps also the woman who answers the door bell earlier in the poem and the telephone later, both sounding off-stage. If "we are at the centre of the world", that "we" is figured not in the first person's relationship with "a woman's impression" but in "all men" following the instance of Charles Olson and Robert Creeley, whose sense of a shared *project* for all the difference in scale, is conveyed amply through the ten volumes of their published correspondence.

While the problem of how a viable and ethical 'we' is constituted on its specific terrain drives the drama of *The Maximus Poems*, Creeley's poetry of the period 1950–60 is so sparing of that pronoun as to draw attention to its absence and to the mechanisms which substitute for it. One is the generic 'he' as in 'A Song', "Which one sings, if he sings it, with care." Another is "a man" as in the Preface to *For Love*: "a sudden instance of love, and the being loved, wherewith a man also contrives a world (of his own mind)."[160] 'A man' and 'the man' occur more frequently than 'men', and 'man' as an abstraction does not seem to appear at all whereas 'woman' often does; to read Robert Creeley's poems in any number is to notice that the world is actuated by 'a man', his perception of the world and his acts upon it, that world having grown to include 'woman' even if structured by her originally. But specifically, the effective substitutes for 'we' are line-breaks and commas, as evident in the demonstrative stumbles of the final stanza of 'The Awakening', where they admit the self-consciousness which first identifies 'you' as an aspect of the split self, and then enjoins 'you' the reader into a union with the exemplary (male) self. The pause enforced rhythmically and by enjambment prior to 'the awakening', a phrase prefigured in the poem's title and therefore a realised portentousness, creates a space for the awakening of an immanence of the other in the self, a recognition evoking the world in a quasi-divine way. The world then is the precipitate of self-recognition. It is on this ground that 'you' come into being, through the exemplary acts of a stumbling poet, whose purposeful breaks give you utterance: Creeley gives you a break.

Just so with the beautiful lyric 'The Rain' where Altieri claims "we find poetry pursuing a form of resolution quite distinct from the imaginary satisfactions sought by confessional poetry" while bracketing off the final words of the poem with the curiously evasive phrase (for a critic not notably reluctant to moralise) "whatever "decent happiness" can be."[161] The poem's final two stanzas read:

> Love, if you love me,
>     lie next to me.
> Be for me, like rain
>     the getting out
>
> of the tiredness, the fatuousness, the semi-
>     lust of intentional indifference.
> Be wet,
>     With a decent happiness.[162]

Altieri is right on the button in identifying the frank sexuality of "Be wet", and it is an instance of Creeley's rigorous attention to his own moral state that he can ask help in overcoming "the semi- | lust of intentional indifference"—one might indeed feel that a 'we' appears on the horizon here, yearned-for and almost conceived, were it not for the phrase which stumps Altieri. But not this only, for multiple devices of objectification and subservience come into play: the injunction (Be wet), the line-break, the comma, and most strikingly, the initial capital letter after the comma. "With a decent happiness" operates then as a form of dismissal, "decent happiness" being a happiness fitting to the speaker's needs, only the speaker being present to judge her decency in the instance of such unselfconsciousness. Hence the poem enacts for the speaker his moment of potentially unselfconscious union in orgasm followed by a turning away. With this break and comma and capital letter to follow, the wetness appears less the evidence of female sexual arousal than the residue of male sexual arousal, since the poem earlier has referred to "the ease, | even the hardness, | of rain falling" as representing the suspension of self-consciousness to which the too-persistently self-scrutinising poet aspires, the achieved Lawrencian phallicism.

In an interview published in 1971 Robert Duncan talked of Creeley's "practised stumbling" as symptomatic of castration and impotency, the halting of self-consciousness being his privilege and his shame—yet Creeley surely expecting to be forgiven in the understanding that he must go his own way, bound henceforward to survey the earth for its adventitiousness. How could prosody be more exacting, more controlled than by such footfall? Nathaniel Mackey mentions Duncan's phrase when citing lines from Creeley's slightly earlier poem dedicated to his Black Mountain colleague, 'The Door': "The Lady has always moved to the next town | and you stumble on after her".[163] The Lady here comports herself as a particular case of generic 'woman' because she is unmistakably The Muse, and following Duncan's lead Mackey identifies this poem's indebtedness to a poem of the same name by Robert Graves. The late romantic manner also constitutes a homage to Duncan, albeit Duncan's muse-worship showed no propensity to subordinate the muse whereas Creeley interrupts this rhetoric with self-conscious commas and line-breaks calculated precisely to reclaim creative agency from Lady to poet. The most salient lines of Creeley's poem read:

> So I screamed to You,
> who hears as the wind, and changes

multiply, invariably,
changes in the mind.

Running to the door, I ran down
as a clock runs down. Walked backwards,
stumbled, sat down
hard on the floor near the wall.

Where were You.
How absurd, how vicious.
There is nothing to do but get up.[164]

Although there is nothing to do but pursue The Lady, the Lady's task
amounts merely to setting the direction of travel; whilst what engenders poetry of value is exactly that stumbling whereby world, body and
the perceiving of their relatedness, a perceiving out of which world,
body and poetry are born—proprioception—, here fall into place. For
Olson the work of place may be social, economic, mythic and geological,
and collectively proprioceptive, but for Creeley the adamant place of
"the floor near the wall" is conjured through his stumble. Writing of
Creeley's prose, Mackey observes that "a certain "surefootedness" char-
acterizes women as portrayed by Creeley, as opposed to insistent
awkwardness, a tendency to stumble, on the part of the men" and
acknowledges "a binarism that is not innocent of sexual equations
(man = mind, woman = matter)".[165] The surefootedness is doubtless
related both to the singularity of 'woman' as entity in the poems, and,
ironically enough, to the lack of selfconsciousness to which the poet
aspires in 'The Rain' and more so in another poem admired by Altieri,
'Something.' Here watching a woman piss in a sink after having sex,
Creeley reflects (and what can a man do but reflect) "What | love might
learn from such a sight." Singularity then, makes women 'woman' as
well as making woman whole, as distinct from the special role of men in
the plural, especially Black Mountain poets, even one as habitually cool
and unstumbling as Edward Dorn: "Well, I think there's only one
Woman, anyway. It seems to me that men are multiple and women are
singular."[166]

While Creeley's enterprise may be conative, as Altieri characterises it,
Mina Loy's might be held to be wilful more in the sense of obstinacy and
unwillingness to accept convention or authority, to the extent that decisively adopted positions of challenge and refusal in turn become the
objects of denial, even of revulsion. This characteristic has confounded

attempts to read Loy as feminist according to its late twentieth century formations, much as it restrained her from throwing in her lot with any particular group in the contemporary women's movement, despite being recognised as an embodiment of 'new woman' in the popular press as well as by literary contemporaries like William Carlos Williams (with admiration) and Amy Lowell (with horror).

Such restiveness requires its proper form of expression. It is more than irksome that the eighth edition of *The Norton Anthology of English Literature* canonises Loy's 'Feminist Manifesto' (probably 1914), which went unpublished at its time with good reason, while passing over her poems. Discussing the Futurist manifestos which were Loy's model for the 'Feminist Manifesto', Marjorie Perloff celebrates Marinetti's innovative embedding of statements and directives in a narrative context so compelling that the banalities and contradictions of his "cult of energy, aggressiveness, violence and heroism" go unnoticed.[167] Wholehearted buffoonery can wow the most unlikely audience (as well understood by Hugo Chávez, the present-day master of the mode); a manifesto should elicit, at least imaginatively, a commentary of roars and gasps rather than critical analysis. Although Loy's manifesto starts with Futurist brio, it makes the fundamental error of confusing a manifesto with a wish-list. Rhetorically this produces bathos; after the great line which brings the second paragraph to a head, "Are you prepared for the WRENCH?", the text descends to the flaccid prose of "Another great illusion that woman must use all her introspection, innate clear-sightedness, and unbiased bravery to destroy is the impurity of sex—for the sake of her self-respect", so adding afterthought to afterthought in a discouraging sequence.[168] As for content, Loy's inability to stay single-minded leads her to temper her assault on men by acknowledging the mutual deformation of men and women in the master-slave dialectic, and scornfully to admit "the advantages of marriage" for women. This is much too reasonable, and buffers the shock-value of the demand for "the *unconditional* surgical *destruction of virginity* throughout the female population at puberty". For a manifesto, equivocation is far more damaging than contradiction.

The weakly-linked exposition into which the 'Feminist Manifesto' declines, contrasts to its great disadvantage with the abrupt expostulations comprising 'Love Songs to Joannes'. Since the shocking opening of the sequence has attracted much analysis, this example is taken from close to the end and is relatively decorous.

31.

Crucifixion
Of a busybody
Longing to interfere so
With the intimacies
Of your insolent isolation

Crucifixion
Of an illegal ego's
Éclosion
On your equilibrium
Caryatid of an idea

Crucifixion
Wracked arms
Index extremities
In vacuum
To the unbroken fall[169]

The "longing" here bears no resemblance to the conative 'longing' of Olson and Creeley, extending phallically from where 'a man' stands; and the difference in longingness is felt at once through Loy's distinctive prosody. Even in this poem, among the most densely-woven and linguistically consistent of the sequence, every line starts with an effort of resumption from which rhythmically it falls rapidly away. This is yet more marked owing to Loy's propensity for offending against the most basic precepts of verse writing by starting a line with a customarily forceless conjunction such as 'of' or 'with'. The act of conjunction is thereby asserted as the central performative task of verse, reinforced by the formal decision to retain the initial capital of traditional verse lineation while suppressing the punctuation which would bring a line to a close, or at least to a lengthened pause (for the stanza here conforms to a sentence or a colon-divided period). "Nor does she enjamb lines to modify semantic or syntactic significance", as Maeera Shreiber observes; enjambment recruits the force necessary for resumption.[170] The pauses in this poem occur at the start of its lines, not at their ending. While the third stanza cannot be read except with a powerful emphasis on each line's first syllable, the first stanza's greater grammatical fluency is disturbed by the weakly dactylic line-endings: indeed, the poem's every line could be read as an extended dactyl. Short lines, the emphasis on conjunction, and extreme intricacy of internal rhyme as a kind of syllable-shuttling, distinguish Loy's verse which, as Perloff notes in a brilliantly anachronistic association, is so far removed from anything that might be called 'free verse' that it recalls the 'skeltonics' of the Tudor poet John Skelton.[171]

Loy's syllabic intricacy is such that her lines risk falling over their own feet, as in the phrases "Of an illegal ego's" and "Index extremities". Their resumptions then sound like continual new starts pitched against a syntax approaching discursive regularity, borrowing strength from such regularity and the prominence of conjunction so as to prevent the lines from either trailing away or fragmenting into discrete entanglements. They would be left-hand jabs but cannot connect with the man shrugging them off. Rather than a conative pressure, "longing" denotes a kind of battering at the fixity of the loved object's "insolent isolation", epitomised in his "streetcorner smile" of poem 24—a phrase capturing perfectly the male narcissism of 'hanging out' with a smile both self-satisfied and appraising.[172] No wonder these lines so nearly balk.

To fall over your own feet is not the same as to stumble. Stumbling induces self-consciousness whereas falling over your own feet is a product of self-consciousness; it is the fault of a "busybody" rather than of a man going about his business and surprised by stumbling, that sudden unmeshing of the unconscious accord between body and environment. The crucifixion of this poem reduces (or multiplies) the body to limbs, whereas the narcissistic male lover's projection of the speaker is as the "Caryatid of an idea", a draped and therefore limbless female statue. While it might seem perverse to disregard Christian iconography by departing from others who read Loy here as claiming a Christ-like suffering, I believe such a reading mistakes the nature of Loy's appropriations. These tend to be arbitrary as to cultural and symbolic association; that is, the poet arbitrates by immediate context. "Crucifixion" for Loy's present purpose is more like being pinned by an entomologist than self-sacrifice in pursuit of human redemption; it involves being ascribed within a taxonomy according to the configuration of limbs or lines: "Crucifixion | Wracked arms | Index extremities". In such tightly-wound verse, cultural resonance is far less powerful than local intensities of abutment and exchange—and it therefore departs much further from symbolism than Pound's.

This poem's prosody grants resonance only to the final phrase, to "unbroken fall", which dangles unbound from the intricate sound-texture. Such a terminal irresolution plays back across the preceding poem, and introduces (if not suspected previously) the possibility of a deep ambivalence. As against Rachel Blau DuPlessis, whose essay '"Seismic Orgasm"' is far the most precise and intelligent published account of 'Love Songs to Joannes', I disagree that this poem treats "specifically her "crucifixion" as the bearer of a new and controversial idea (she is the "Caryatid of an idea"): that women should freely bear the children of their lovers, and that superior women will bear superior children in a eugenicist sense."[173] This construction rests on too linear a reading of the sequence, and takes Loy's eugenicism as internally uncontested. It is a reliable principle in reading Loy to expect contradiction at every turn. Her contrariness on eugenics is vivid for instance in poem 29, which lends itself to strongly opposed readings. A sentimental and wounded voice objects to "unnatural selection", Darwinianism as a kind of phylogenetic, random miscegenation producing "Uninterpretable cryptonyms", its irresponsibility attributed to masculine revulsion against the self's engrossment by another, intolerant of "own-self distortion".

But this poem is strikingly unspecific as to gender, describing "sons and daughters" as alike set into motion sexually by evolution, an evolution curiously responsive to human lack—the "human insufficiencies" of the second stanza prompting emergence from the sea and adoption of upright posture. A reading pitched against the sentimental voice might recognise the lure of "uninterpretable cryptonyms" (hard to deny in poems such as these), leading to a final stanza appearing to challenge eugenics in a negative version as merely "Own-self distortion", contrasting it with genetic diversity and mutation and their wider potential ("far further | Differentiation"). Where is the eugenic position in this poem? Does it reduce simply to romantic love, a coupling with Joannes promising utopia in a zygote? Or does it revise natural selection as the workings of a collective will, sentimentally misconstrued in terms of "snowdrops or molasses" (stanza 2) while infallibly perfecting the race?

A stabilised reading of poem 31 is no more sustainable, but DuPlessis tends to seek resolution, thereby missing prosodic cues. Contrary to her account, "Unbroken fall" can be read as suggesting that Christ's crucifixion failed to fix anything, that mankind's fall continues unimpeded since expulsion from the Garden of Eden; and more radically as celebrating what that continuing fall implies and portends: that human beings have responsibility for their own future—which may have entailed eugenicist policies in Loy's view at the time, but no more made her verse consistently eugenicist than it was consistently feminist.

However, if Christ was crucified to no good purpose except negatively in a busted eschatology, that may not apply to Loy's crucifixion. It is at least an allowable question, whether crucifixion in the nailed lines of this poem is not a fate more exemplary, more potent, than either that of the marmorealised "caryatid", a smooth-surfaced and sexless representation of female sensibility, or the "insolent isolation" of the phallic master. If that is the case, the phallic master has a value in ordaining the "equilibrium" provoking the "illegal ego's" development (its "éclosion", that is, its nesting), rather like the justification for Judas in his act's outcome but contrariwise, in that here it is the fall that matters. "A busybody", "an illegal ego", "wracked arms" and "index extremities" engage in an immense tension forced by the poem's conjunctions and a sentence structure overcoming a continual risk of falling mute, or halting and shying in the face of "your equilibrium". This compages of force makes the parataxis of the contemporary imagist poem look slack, and too prissily aestheticised in its suspension and invitation to commentary in the circumtextual space.

What of "Longing to interfere so | with the intimacies | Of your insolent isolation"? Loy's longing does not organise the world from a phallic vantage but rather, in a present-day phrase, mixes it with the world. "The intimacies | Of your insolent isolation" seems linked to the sequence's use of slang terms for masturbation, apparently unremarked hitherto. To "pull a weed" (poem 1) is to masturbate, to "pull the wire" also (poem 6)—and although the later is recorded as current in the late sixties, it was already considered quaint (fathers' era) when I was at boarding school at the close of the fifties and therefore probably had a long history. The "one eye" in poem 6 is reminiscent of the Australian sexual slang 'one-eyed trouser snake'. In writing about Loy of all poets, it must be permissible to state that she frequently regards Joannes as a wanker, and that his "intimacies" amount to little more than self-gratification—hence the 'clockwork mechanism' of poem 2, associated with Italian Futurism and Loy's recent sexual relationship with Marinetti, and contrasted with female sexual insatiability and tenderness ("My fingertips are numb | From fretting your hair").[174] It is contrasted too with the timeless instantaneity of wholly joined sexuality, neither masturbatory nor distracted: "You could look straight at me | And Time would be set back". That said, Loy can be brisk in response to sentimentality about sexual activity, celebrated and reduced as "Only the impact of lighted bodies" (poem 14), and associating tenderness with a vulnerability perhaps post-coital or impotent—"I had to be caught

in the weak eddy | Of your drivelling humanity | To love you most"
(poem 15). "Drivelling" seems to belong to a word-cluster connected with
Loy's reflex of disgust against non-reproductive sex, often after descrip-
tions of unselfconsciously 'good sex' have tended by negation towards
the inhuman and mechanical, and staged again through poems 25–27:
her poems are driven by such unresolvable contradictions and flex
about their skeleton.

Longing figures in Loy not as a narrative project strong enough to
brush aside opponents and persist through setbacks, but as a polyvalent
force sustaining at its tensest (as in the crucifixion poem) an improvised
and somewhat ramshackle structure, much as might be said of cubist
collage, and at its strangest a three-dimensional and timeless figure
where events coexist in an occult but proclaimed intimacy—more,
perhaps, like a harder-edged variety of the Surrealist painting of Yves
Tanguy. Nodal words in 'Love Poems to Joannes' undergo radical reorientation, donning and shrugging off historical associations at will; in
this way (for example) 'white' and 'coloured' become as critically
contested as the pronouns 'you' and 'me'. The relationship between
their contradictory usages is pressured, but reconciliation is neither
attempted nor even seen as called-for. The comparison with painting or
collage holds; this is a poetry of space, perhaps of an inner space within
which entities coexist, and one single entity may split into positive and
negative part-objects, turning round to bite after leading on.

The first dab of white appears in poem 7, where "the scum of the
white street" is transmuted through lungs and nostrils into "Exhilarated
birds | Prolonging flight into the night". Here the negative connotations
of "scum" and its echo of 'sperm' link the phrase "the scum of the white
street" to the masturbator of the previous poem, and the wind performs
fellatio. At that instant "the white street" with an upward cadence
unusual in these poems, breaks into radiance and prepares to release its
soaring birds. "Prolonging flight into the night" converts the scum, the
day's residues, into dreamwork; or maybe this is the expression of
female sexuality, of repeated orgasm, of "Never reaching", that is, never
being spent. Or again, it may speak of the delirium of fully shared
sexual expression. Whiteness may be male, female, positive, negative,
vacant or entire, cold or hot, perfect or diseased, and it recurs in poem 9,

> And spermatozoa
> At the core of Nothing
> In the milk of the Moon

in poem 23,

> Rot
> To the recurrent moon
> Bleach
> To the pure white
> Wickedness of pain

and particularly in poem 28, here given in full:

> The steps go up for ever
> And they are white
> And the first step is the last white
> Forever
> Coloured conclusions
> Smelt to synthetic
> Whiteness
> Of my
> Emergence
> And I am burnt quite white
> In the climacteric
> Withdrawal of your sun
> And wills and words all white
> Suffuse
> Illimitable monotone
>
> White where there is nothing to see
> But a white towel
> Wipes the cymophanous sweat
> —Mist rise of living—
> From your
> Etiolate body
> And the white dawn
> Of your New Day
> Shuts down on me
>
> Unthinkable that white over there—
> Is smoke from your house[175]

"Illimitable monotone" maybe, but it would be difficult, apart from the stagey oxymorons of the baroque, to imagine a monotone more comprehensive of contradiction and variety. To begin with, white can be "the core of Nothing" or the final incorporation of all colour. In poem 28, whiteness confronts the reader in marble or in Busby Berkeley icing-sugar at the foot of a sweep of stairs, divides into the colours of the rainbow and recombines into "synthetic | whiteness", a whiteness which is the nuptial or heavenly restoration of virginity, the flower of a synthetic new "emergence". The lineation proceeds by steps, adding dab to dab until it reaches beyond synthesis with the astonishing lines "And I am burnt quite white | In the climacteric | Withdrawal of your sun". To be "burnt quite white" is to be subject to a radical negation, to the extinction of personal qualities and personality within a consuming solar dazzle. These lines unite total loss with total ecstasy, fulfilment with abasement. "Climacteric" is a brilliantly polyvalent usage; critical, ripened to fulfilment, and condemned to infertility, all radiate from the pivot of this one word, and all are subsumed in a universal climax, an orgasm. What follows is nothing less than white-out, where white over-lays white as in a painting by Robert Ryman. With "words all white", writing as well as its referents should be indiscernible, but the white-ness of script and of will "suffuses" the whiteness of dazzle, and breaks down "Illimitable monotone" into textures—actually into a textile at first, a white towel. Absorbent white wipes the laden white of mist, and the encounter of white with white, the full varietal range of whites, concentrates in "cymophanous mist", "cymophanous" meaning 'opalescent'—from the Greek signifying 'shining billows' but with 'billows' pertinently evolved from a root-word for 'pregnant.'

White now has condensed from dazzle and burning heat into mist, sweat and discriminable textures. Whiteness also tracks an incarnation, whereby "your sun" returns "where there is nothing to see" as an "etio-late body", "etiolate" here indicating loss of colour as much as gaunt-ness, white towel wiping white sweat off a white body in white mist. What then does a "white dawn" display? What else but what this poem unfolds and spills, mops up and abruptly breaks from—what André Green has termed a 'psychose blanche', as here summarised on the website of the *Association lacanienne internationale*:

> ...his concept of "blank psychosis": "A hypochondriacal negation of the body, especially the head, with the impression of empty-headedness, of a hole in mental activity...accompanied by ruminations, compulsive think-ing, and near-delirious mental wandering".

> But in the end one comes back, just as this author does, to the concepts of primary fusion and of an indeterminacy between subject and object. He insists on the importance of limits for any subject, evoking different kinds of limit, more or less permeable, such as fear, skin or other bodily

tissues comprising surfaces—a psychic envelope for the subject, organising the relationship with objects.[176]

Primary fusion with its effacement of all entities and distinctions, swirls
mistily as the terrifying threat this poem faces, succumbing repeatedly
and as often pulling back to re-identify objects and re-identify the psychic
boundaries of both 'me' and 'you' as distinct from each other and as
distinct from amniotic illimitability and sepulchral mephitis. Never has
a "New Day" sounded more like a groaning slab drawn over the mouth
of a funeral vault; the marble step which opened the poem now recycled
in a bid to solidify indistinctness itself into death's seal. "The word *blanc*
represents, then, the *invisible* whereas its semantic opposite is the dawn
of light" writes Green in a discussion of whiteness and blankness.[177] 'Me'
at this ground zero is no more than a hole in mental activity. Once
again Loy has recourse to a vicious parody of the Christ myth: the tomb
is empty because it contains the nothing which is *me*, while *you*, having
obliterated me and all the world, casually climb down from your cross
and walk home. Consequently this departure, by another irony, delivers
my salvation owing to the distance it introduces, for my renewed ability
to point to "that white over there—" heralds the first step back towards
the prismatic decomposition enacted in the poem's first lines. "White
smoke" signifies the ex-lover's disinterest and domestic comfort, as well
as a last onanistic ejaculation, a sign of departure as mournful as a puff
from a steam-engine. "Moreover", writes Green, "the *Dictionnaire érotique*,
by Pierre Guiraud, gives two meanings for white: (1) sperm, no doubt,
says the author, in the sense of 'egg white', and (2) a woman's sexual
organs, which links up with psychoanalytical conceptions on feminine
castration and the vagina."[178] White obliterates the dawn, and preg-
nancy foretells a stillbirth or abortion.

The "New Day" shutting down may read as one more contemptuous
dismissal of the promise of religious salvation, reaffirming the grace of
the quotidian in the almost Wordsworthian cottage where 'you' are now
relegated; but it surely carries a bitter overtone of the 'New Woman'
which Loy discovered herself to represent. Loy's compulsion to shed
doubt is once again in evidence, and her passionately-driven contrariness. The force of Loy's feminism derives from the force of her desire for
submission; and the force of her desire for a perfectible futurity from
the force of her disappointment with the temporising of practical politics and with her body's longings. In every direction, blockage or obliv-
ion, or a false identification would shut her trap.

Yet such twists and turns make this poetry considerable; its "wills and words" are concentrated with rare vehemence. What has to be learnt in reading 'Love Songs for Joannes' is first the necessity to follow the writing with the kind of alertness one would bring to Celan, a poet who furrows where Loy tacks; then to take account of the "dance of intelligence among words and ideas" Pound saw in Loy's writing, entailing a restless back-tracking and side-glancing, and recognition of a kind of skittish scepticism not to be found elsewhere—until the poetry of Marjorie Welish, at any rate.[179] To play with this logopoeically, Loy's cognitions are always subject to further recognition. But this skittishness is serious and actuated by an extraordinary truthfulness, the recognition of each position as provisional, potentially self-serving, potentially serving others' interests, potentially a way-station towards a more provocative mark of position. And Loy is provocative in the best sense, of calling-forth, of challenging, then dancing beyond reach, wry and exacting.

To use the word 'truthfulness' in talking of a poet whom it is hard to imagine knowing where any of her poems might end up, is of course to presume a particular test of truth, and one which is highly contingent; nothing could be further from Laura (Riding) Jackson's brand of truthfulness, for instance, whereby truth is universal, unaffected by experience, and precisely non-contingent. Jennifer Ashton associates (Riding) Jackson's' 'truth' with the wholly autonomous work of art, explaining that "everything about a poem that, in [I.A.] Richards's account, should captivate our attention is, in (Riding) Jackson's account, the source of ruinous distraction from the truth ... Because the physical effects of "rhythm and harmonic sound-play" are inevitably personal and idiosyncratic, varying from reader to reader, they cannot fulfil the promise of a universal truth."[180]

But the comparison with Robert Creeley is a fair one since Creeley's poems attend so intently to their own manoeuvres, and claims a truth through the minutest fluctuations of perception. After reading Loy, the continuity of perceptual movement in Creeley becomes problematic; the test of truth becomes exactly self-interested, subordinate to the continuity which is never put seriously in jeopardy. Loy's self-consciousness forever makes her tongue-tied, but does not lead her to privilege self-consciousness as a basis for self-esteem through the reflexive estimation of a projected other. Because she balks before she utters, and fails at the thought of a course ahead, Loy cannot rest satisfied with any position, or the promise of salvation or extinction—she cannot adopt a line; even the "terrific Nirvana" of poem 13, "terrific" in both of its obvious and power-ful senses, leads to the formula "Me you-you-me" which makes at least three persons out of the instant of depersonalisation and possibly six. "Myself" is but a "nascent virginity" (p14), and virginity was not a state Loy admired or aspired to mimic.

Twentieth-century taste in lyric poetry tended to favour either a mystical dilation of significance around the sphinx-like object, or the felt authenticity of nearly-tangible and embodied voice. Robert Creeley's poetry does not belong entirely to either of these traditions, although Altieri's revisionism in associating him with the latter can be illumi-nating. Creeley's invention is to make of his errors a finely responsive linguistic and emotional environment, an *envelope* as Green would have it, within which sexual clumsiness and stumbling words can be safe and yield for him, in the psychological cliché, an enormous secondary gain. Mina Loy's poetry has more in common with the poem as object than first appears, since its forthrightness makes the initial impact, but the status of the poem as an achieved thing is never allowed to rest; in this regard, the 'Love Songs to Joannes' point towards the serial poems of Jack Spicer, a logopoeic poet if ever there was one.

When Loy halts it is because the ground is uncertain, it is because the 'she' who would occupy the ground is unreliable, and it is because the very idea of occupation is questionable. The 'Love Songs to Joannes' are opinionated, but they are poems, and their opinions are applied, donned and foisted at will and at necessity. Constructive strategies such as reading the sequence as the history of an abortion, or foregrounding Christian and Classical mythical derivations as Shrieber does in her essay, work only to a point, for throughout its course the sequence wages war with all its preoccupations.

> We might have given birth to a butterfly
> With the daily news
> Printed in blood on its wings

Wit and precision are indefatigably deployed against introspection, and nowhere more movingly than in this stanza. The second the conven-tional image of the soul of the new-born is given birth, its ephemerality is asserted, and the image becomes material. Simultaneously the lines present a horrifying picture of a back-street abortion, and a vividly specific description of a butterfly's wings, with its fractal markings the announcement of its short life. Each line end-stops and resumes effortfully as a reconsideration of the place arrived at, a new utterance and a new birth into unforeseen conjunctions. Each line goes as far as it goes, but another tack follows. This is what Mina Loy does, and her writing remains news at every turn, at every stress-point—news that a new generation of poets and readers might be among the first to read, and to take up in their writing.

# Faktura: The Work of Marjorie Welish[181]

How welcome to the admiring but often more than slightly baffled has been the Slought Foundation's issue of a handsome volume aiming to guide with various criticism, appreciations, interviews, and archival matter, the reception of Marjorie Welish's work in paint and in language. What's more, the volume's high-quality if small reproductions of Welish's paintings are complemented by a substantial gallery at the Slought Foundation's website (http://slought.org). And more again, Coffee House Press's publication in 2000 of *The Annotated "Here" and Selected Poems* has been followed by a new collection *Word Group*, gathering several chapbooks. On screen and table the showing declares that the work of Marjorie Welish is gathering attention both in North America and in Europe, and that the contractual terms of that attention are being drawn up. These terms are of more than usual interest where this artist is concerned, for her work is much preoccupied with what she has called "a conceptual painting by visual means", abjuring the pursuit of unmediated visual impact. Indeed, if there is a convergence between her verbal and visual practice, it may resolve in the explicit diagram. "Drawing to be read"—or what will do as well in her case, "painting to be read"—is the protocol, and has its reciprocity in verbal schemata to be read graphically while still in the hearing of a lyric tradition.

The apparatus for receiving Welish's work has already been informed with great intelligence. In her 2001 review (in *Jacket* 15) of *The Annotated "Here" and Selected Poems*, Chris Tysh writes: "Welish problematizes the dialectical relationships between text and supplement, by sending up the notions of source and origin as emblematic of patriarchal authority, but also by relinquishing the outmoded telos of originality." Ironically, this has become a routine account of innovative writing by women: "problematizing" bids fair to become a familiar topos and hence no problem at all. Tysh's encapsulation would apply just as well to the work of Susan Howe for instance, while a reader passing through writings by Howe and Welish would encounter quite different textures. Nonetheless Tysh's generality is precise and must be the starting point for discussing the unprecedented range and quality of poetry by women during the past three decades in North America, a cultural efflorescence whose now manifest extent reduces to size the period's old-school-avant-garde formations.[182] Still, the general applicability of Tysh's critique calls for distinctions: why, within the larger endeavour, does Welish's poetry look so very odd, and what rewards can the thoroughly problematized reader expect?

*Of the Diagram* is a great help. This 300-page volume in the Slought Foundation's Contemporary Artists series, edited by Aaron Levy and Jean-Michel Rabaté, establishes a ground and context for the reception of an artistic practice pitched to summon ground and context into the centre of its action. Of first importance are the interviews with Welish, who is a breathtaking interviewee, dodging, feinting, counter-punching, erudite, funny, and serious—and these are transcripts of live interviews, not authorial statements masquerading as off-the-cuff brilliance. The essays by Norma Cole, Frances Richards, Kenneth Baker, Ron Janssen, and Keith Tuma are particularly valuable, with Tuma's close attention to the opening poem in *Word Group* an exemplary act of critical exposition.

Considered as an entity, *Of the Diagram* seems haunted by a particular word which becomes either the nub or the horizon of its discussions of Welish's painting and poetry: Constructivism. Welish's response to Bob Perelman's question about the centrality in her recent paintings of the colour yellow, entails a disquisition on the historical reception of Soviet Constructivist art in New York (36), while Joseph Masheck asserts that "a painting by Marjorie Welish presents itself forthrightly as an image, a distinct and complete visual construct, but never as a picture" (67).[183] Tuma describes Welish's poetry as a practice which "folds self-reflexive activity within a Constructivist poetic" (179). All which raises the following question: What does it mean to describe the work of a New Yorker in the twentieth and twenty-first centuries as Constructivist?

Though now little more than a set of stylistic referents, Constructivism, as with Dada, once represented a radical challenge to the separation of art and life. In its origins in the Soviet Union of the early 1920s, Constructivist 'fine art' was framed as laboratory work both for industrial production and more radically as an example of Bolshevik precepts: collective rather than individualistic, functional rather than decorative, efficient rather than self-indulgent. Of particular importance was the use of prefabricated components—whether directly in sculpture, through appropriation in photomontage, or in the disposition of geometrical shapes on canvas or other surfaces. Such use of what lay ready to hand was related to a scarcity economy and to a cult of the machine driven by industrial-economic pragmatism and a romance with speed and precision shared with Italian Futurism. Very rapidly the Constructivist project became aestheticized, due to the resistance of industry and party apparatchiks and the backsliding of bourgeois artists, although not without at least a prototyping phase producing propaganda kiosks and now-desirable crockery.

Constructivist precepts also proved remarkably adaptable to idealism and religiosity. While Alexander Rodchenko and Vladimir Tatlin struggled to implement their program of artistic modernization in a traumatized Soviet Union, in the Netherlands Piet Mondrian developed a stripped-down visual vocabulary, which he described as the synthetic climax of Western art, a distillation of the synthetic spirituality he espoused through his theosophy. Intent, performance, and historical fate never correspond, and in Welish's reading the rigors of cubism were taken to radical extremes by De Stijl, the movement of which Mondrian was the indispensable proponent. Mondrian's penetration into structure, later ramified through the street grid of Manhattan and the syncopations of jazz, remained keyed to a visionary reality, unlike Constructivism, which renegotiated that reality in actual social space.

It is been a remarkable turn of events that has rendered Soviet Constructivism a décor choice whose traces flicker across the interiors reproduced in *Elle Deco*, while the heirs of the later Mondrian have also amused themselves into an historical farce in the 'life-style' severity that connotes extreme wealth. The irony is particularly bitter when art historical narrative asserts as an obvious truth that the turn from Abstract Expressionism to serial works in the strict minimalist mode deriving from Mondrian, represented a head-on struggle with US capitalism, imperialism, and militarism.[184] Rodchenko's abandonment of art for advertising, to which Welish alludes, may have been premonitory of his art's fate; but when Welish protests that "Mondrian's conceptual configuration of red, yellow, and blue is very different, utterly different" (36) she is unlikely to have in mind the naïve positivism of a left romantic historiography or the implications of formalist cool and indifference that make style sociopathic. Indeed, one of Welish's most engaging characteristics is her insouciant disregard for the revolutions proclaimed tirelessly by the art industry on both its oppositional and commercial flanks.

In *Of the Diagram*, Kenneth Baker describes Marjorie Welish's painting as having "the air of an abandoned game" (96)—a happy phrase that indicates each painting's irresolute position within an irresolvable series; Joseph Masheck invokes chess, and Welish herself talks of her "'play' activity": "Generating games and improvising rules for the 'pieces' of other games had fed an insatiable conceptual appetite for non/narrative— that is to say, those temporal orders built of convention, contingency, but not of causality" (139). Welish's is an unusual game, however, in two respects. The pieces she deploys are patently adopted from elsewhere, chiefly from Mondrian but with some passages and constructional principles reflecting Jasper Johns—a painter to whom she returns repeatedly in her art criticism.[185] As in Johns, the game's rules, agents, and pieces do not necessarily forswear gestural painting. Since Abstract Expressionism if not well before, gesture itself has become a given bit of the language of art which, along with unpainted tracts of blank canvas, is characterized in Welish's work by no particular poignancy, transcendentalism, or materialist pedagogic intent. Passages 'abandoned' to canvas or subject to gesture contribute, as Masheck emphasizes, to an unbalanced dimorphism or occasionally a quartering reminiscent of Johns but once again with at least one quarter radically out of balance.

The paintings of Welish's reproduced in *Of the Diagram* reveal a major departure from Mondrian: if at first glance they seem dominated by primary colours straight from the tube, it rapidly becomes clear that at least part of Welish's project concerns the effects of colour variation around the primary red, yellow, and blue. Her painting simultaneously investigates mismatches and accidents in the relations between painting and drawing—an investigation that includes painting in blocks undisciplined by a drawn grid, imposing drawn grids in a variable relationship with painted blocks, and more painterly passages invasive of blocks. 'Indecidability of the Sign: Frame 2', the painting from 2002 reproduced on the cover of *Of the Diagram*, is an elegant work in two yellows with black verticals and a caesura of its own ground, articulating a language of difference and differentials that cannot be resolved through sight alone. With spare means it invokes the slashes and girders of Soviet Constructivism (but in white, or absences) and the characteristic double-line verticals of late Mondrian, here on the far left of the painting wittily pulled open and provided with a few horizontals reminiscent of a filmstrip. In the middle of the right side of the implied diptych is a truncated and slightly wider reflection of the double strip.

Without seeing this painting (or its reproduction) it would be difficult to imagine that a painting so minimalist in manner could be so richly allusive. One way to think about it would be as a post-minimalist painting: the characteristics of easel painting are reintroduced sparingly in order to register as precisely as possible their effect within a zone marked out with drawings that do not correspond to the painted areas. Given their confinement, the light yellow blocks ask a question regarding their relationship to the much larger dark yellow areas: do they represent their representation of the represented dark yellow, spruced up and optimistic? Do they naïvely reconcile dark yellow and white? What is the relationship between the pencil marks and the black vertical lines? Do pencil lines propose a plan for a construction elsewhere? When is a line thick enough to become painted rather than drawn? Are the white girders interruptions or impositions? And then, what might be brought into the argument by other paintings in this series?

An uncouth rejoinder to these questions would be to ask why anyone other than a painter or art historian should care, especially if one were to agree with the painter Osvaldo Romberg, who writes: "when I saw her work recently at Baumgartner I was mesmerized by her lack of beauty" (124). One may follow Romberg and suggest that "This lack of beauty in fact makes her work profoundly sensitive and tragic" (124) but the real value of the uncouth challenge is that it re-poses the question of Constructivism. What is the significance of this new work produced in a Constructivist tradition? Romberg probably means that Welish's painting has nothing of the sublime about it, and this decidedly is worth saying. American painting has had more than enough sublimity. The sublime can (un)safely be left to CEOs, Secretaries of State, pastors, genetic engineers, and neocons: for artists to join in wonder-filled aspiring at this time would be monstrous. That said, does Welish's painting then require assent to Masheck's ludic account of painting, where chess is not merely a partial metaphor for artistic activity, but an adequate analogy? For Masheck art follows the rules of a game, even if its rules are subject to periodic revision, and "it is quite possible for art to stand respectably in Schopenhauerean-compensatory disjunction with life, rather than in metonymic continuity or reflexive relation with it" (74). Maybe so, but Romberg's tragic view of Welish's painting seems more apt; while 'Indecidability of the Sign: Frame 2' is notable for its wit, Welish's denser paintings often suffer violent attacks—from elements within their boundaries failing to keep to their place ('Small High Valley' series), from incipient figuration ('The Without, 1'), from incursions from outside the frame ('Small High Valley 66'), and from periodic abandonment of territory into unpaint ('Indecidability of the Sign: Red, Yellow, Blue, 1').

Welish's painting therefore does not so much provoke the 'problematizing' hailed by several contributors to *Of the Diagram*, as address the real problems of Constructivist faktura; that is, her paintings suggest the ways in which the restricted space of the canvas, a restricted palette, and a restricted set of shapes can be manipulated without recourse to spurious novelty or to spurious reproduction, thereby sustaining a doubly critical practice. Welish's painting is subject to crisis in its own variously repeated re-emergence into image. It critically prises the sealed products of art history from incessant replication. In his valuable discussion of Welish's diptych structures, Masheck registers exactly Welish's ambivalence about duplication, that is, replication: such structural disturbance, going beyond asymmetry into parody or defacement, cannot be held securely within a separate aesthetic domain. Welish might be recognized as a successor to the Polish Constructivist Wladyslaw Strzeminski: for both, painting models a practice of reason that demands constant tending and shoring, one that is threatened principally by its own lapses, submissions and indulgences. Respect for past achievements as a resource rather than authoritative source; a decisive refusal of the novelty demanded by the market; strenuous restriction on self-expression; a critical attitude at all times; love of materials; concision: these are some of the characteristics of Welish's art.

If these characteristics are to be regarded as exemplary in a Constructivist sense, how do they determine Welish's art in a different domain, that of lyric poetry? It is a commonplace that post-Romantic lyric poetry has become wedded, through its gradual decadence, to self-expression of the most naïve kind. Such an account neglects the travails of the sentimental project (in Schiller's sense—that is, self-reflective and alienated from nature while seeking or finding a plenitude in human society) from Shelley to Frank O'Hara and stops at the laboratory doors marked L=A=N=G=U=A=G=E. The blurb on the back of *Word Group* locates the poetry by reference to both the sentimental and the denaturalizing: "With the resources of Language School poetics and New American Poetry, this collection breaks new ground by engaging the critical strategies necessary for creating a lyric poem." This is exactly poised. As Marjorie Perloff has observed, New York poets such as O'Hara, Ashbery, and Guest did not "call into question the centrality of painting and lyric poetry among the media."[186] Neither does Welish; rather, she takes painting and lyric poetry to be exemplary practices requiring incessant attention and critique if they are not to lapse into commodity fetishism or narcissism. To abandon the field of either would be catastrophic, a betrayal of the work of generations; and the notion that the threats both arts face can somehow be side-stepped through 'interventions' in other media looks simple-minded.

The word 'resources' is important when considering Welish's lyric poetry (or her poetic writing with designs on lyric). An analogy with the resources deployed in Welish's painting is not quite tenable; for this to work, the elements would have to be as recognizable for the poetry reader as her citation of elements from Rodchenko or Mondrian might be for the aficionado of modernist visual art. Such a practice is imaginable, but does not correspond to the work presented in *Word Group*, whose discourse draws less on the familiar resources of a modernist poetic than on the resources of prose theory—whether art theory, linguistics, anthropology, or literary theory (with Roland Barthes a favourite). Although her literary resources often receive specific citation or might be recognized by a reader well-read in theory, the question as to what Welish is doing with the lines she adopts is not so urgent as with the allusiveness of her paintings.

The risk is that poems constructed using the language of theory might be read as demonstrations of the now banal idea that the secondary/ primary writing distinction has been superseded: that is, that the poems conduct theory war by other means. This is decidedly not the case with Welish. The chief distinction between her paintings and poetry is that the paintings' Constructivism accepts for its components the vocabularies and practices of what has become a distinct stylistics, a third-generation Constructivism if you like; whereas the poems take their material from the linguistic world within which poems are manufactured rather than the vocabularies and practices of lyric poetry. Manufactured with a conspicuously collective social lexicon, the poetry puts early Soviet Constructivism and its structural poetics in the same space as the theory subsequently elaborated to investigate the cultural assumptions of these ideas and practices.

It is difficult to discuss Marjorie Welish's poetry without showing in some detail how one of her poems works. Since Keith Tuma has journeyed so compellingly alongside 'Else, in Substance' the decision here is to consider a poem published in both *Word Group* and *Of the Diagram*, 'Clans, Moieties and Other'. A first and maybe irritatingly obvious point about this poem is the fact that it consists of lines and stanzas. Nothing obtrudes on the lineation of poetry like lines that necessitate breaking to fit on the page. What standard page could accommodate a line such as "image, music, text. After a few uniformities, traps and axes acquire traits of amphitheatres and tribunes"? Impossible. This is a poem in four stanzas of four lines, with a supplementary line as envoi. But even as it asserts its construction with lines and stanzas, this poem's form declares a conformity with lyric tradition, reassuring after a title so disconcertingly technical.

It may be helpful to gloss the title, not least because Welish never uses technical language merely for decorative or refractory purposes. Once "clan" is set alongside "moiety" it assumes a precise anthropological sense and means a unilineal descent group whose members do not trace genealogical links to a supposedly historical founding ancestor; in contrast, "moiety" refers to a more unusual form of unilineal descent, which involves the occurrence of descent groups in linked pairs. Each moiety (or half) of a pair will almost always be exogamous and take its husbands and wives exclusively from the matched group.[187] "Exogamy" occurs later in the poem, closing the circuit of the poem's unfamiliar terms. Certain phrases may alert some readers to the original resources; for instance, in the long line quoted above, the opening phrase "image, music, text" is the title of Stephen Heath's English-language selection of Roland Barthes's essays. But although this recognition helps to confirm what might be happening in the first stanza, it is unnecessary to recognize the allusion. Such usage therefore differs from Welish's paintings, which require a familiarity with the historical grounding of their syntax.

> The first stanza maps a linguistic territory:
> Used and out-of-print books classified as steppe. Fish were an
>     important supplement.
> Only printed words. Forty-two children's .... Territory there in
>     the archive frequents an inkling
> or inking: Eskimo, harpoon, seal; Australian aborigine, boomerang,
>     kangaroo—throughout
> image, music, text. After a few uniformities, traps and axes acquire
>     traits of amphitheaters and tribunes.

In the 'real' world, an inkling or an inking would "frequent" the territory, but this poem performs archive work on "used and out-of-print books classified as steppe". The witty following phrase might suggest that the supplement to the *OED* is a flounder or mullet; but the supplement is the world insofar as it is English-language territory. The pun on inkling/inking encapsulates a straightforward signified/signifier lesson but with some post-colonialist asperity in the mix: those musical words in line three assimilate an indigenous Australian word such as "boomerang" to English along with the Latinate reference to discarded origins in "aborigine". Imposing "a few uniformities" swallows the hunter economies of Eskimo and Australian aborigine alike; the "traps and axes" used in their clans are succeeded by modern and hierarchical societies with grand legal and legislative institutions ("amphitheaters and tribunes"). On the steppe of language clans may be more assimilable than moieties because their kinship terms are translatable directly into English. Undoubtedly the anachronistic words strung here assert their music: in this stanza there is "image, music, text," but perhaps music is only a phylogenetic remnant? This may link with "Forty-two children's...." and the stories of idealized Arctic and Outback ways of life continuing to delight American and European children.

The poem tacks hard into the second stanza and at once invokes Mondrian's most characteristic colours:

> Where is the true red, yellow or blue? is wearing a stubbornness in which
>    two reds, two yellows,
> two blues, vie for that distinction. Who's Afraid of Nouns, Verbs, and
>    Adjectives?
> Band exogamy: in exchange, hunting, dancing, gambling. Whereabouts
>    of the winter encampment,
> whereabouts of less strongly tied margins of error. A fish weir similar to
>    ours.

Here, the persistence of traditional "hunting, dancing, gambling" is tied to moieties and their rules of exogamous permutation—cultures as resistant to assimilation as their kin terms into English. Two moieties are at once locked in mutual dependency and fiercely distinct, much like the reds, yellow, and blues in one of Welish's diptychs—and unlike in Mondrian, where red, yellow, and blue proclaim their truth as ideal, even spiritual wavelengths. Nonetheless, red, yellow, and blue remain shared and fundamental, whatever the obstructions to translation incurred through varying internal relationships. Despite or even because of such obstructions, the marks of difference in the moieties from the Other, which is "us", cannot be reduced to exotic vocabularies. A desire for survival is shared; what is signified beyond language's ripple of signifiers may align across cultures: "A fish weir similar to ours." The question "Who's Afraid of Nouns, Verbs, and Adjectives?" then marks a concession to functionalist as opposed to Saussurian linguistics.

This seems far from early Language School poetics. Welish, however, does not reinstate the pre-Language lyric ego; her poetry's fierce focus on connections, joints and articulations, on logical argument and its workings, mark it as post-Language and Constructivist. 'Clans, Moieties and Other' does not exhibit the extraordinary highlighting of connectives found elsewhere in *Word Group*, where the pressure on phrases such as "as if" and "insofar as" (for instance in '1A') conjures images of ball-and-socket joints, lines as steel struts: the mid-1960s sculpture of Anthony Caro. The poem does display in a relatively nontechnical way Welish's uniquely expository and argumentative rhetoric, which in *Word Group* often deploys logical and mathematical terminology. The rest of the poem brings image and music back to the fore:

> Where red, yellow and blue is a commonplace diving under yellow
>     in some scheme of left and right
> counter tops, to be sent up to be as sky to the earth's black and white,
>     ivory black and/or
> lamp black. Lamp and mirror shade to keep away composure: blues
>     will do it, as will jazz blues,
> Orpheus! The deceased were burned and buried, or bound and buried,
>     the former in the low lands.

The word "commonplace" is here rescued and refreshed. The implicit assertion that the formal relationships of red, yellow, and blue stand in relation to painting as black and white do to language is, of course, highly contentious. It is not allowed merely to rest, however, and even though the idealism associated with Mondrian's red, yellow, and blue is mocked gently it is not repudiated. The earth may be black and white—that is, text—but text's own materiality here undoes its own dichotomous display, much as the dialectics of black and white, of life and death in Frank O'Hara's *Odes* invert, unpick, and mix the dichotomies of Romanticism. So black becomes "lamp black" and therefore illuminates despite its dark and sooty residue. "Lamp and mirror shade" delivers a multiple pun that in best Language fashion serves to "keep away composure". Perhaps poetic music, even the blues, may trouble composure, despite the narcotic dangers feared by a moralizing avant-gardism, in the tradition of Lenin's self-denial of music to protect his revolutionary fervour. Much by Ashbery might say so. Then the stanza terminates with ethnographical data on burial practices, a tip of the hat to *The Waste Land* in this approved reflexive and modernist ending, making distinctions all the way to the grave, while Orpheus loiters at the gates of death, longing for Eurydice, his vanished beauty.

The poem's envoi—"Baseball. Prehistoric football, AND, OR, BUT NOT unlike surpluses"—insists that lyric poetry is a serious game, and must be conducted within available resources, "a fish weir similar to ours". This is unashamedly a moral and political injunction. Conjunctions in capitals refer to linkages, and the third person pronoun "ours" now sounds like a place we should head for rather than an easy assumption. But 'our' world, the owned and administered world, is rather the world of surpluses. The game of lyric poetry might then aim to use existing resources to create light from the "lamp black". While poetry's moiety may have a problematic relationship with the moiety of the signified or mirrored world, it should not compensate by devouring the world. The "commonplace" should not be disdained and subverted in the name of a radicalism which finds itself excitedly complicit with the disembodied flows it deplores. But then, the commonplace can be recognized only through language's constructions, pointers, and frames rather than any direct and unproblematic access. Marjorie Welish's poems perform acts of intricate, nearly miraculous alignment:

> The reader leapt through the index
> To save time
>
> the reader leapt through the scrim.
>
> This is a test, a breakthrough for readers in reading rooms.
> They have leapt through many Kraft paper screens
>
> have broken through colloquially—a hiatus!

This passage comes from 'Delight Instruct', an injunction which Welish's poems fulfil, and a sequence improbably 'about' indexing. It accords well with Welish's Constructivist aesthetic to conclude this introduction to her work with Charles Harrison's uncannily pertinent response to Art & Language's 1972 gallery installation 'Index':

From the point of view of the notional spectator, the exhibition of the Index was also the first occasion on which Art & Language achieved a form of coincidence between attention to the materials of presentation and attention to the form of the work, such that neither was in the end left as a remainder of the other. This coincidence was achieved in part by conceiving of the spectator as a reader and potential interlocutor—and thus as the type of an engaged and intellectually versatile public quite distinct both from that constituency of detached and self-sufficient beholders which was predicated in mainstream Modernist art and theory, and from that constituency of professional and knowing curators which had identified itself with Minimalism.[188]

Marjorie's Welish's painting and poetry call to this "engaged and intellectually versatile public", soliciting its attention as the daughters of Danaus were called by Orpheus from their ceaseless sieving of water, to be caught in the nets of art.

.

# Notes

1 J.H. Prynne, *Not-You*, Cambridge: Equipage 1993.

2 If I had kept my eyes open or if this article had been written during the internet age, this particular reader would have known that 'lithium grease' is a perfectly ordinary lubricant sold for use on bicycles, as well as for more specialist uses. However, as a website devoted to lubricants concedes, so allowing me a shred of dignity, the term Lithium Grease is misleading since the lithium content is simply used to thicken the oil content to make it a grease as opposed to an oil.

3 *ORIGINAL: CHINESE LANGUAGE-POETRY GROUP*, translated by Jeff Twitchell, edited by J.H. Prynne, *Parataxis: modernism and modern writing*, number 7 (1994).

4 Andrew Crozier, *Duets*, Guildford: Circle Press 1976.

5 Iain Sinclair, 'Vermin Correspondence'. Review of Ben Watson's *Frank Zappa: The Negative Dialectics of Poodle Play* and J.H. Prynne's *Her Weasels Wild Returning*. *London Review of Books* Oct 20 1994: pp.41-2.

6 Iain Sinclair, *Radon Daughters: A Voyage, Between Art and Terror, from the Mound of Whitechapel to the Limestone Pavements of the Burren*, London: Cape 1994.

7 A review of J.H. Prynne, *Poems*, Fremantle Arts Centre Press (Western Australia) and Bloodaxe (UK), 2005.

8 Devin Johnston, 'Prynne's Poems', *Notre Dame Review* 10, Summer 2000, downloadable from the *Notre Dame Review* website. The first issuance was *Poems*, Edinburgh & London: Agneau 2 [subsequently Allardyce, Barnett], 1982, while the second issuance was published in the UK by Bloodaxe in 1999.

9 Although in both British and US reviews this edition is universally credited to Bloodaxe Books, a UK publisher, the primary publisher of both editions is Fremantle Arts Centre Press, Western Australia. As for sales, the first edition of *Poems* (1999) sold 2028 paperback and 341 hardback. This figure excludes sales made by Fremantle in Australia. Once it had sold out, the book was unavailable for some time because the Bloodaxe contract was for one printing only. However, while the author was not willing to agree to a reprint, he was willing to allow an

enlarged second edition to be published later. For this second edition under review (2005), the Bloodaxe contract permits them to print 3000 copies in paperback and 500 in hardback, and they may reprint a further 3000 paperbacks. Thanks to Neil Astley of Bloodaxe for this information.

10 As quoted, unsurprisingly, on the Bloodaxe webpage devoted to the new edition.

11 Ed Randall Stevenson, *The Last of England? The Oxford English Literary History Volume 12 1960–2000*, OUP 2004. The spat can be followed through a series of articles accessible via the Books section of *The Guardian*'s website (http://books.guardian.co.uk) by typing in the search term 'Prynne'.

12 The representative figure here, excoriating the 'postmodernists' and 'academic' poets on behalf of a conference of the comfortably tenured and subsidised, is Don Paterson. Andrea Brady's article 'Meagrely Provided' (*Chicago Review* 49:3/4 & 50:1, Summer 2004, pp.396–402) has his measure, and how! The following issue (*Chicago Review* 50:2/3/4, Winter 2004/5, pp.377–379) contains a thoughtful letter from Andrew Duncan reviewing the politics and sociology of this poetry war.

13 The style '*Poems* 2005' is adopted throughout to prevent confusion with the two earlier books by J.H. Prynne entitled 'Poems': *Poems*, Agneau 2, Edinburgh & London 1982, and *Poems* 1999.

14 For instance those issued by QUID magazine: see http://www.geocities.com/barque_press/quidcd.html

15 Kevin Nolan, 'Capital Calves: Undertaking an Overview', *Jacket* 24, http://www.jacketmagazine.com/24/nolan.htm

16 Anthony Mellors, *Late Modernist Poetics from Pound to Prynne*, Manchester University Press 2005.

17 http://ronsilliman.blogspot.com/, with no competitor for the most tireless, constantly intelligent and provocative English language poetry blog.

18 Gerald L. Bruns, *The Material of Poetry: Sketches for a Philosophical Poetics*, Athens GA: University of Georgia Press 2005.

19 Bruns p.29.

20 There is a real problem in referencing lengthy internet texts with no internal divisions. The only way to find passages in 'Capital Calves' is to use a browser's search function.

21 Jay Basu, 'The Red Shift. Trekking J. H. Prynne's *Red D Gypsum*', *The Cambridge Quarterly* Vol.30, No 1, 2001, pp.19–36.

22 The dedication of the *Furtherance* collection, opened by *Red D Gypsum*, is to Marjorie Welish, author of *Begetting Textile* (Equipage, Cambridge 2000) and the subject of an essay in this volume.

23 The signal exception to the redemptive tone of the Prynnian closing stage comes at the end of the utterly bleak *Down where changed* (1979), whose parting tribute to hospital food is "stuff it".

24 *Poems* 2005, p.572.

25 The line is from Lyn Hejinian, *A Border Comedy*, New York: Granary Books, 2001, p.127.

26 '(cough)' in John James, *Collected Poems*, Cambridge: Salt Publishing 2002, p.156, recycling lines from 'Talking in Bed' p.109. I am indebted to Drew Milne for his stringent comments on an earlier draft, which helped me to focus the opening sections of this essay.

27 A study of the responses of James and Brinkmann to New York poetry, and of their poetic dialogue, would be valuable.

28 "David Lehman has described how O'Hara, on a ferry on his way to read in Staten Island on a shared bill with Robert Lowell (whose poetry O'Hara disliked intensely), quickly penned his poem. "On the way to the Staten Island Ferry, O'Hara bought the *New York Post* and on the choppy half-hour ride he wrote an instant meditation on the tabloid revelation that Hollywood actress Lana Turner had collapsed…O'Hara read the poem that afternoon, making it clear that he had written it in transit. The audience loved it; Lowell looked put out." Such a story, retold by Berrigan and others so often that it became legend, possibly—if partially—accounts for the consistent referrals that poets at St. Mark's Church made to the relatively short time it took them to write poems." Daniel Kane, *All Poets Welcome: the Lower East Side poetry scene in the 1960s*, Berkeley: University of California 2003, p.168. However, O'Hara's one-time lover Joe LeSueur was concerned to correct "a misunderstanding about Frank's attitude towards Lowell; he didn't like the guy's poetry but he had nothing against him personally. Thus, and I'm quite sure about this, at their joint reading he didn't try to show Lowell up or tweak his nose by reading the Lana Turner poem he'd written on his way to the reading. It's simply not the sort of thing Frank would have done." Joe LeSueur, *Digressions on Some Poems by Frank O'Hara*, New York: Farrer, Strauss and Giroux 2003, p.265.

29 *The Collected Poems of Frank O'Hara*, ed. Donald Allen, New York: Knopf, 1972, p.449 (and bibliographical note p.554). A recording of O'Hara reading the poem can be found at http://www.epc.buffalo.edu/sound/mp3/sp/dial_a_poem_poets/big_ego/34-ohara.mp3.

30 Robert Lowell, *Collected Poems*, ed. Bidart and Gewanter, New York: Farrar, Strauss and Giroux 2003, p.325. See also notes pp.1057–1058.

31 Ted Berrigan, *So Going Around Cities: new and selected poems 1958–1979*, Berkeley: Blue Wind Press 2003, p.216.

32 Berrigan, *So Going Around Cities* p.201.

33 Roy Carr, 'MELANIE ON: LIFE LOVE—WOODSTOCK DYLAN—MOON AND HER NEXT ALBUM' in *New Musical Express* 3rd April 1971, reproduced at http://ourworld.compuserve.com/homepages/David_Boldinger/rc030471.htm

34 Dore Ashton, 'Parallel Worlds: Guston as Reader' in *Philip Guston Retrospective*, Forth Worth: Modern Art Museum of Fort Worth in association with Thames & Hudson 2003, p.86.

35 The point is made by Stephen Paul Miller: 'Whereas O'Hara cultivated a community through his notoriety and collaged his personal experiences into his

poems, Berrigan cultivated a community through enthusiasm about poetry and his formal and informal role as a teacher.' 'Ted Berrigan's Legacy: Sparrow, Eileen Myles, and Bob Holman' in ed. E. Foster and J. Donahue, *The World in Time and Space: Towards a history of innovative American poetry in our time*, Jersey City, NJ: Talisman House 2002, p.219. While Miller's description of Berrigan's public role rings true, the description of O'Hara's work fails to register its characteristically interpersonal, conversational quality.

36  It is not strictly true that only the finished text can be delivered through a book; the productions of Bob Cobbing's Writers Forum press exploited the approximate reproduction of stencil duplication, a technology close to screen printing. But that's an exception that proves the rule.

37  The quotations are from 'War' in John James, *Collected Poems*, Cambridge: Salt Publishing 2002, p.150 and 'Talking in Bed', p.109.

38  James, *Collected Poems* p.131.

39  Contrary to James's assertion in the 'Author's Note' at the beginning of the Salt *Collected Poems* that "Where poems were subsumed into larger volumes they have been separated out, omitted from the later collection and returned to their status as separate publications". Absolutely not.

40  James, *Collected Poems* p.235.

41  Berrigan's habits of appropriation are noted by Raphael Rubenstein in his essay 'Gathered, Not Made: A Brief History of Appropriative Writing' where he describes Berrigan as "a kind of editor-plagiarist" (http://www.ubu.com/papers/rubinstein.html) and discussed by Daniel Kane, *All Poets Welcome* pp.46-47.

42  from 'War', James, *Collected Poems* p.141. James Osterberg is better known as Iggy Pop. I imagine that the Veronica lines reproduce a snatch of dialogue with the poet Veronica Forrest-Thomson (1947-1975).

43  James, *Collected Poems* p.208.

44  The line is from 'A Theory of Poetry', James, *Collected Poems* p.138.

45  A review of Denise Riley, *Mop Mop Georgette: New and selected poems 1986-1993* (Reality Street, 1993).

46  Nigel Wheale, 'Colours—Ethics—Lyric, Voice: Recent Poetry by Denise Riley', *Parataxis* 4 (Summer, 1993), pp.70-77.

47  James Keery, 'Well, There Was, And Wasn't, And There Is: The Third Cambridge Conference of Contemporary Poetry', *PN Review* (January-February, 1994), pp.11-15.

48  Stephen Frosh, 'On narcissism', *Free Associations* 18 (1989), 20-47. I draw on this excellent survey article on recent psychoanalytic accounts of narcissism throughout this essay.

49  Quoted by Frosh, 'On narcissism', p.41.

50  See my review of Oliver's *Penniless Politics*, 'Hoodoo Bozo Talks that Rainbow Jive', *Angel Exhaust* 8 (Autumn, 1992), pp.110–113.

51  Frosh, 'On narcissism', pp.36, 37.

52  Denise Riley, *'Am I That Name': Feminism and the Category of 'Women' in History*, London: Macmillan, 1988, p.16.

53  Denise Riley, *Four Falling*, Cambridge: Poetical Histories 26, 1993.

54  A review of Barry MacSweeney's section of Thomas A. Clark, Barry MacSweeney, Chris Torrance, *The Tempers of Hazard*, London: Paladin 1993.

55  Two notable obituaries provide excellent summaries of Oliver's richly varied life, and of his literary work. Nicholas Johnson's for *The Times* has been made available on the website for the journal *Exquisite Corpse* [www.corpse.org/issue_5/burning_bush/oliver.htm], while Andrew Crozier's for *The Guardian* with a further appreciation by Greg Chamberlain can be found online at www.guardian.co.uk/obituaries/story/0,3604,217852,00.html.

56  Two largely overlapping collections were issued, both including *The Infant and The Pearl*, Lewes: Silver Hounds, for Ferry Press, 1985; *Kind*, London: Allardyce, Barnett, Publishers, 1987 and *Three Variations on the Theme of Harm*, London: Paladin, 1990. Both are unavailable. A *Selected Poems* is published in the US by Talisman House.

57  This should be substituted for Brenton's in any reissue. Alice Notley, 'Douglas Oliver's New York Poem', *Chicago Review* 45:1 (1999), pp.79–88.

58  The best short account of this history lies in Deborah Wallace and Rodrick Wallace's pioneering work of urban ecology, *A Plague On Your Houses, How New York Was Burned Down and National Public Health Crumbled*, London: Verso 1998. See especially Chapter 2.

59  Edward Fairfax's wonderful contemporary version published in 1600 (the original Italian was published in 1581) can be found in full at http://sunsite.berkeley.edu/OMACL/Tasso/.

60  The debate is rehearsed fully in Andrea T. Baumeister, *Liberalism and the 'Politics of Difference'*, Edinburgh: Edinburgh UP 2000.

61  On reading a draft of this essay, Alice Notley commented: "the refrain from White Crossroads that you still dislike was taken down verbatim from a man walking down the street shouting. Doug was shocked by the speech he heard in New York and that refrain also registers his shock." An author cannot abrogate from what he puts down, but then a reader should be prepared to think on his or her embarrassment.

62  Works by Tom Raworth cited in this article are: Tom Raworth, *Ace*, 3d ed. Washington, DC: Edge, 2001; *Act*, London: Trigram, 1973; *Collected Poems*, Manchester: Carcanet, 2003 (cited as *CP*.)

63  John James's poem *War* (1978) and two succeeding semi-published works, *A Former Boiling* and *Toasting*, together with some of Barry MacSweeney's *Odes* (1978), are the most notable examples of British poetry influenced by the punk

and reggae moment. James's poems have now been reissued in his *Collected Poems* (Cambridge: Salt Publishing, 2002). My thanks go to Drew Milne, Geoff Ward and Anita Sokolsky for their helpful comments on a draft of this essay.

64 An interesting discussion of music, time and studio technology which prompted some of these thoughts is to be found in Peter de Bolla's *Art Matters*, in the chapter entitled 'Clarity: Glenn Gould's Goldberg (1981)'. Peter de Bolla, *Art Matters*, Cambridge, Mass.: Harvard University Press, 2001.

65 See the end of 'Tracking (Notes)': "but there is print through", followed by a diagram of forward rotation producing "image blur" (Act, 47). "Print through" refers to the audio ghost produced by incorrect storage of tape reels, and which fractionally anticipates the full musical presence.

66 'Eternal Sections' may be the late exception, but the eternal cannot be architectonic.

67 Raworth's poetry from 'Tracking (Notes)' onwards offers ample permission for a reading as an exemplary poetry of cocaine. Both Ace and Bolivia (the latter title a bit of a giveaway) are littered with the language of cocaine use, often redirected in order to converge with the light/freezing/cutting of film. These pages have more white crystals embedded in them than a dollar bill.

68 *ed.* James Acheson and Romana Huk, *Contemporary British Poetry: Essays in Theory and Criticism*, Albany NY: SUNY Press, 1996. Keith Tuma, *Fishing by Obstinate Isles, Modern and Postmodern British Poetry and American Readers*, Evanston, IL: Northwestern, 1998. *ed.* Romana Huk, *Assembling Alternatives: Reading Postmodern Poetries Transnationally*, Middletown, CT: Wesleyan, 2003.

69 See Milne's important essay 'Agoraphobia and the embarrassment of manifestoes: notes towards a community of risk', Cambridge, *Parataxis* 3 (1993), pp.25–40. Available on line at http://jacketmagazine.com/20/pt-dm-agora.html.

70 Denise Riley, *Impersonal passion: language as affect*, Durham NC and London: Duke UP, 2005.

71 J.H. Prynne, *To Pollen*, London: Barque 2006, p.25.

72 Penn Sound Close Listening Edition #14, first broadcast May 22 2006, http://ps1.el.net/web/archive/metafiles/ram/sbperclose_14upenn_milnetalk.ram.

73 The claim is based on Douglas Oliver, *Poetry and Narrative in Performance*, New York: St. Martin's Press 1989.

74 See D.S. Marriott, *Of Black Men*, New York, Columbia UP 2000, and *Incognegro*, Cambridge: Salt Publishing 2006.

75 Allen Grossman, 'Summa Lyrica' in Allen Grossman with Mark Halliday, *The Sighted Singer: Two Works on Poetry for Readers and Writers*, Baltimore: Johns Hopkins 1992, p.278.

76 Andrea Brady, *Embrace*, Glasgow: Object Permanence 2005; Keston Sutherland, *Neocosis*, London: Barque Press 2005.

77  Susan Stewart, *Poetry and the Fate of the Senses*, University of Chicago Press 2002, p.152.

78  Allen Grossman, 'Summa Lyrica' in Allen Grossman with Mark Halliday, *The Sighted Singer: Two Works on Poetry for Readers and Writers*, Baltimore: Johns Hopkins 1992, p.238.

79  http://jacketmagazine.com/29/morris-brady.html

80  J.H. Prynne (Pu Ling-en), 'Keynote Speech at the First Pearl River Poetry Conference, Guangzhou, China, 28th June 2005', *QUID* 16, Brighton 2005, pp.7–17.

81  Richard Goldstein, "Bitch Bites Man!', *The Village Voice*, May 10th 2004, at http://www.villagevoice.com/news/0419,goldstein2,53375,6.html

82  Laura (Riding) Jackson, *The Poems of Laura Riding*, Carcanet New Press, Manchester UK, 1980.

83  Laura (Riding) Jackson, *The Telling*, The Athlone Press, London 1972, p.14.

84  Laura (Riding) Jackson, *The Telling*, The Athlone Press, London 1972, p.149.

85  A slightly revised version of a paper read at the Philosophy of Literature Conference, University of Warwick 1986, alongside contributions from Anthony Barnett and Peter Riley.

86  This paper was presented in the staff/student seminar series at the Department of English, University of Swansea in January 1994. The seminar began with a reading of the poem 'Facing Port Talbot', since published in *Torn Off A Strip* (Equipage, 1994)—but the talk assumes the reading supplied only an impression of texture, and does not rely on close analysis. 'Facing Port Talbot' is reprinted in revised and abbreviated form in *Effigies Against the Light*, Cambridge: Salt Publishing 2001, pp.113–126.

87  Wieners, J., ed. Foye, R., *Selected Poems 1958–1984*, Santa Barbara: Black Sparrow 1986. p130. This paper is particularly indebted to L. Sass, *Madness and Modernism*, Cambridge MA: Harvard University Press 1994, and benefited also from comments by Drew Milne and D.S. Marriott on an earlier version. The paper was first presented at the 1996 Assembling Alternatives conference at the University of New Hampshire.

88  Wieners, *Selected Poems 1958–1984*, p.278.

89  S. Freud, tr Strachey, 'The Unconscious' in Freud, *On Metapsychology*, The Penguin Freud Library vol.11, Harmondsworth 1984, pp.159–222.

90  Charles Bernstein, 'from The Manufacture of Negative Experience', *Salt* 8, 1996, Applecross, Western Australia, pp.6–12.

91  S. Freud, tr Strachey, 'The 'Uncanny'', in Freud, *Art and Literature*, Harmondsworth: The Penguin Freud Library vol. 14, 1985, pp.335–376.

92  A talk given at Queen Mary College, London in 2000, at the invitation of Annie Janowitz.

93  The poems discussed in this talk, at that time titled 'Dew on the Knuckle, Due on the Nail', were eventually published as 'Case in Point' in *Contrivances*, Cambridge: Salt Publishing 2003, pp.125–180.

94  A review of three anthologies: Ed. Keith Tuma, *Anthology of Twentieth-Century British and Irish Poetry*, OUP US, 2001; ed. Edna Longley, *The Bloodaxe Book of 20th Century Poetry*, Bloodaxe, 2000; and ed. Simon Armitage and Robert Crawford, *The Penguin Book of Poetry from Britain and Ireland since 1945*, Viking, 1998.

95  See the discussion of this tendency in Drew Milne's manifesto article 'Agoraphobia and the embarrassment of manifestoes: notes towards a community of risk,' *Parataxis*, 3 (1993), pp.25–40.

96  The major exception, and strongly influential on Tuma's Preface, is Veronica Forrest-Thomson, *Poetic Artifice*, Manchester UP 1978. Tuma also prints Forrest-Thomson's wonderfully funny celebration of poetic artifice, 'Cordelia: or, 'A Poem Should Not Mean, But Be''.

97  A *Collected Poems* (but not a complete poems, since it selects from unpublished collections while reprinting the published books of poems in full) edited by John Pikoulis was published by Seren in 1998 but withdrawn immediately. See my review of the subsequent Carcanet *Collected Poems*, edited by Patrick McGuinness, in this volume.

98  Credit for such diligence belongs properly to the Canadian scholar Nate Dorward rather than the anthology's editor.

99  ed. Jerome Rothenberg and Pierre Joris, *Poems for the Millennium*, Berkeley: University of California Press, vol.1 1995, vol.2 1998.

100 Examples might include the poetry of Ken Edwards, Peter Middleton and Miles Champion. It is conventional in reviews of anthologies to lament unaccountable omissions, and the failure to represent the poetry of Douglas Oliver deprives readers of a politically and morally engaged poetry not concerned principally with identity politics. One should also lament lapses of judgment in choices from the work of poets included; neither John James nor Barry MacSweeney is represented adequately.

101 Prynne declined to be represented in the Tuma anthology.

102 No anthologist includes an example of his earlier poems, which would make apparent the association with Dylan Thomas.

103 See my 'Counterfactual Prynne: An Approach to Not-You', *Parataxis*, 8/9, (1996) pp.190–202, and in this volume.

104 The possibility exists that a collective practice of reading, facilitated by new technology, might enhance the accessibility of such highly demanding work— particularly where, as in the case of Prynne's poems, the professional knowledge of information scientists, biochemists and others can make an important contribution to understanding. As recording technology has altered the reception of music and assumptions about the level of information which is assimilable, so information technology may make available more highly-concentrated linguistic information.

105 A review of Lynette Roberts, *Collected Poems*, edited by Patrick McGuinness, Manchester: Carcanet 2006.

106 Adam Phillips, 'A Terrible Thing, Thank God', *London Review of Books* 26, no.5 (4 March 2004), pp.22–24. A version of this essay was delivered at the University of Notre Dame on April 13th 2004. Thanks go to Prof Stephen Fredman for his kind invitation, to Neil Reeve for his comments on a draft, so saving me a public pratfall, and to Maud Ellmann for her detailed suggestions for turning a dense paper into something phrased for the occasion.

107 Adam Phillips, 'Being ignored isn't the worst thing that can happen to a poet'. Review of *Poems* (1999). *The Observer* 21 March 1999.

108 Szondi was a friend of Paul Celan and his first major interpreter: his importance as critic consisted in drawing the different close reading practices developed in France, Britain and the US into German currency. After Celan committed suicide in April 1970, Szondi, a concentration camp survivor too, also committed suicide.

109 A transitional object is what an infant carries about to assist in transition from maternal dependence to a degree of independence—the classic example is Linus' blanket in the cartoon Peanuts.

110 'The Use of an Object and Relating through Identifications' in D.W. Winnicott, *Psycho-Analytic Explorations*, ed. Clare Winnicott, Ray Shepherd, and Madelaine Davis, Cambridge MA: Harvard University Press 1989, pp.218–227. 'Reading "Engführung"' in Peter Szondi, *Celan Studies*, Stanford CA: Stanford University Press 2003, pp.27–82.

111 'Engführung'/'Stretto,' tr. John Felstiner, *Selected Poems and Prose of Paul Celan*, New York: W.W. Norton 2001, pp.118–131.

112 Szondi, pp.81–2.

113 George Herbert, *The temple. Sacred poems and private ejaculations*, edited by N. Ferrar, Cambridge: T. Buck and R. Daniel, 1633. Facsimile, Scolar Press 1968.

114 Alfreda Murck, *Poetry and Painting in Song China: The Subtle Art of Dissent*, Harvard-Tenching Institute Monograph Series, 50, Cambridge MA: Harvard University Asia Center for the Harvard-Yenching Institute, 2000, p.60.

115 This and the following paragraph's discussion of poetry as cognition draws substantially on two articles: Simon Jarvis, 'Prosody as Cognition', *Critical Quarterly* 40, no.4 (Winter 1998), pp.3–15; and Keston Sutherland, 'Prosody and Reconciliation,' *The Gig* 16, (February 2004), pp.41–55.

116 Ed. Kelvin Everest and Geoffrey Matthews, *The Poems of Shelley: Volume Two, 1817–1819*, Harlow, Essex: Longman 2000, pp.530–531.

117 This sentence draws on Thomas Pepper, *Singularities: Extremes of Theory in the Twentieth Century*, Cambridge: Cambridge University Press 1977, specifically on the essay 'Afterword: er, or, borrowing from Peter to pay Paul: further notes on Celan's translation of Shakespeare's sonnet 105', pp.227–243.

118 'The Fate of the Transitional Object' in D.W. Winnicott, *Psycho-Analytic Explorations*, ed. Clare Winnicott, Ray Shepherd, and Madelaine Davis, Cambridge MA: Harvard University Press 1989, pp.54.

119 J.H. Prynne, *Biting the Air*, Cambridge: Equipage 2003.

120 Stephen Jonas, *Transmutations*, Ferry Press, London 1966. The preface is reprinted in (ed. Foye) Wieners, *Cultural Affairs in Boston: Poetry & Prose 1956–1985*, Santa Rosa: Black Sparrow 1988, 'As Preface to Transmutations'. Pp.31–33. The milieu is evoked in Raffael De Gruttola's brief reminiscence published in Stephen Jonas, *Three Poems*, Berkeley: Rose Books 1989.

121 See ed. Rosenfield, *The Collected Poems of John Wheelwright*, New York: New Directions 1983.

122 John Wieners, *Cultural Affairs in Boston: Poetry & Prose 1956–1985*, ed. Raymond Foye, Santa Rosa: Black Sparrow Press 1988, p.15.

123 John Wieners, *Ace of Pentacles*, New York: James F. Carr and Robert A. Wilson 1964, p.11. Reprinted John Wieners, *Selected Poems 1958–1984*, Santa Barbara: Black Sparrow Press 1986, p.47.

124 *Ace of Pentacles* p28, reprinted in Wieners, *Selected Poems 1958–1984*, p.62.

125 *Ace of Pentacles* p33, reprinted in Wieners, *Selected Poems 1958–1984*, p.66.

126 Anne Sexton, *The Complete Poems*, Boston & New York: Mariner Books 1999, pp.139–140.

127 from 'Suicide Note', *The Complete Poems*, p.158.

128 for instance, 'Moesta et Errabunda', 'Lesbos', Un Voyage à Cythèthe', and 'Le Voyage'.

129 *Nerves*, reprinted in Wieners, *Selected Poems 1958–1984*, p.148.

130 *Nerves*, reprinted in Wieners, *Selected Poems 1958–1984*, p.151.

131 *Nerves*, reprinted in Wieners, *Selected Poems 1958–1984*, p.112.

132 Edward Dorn, *The North Atlantic Turbine*, London: Fulcrum Press 1967; *Geography*, London: Fulcrum Press 1968.

133 Opening stanzas of 'Newshit', *Selected Poetry of Amiri Baraka/ LeRoi Jones*, New York: William Morrow 1979, p.95.

134 The relationship of Wieners to Charles Olson and Frank O'Hara, and of the latter two poets to each other, is the subject of an important essay by Andrea Brady based on new archival research. 'The Other Poet: John Wieners, Frank O'Hara, and Charles Olson' in *Don't Ever Get Famous: Essays on New York Writing after the New York School*, ed. Daniel Kane, Illinois State University: Dalkey Archive Press 2007.

135 He goes on to say that in this lineage Charles Olson has been succeeded by the Virgin Mary. Wieners, *Cultural Affairs in Boston*, pp.14–15.

136 Wieners, *Selected Poems 1958–1984*, p.296.

137 Edna St. Vincent Millay, *Collected Poems*, Cutchogue, NY: Buccaneer Books, nd, p585.

138 *Nerves*, reprinted in Wieners, *Selected Poems 1958–1984*, p.119.

139 Final stanza of 'The Merry Maid', Millay, *Collected Poems* p.145.

140 Second stanza of 'Love-Life', *Nerves*, reprinted in Wieners, *Selected Poems 1958–1984*, p.160.

141 Opening to 'On This Side Nothing', Jennifer Moxley, *The Sense Record and other poems*, Washington DC: Edge Books 2002, p.9.

142 Geoff Ward, *The Writing of America*, Cambridge: Polity 2002, p.192.

143 Wieners, *Selected Poems 1958–1984*, p.20. An earlier (and completely different) *Selected Poems* was published in the UK only by Jonathan Cape in 1972.

144 John Wieners, *Behind the State Capitol or Cincinnati Pike*, Boston: The Good Gay Poets 1975, p.1.

145 *Behind the State Capitol*, p.2. The poem is reprinted with corrections in *Selected Poems 1958–1984*, p.169.

146 www.crimelibrary.com/spies/mata_hari

147 *Behind the State Capitol* p.170. It would be pointless to employ the convention of '(sic)' for every departure from orthography and grammar; care has been taken with transcription.

148 'Today's Singular' according to the Contents page. *Behind the State Capitol* p.8.

149 'To Allen Hammerschlag', *Behind the State Capitol* p.45.

150 *Behind the State Capitol* pp.114–115, reprinted in Wieners, *Selected Poems 1958–1984*, p.188.

151 See for instance the section headed 'Fashion: "Madam Death! Madam Death"' in 'Exposé of 1935', Benjamin, *The Arcades Project*, Cambridge MA: Harvard UP 1999, p.8.

152 'Cultural Affairs in Boston', in (ed. Foye) Wieners, *Cultural Affairs in Boston: Poetry & Prose 1956–1985*, Santa Rosa: Black Sparrow 1988, pp.183–185.

153 Laurie Anderson, 'Walking and Falling,' *Big Science* (CD), Warner Brothers 1982. But as Stephen Fredman reminds me, Anderson has stuttered unwittingly through imitation: in *Home of the Brave* she tells a story about memorizing her lyrics in Japanese for a concert in Japan. Afterwards someone comes up and says, "Sorry, excuse me, sorry, but you speak English flawlessly; I can't understand why you speak Japanese with a stutter". The Japanese translator she copied impeccably had a stutter. I am grateful to Stephen Fredman and Christine Froula for reading this essay in draft, and for their very helpful comments.

154 See Rachel Blau DuPlessis, 'A Letter on Loy' in ed. Maeera Shrieber and Keith Tuma, *Mina Loy: Woman and Poet*, Orono, Maine: The National Poetry Foundation 1998. [henceforward Shrieber and Tuma], p.501. Also, Ezra Pound, 'Marianne Moore and Mina Loy,' *Selected Prose 1909–1965*, New York: New Directions 1973, p.424.

155  Carolyn Burke, *Becoming Modern: The Life of Mina Loy*, New York: Farrar Straus Giroux, 1996 [henceforward Burke], esp. pp.195–208. See also Eric Murphy Selinger, 'Love in the Time of Melancholia' in Shrieber and Tuma, pp.19–43.

156  Charles Altieri, *The Art of Twentieth-Century Poetry: modernism and after*, Oxford: Blackwell 2006 [henceforward Altieri], p.182.

157  Charles Olson, *Collected Prose* ed. Allen and Friedlander, Berkeley: University of California Press 1997, p.182.

158  The gloss is borrowed from a paper discussing the poetics of the early writing of JH Prynne and their foundation in Olsonian ontology: Keston Sutherland, 'Ethica Nullius', Prague: Litteraria Pragensia, 2006, pp.239–255.

159  Robert Creeley, *The Collected Poems of Robert Creeley 1945–1955*, Berkeley: University of California Press 1982 [henceforward Creeley], p.205.

160  Creeley, p.105. It is remarkable that Creeley chose to reprint this preface in his *Collected Poems.*

161  Altieri, p.189.

162  Creeley, p.207.

163  Nathaniel Mackey, *Discrepant Engagement: dissonance, cross-culturality, and experimental writing*, Cambridge UP 1993 [henceforward Mackey], pp.108–9. What Duncan says is: "Yes, but the figure of Creeley stumbling after the muse, it's a fool stumbling after the White Goddess; the White Goddess is not the figure of a man with no wife at all. It's the wife that undoes you and that leaves you stumbling and actually crippled, isn't it, finally? There is a subdued castration in which your heel is injured, so you're a stumbler, and Creeley's practised stumbling is an embodiment of a castration and impotency which is the experience we have in his poems." Robert Duncan, *An Interview by George Bowering and Robert Hogg*, April 19, 1969, published as A Beaver Kosmos Folio (without date or pagination).

164  Creeley, p.200.

165  Mackey, p.109.

166  Stephen Fredman, *Roadtesting the Language: An Interview with Edward Dorn*, Documents for New Poetry I, Archive for New Poetry, San Diego, University of California, 1978, p.11.

167  Marjorie Perloff, *The futurist moment: avant-garde, avant guerre, and the language of rupture*, Chicago UP 2003 (first edition published 1986), p.89.

168  Mina Loy, *The Last Lunar Baedeker*, ed. Roger L. Conover, Manchester: Carcanet 1985 [henceforward Loy I], pp.269–271. Variant readings from Mina Loy, *The Lost Lunar Baedeker*, ed. Roger L. Conover, Farrar, Straus, Giroux 1996 [henceforward Loy II] will be shown for all quotations. For the 'Feminist Manifesto' Loy II deploys a typographical resourcefulness characteristic of the Futurist manifesto and removes the uniform paragraphing of Loy I. No explanation is given for this editorial decision. The relevant passages read "–are you prepared for the Wrench–?" where "Wrench" is in outsize type; "Another great illusion that

woman must use all her introspective clear-sightedness and unbiased bravery to destroy–for the sake of her self respect is the impurity of sex'; and "the unconditional surgical destruction of virginity through-out the female population at puberty–."

169 Loy I, p.106. Loy II uses roman numerals to identify the poems and Poem XXXI has 'busy-body' and 'Eclosion' (no acute accent). For Loy II Conover seems to adopt an undiscussed compromise between new manuscript or first-appearance evidence and the exigencies of conventional publishing–so, for instance, while punctuation is no longer regularised, he refrains from isolating Poem XVII in the centre of the sequence as Loy wished.

170 Maeera Shrieber, '"Love Is A Lyric/Of Bodies",' Shrieber and Tuma, p.90.

171 Marjorie Perloff, 'English as a "Second" Language,' Shrieber and Tuma, pp.136–7.

172 Loy I, p.102. Loy II has 'street-corner'.

173 Rachel Blau DuPlessis, '"Seismic Orgasm",' Shrieber and Tuma, p.63.

174 See Burke, p.164, citing Loy's description of her absconding with Marinetti from her first marriage: "She felt herself slipping into his world, she recalled, "where everything seemed to be worked by a piston." Hiding away from the past in his jacket, she continued (speaking of herself in the third person), "she was caught in the machinery of his urgent identification with motor-frenzy." See also Linda A. Kinnahan, *Poetics of the Feminine*, Cambridge UP 1994, p.56, for this clockwork as "the male's libidinal experience from a woman's perspective".

175 Loy I, pp.103–104. Loy II has "Unthinkable that white over there |–Is smoke from your house". The previous two quotations are unchanged in Loy II.

176 'Objet clinique non identifié,' posted by Jean-Jacques Tyszler 04/04/2005, www.freud-lacan.com/articles/article.php?url_article=jtyszler040405 and translated by the author.

177 André Green, *Life Narcissism, Death Narcissism*, London: Free Association Books 2001, p.112.

178 Green, *Life Narcissism, Death Narcissism*, p.112.

179 See my article 'Faktura: The Work of Marjorie Welish,' *Chicago Review* Vol.51 No.3, Autumn 2005, pp.115–127, and in this volume.

180 Jennifer Ashton, *From Modernism to Postmodernism: American Poetry and Theory in the Twentieth Century*, Cambridge University Press 2005, p.115.

181 A review of Marjorie Welish's *Word Group* (Minneapolis: Coffee House, 2004); and *Of the Diagram: The Work of Marjorie Welish*, ed. Aaron Levy and Jean-Michel Rabaté (Philadelphia: Slought, 2003).

182 For a survey see Jed Rasula's essay "Women, Innovation and 'Improbable Evidence'" in his *Syncopations* (Tuscaloosa: U of Alabama Press, 2004).

183 All critical quotations in this review are taken from *Of the Diagram* unless otherwise noted.

184  See Brian M. Reed's "Twentieth-century Poetry and the New York Art World" (especially pp.127–128) in *A Concise Companion to Twentieth-Century American Poetry*, ed. by Stephen Fredman (New York: Blackwell, 2005). Alongside some offensive rhetoric at the expense of a straw-man Abstract Expressionist ("a lollygagger sharing passing ecstasies and complaining of purely private traumas") Reed asserts of the work of Donald Judd, Carl André, Sol LeWitt, "and others" that "A museum is thereby exposed as an extension of, not a refuge from, the 'military-industrial complex' of American capitalism". It would be interesting to test this proposition with the day-trippers to Dia:Beacon or MASS MoCA.

185  See Marjorie Welish's *Signifying Art* (Cambridge: Cambridge UP, 1999), which includes three essays on Johns.

186  Marjorie Perloff, 'How Avant-Gardes Rise, Fall, and Mutate: The Case of Language Poetry' (http://wings.buffalo.edu/epc/authors/perloff/articles/avant_garde.pdf).

187  Definitions    from:    http://www.umanitoba.ca/faculties/arts/anthropology/ kintitle.html

188  Charles Harrison, *Essays on Art & Language* (Cambridge MA: MIT, 1991) p.67.

# Index

Printed in the United Kingdom
by Lightning Source UK Ltd.
122019UK00002B/64-81/A